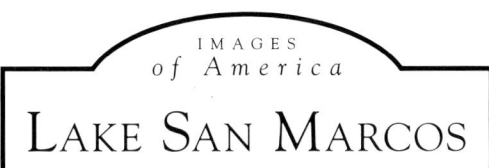

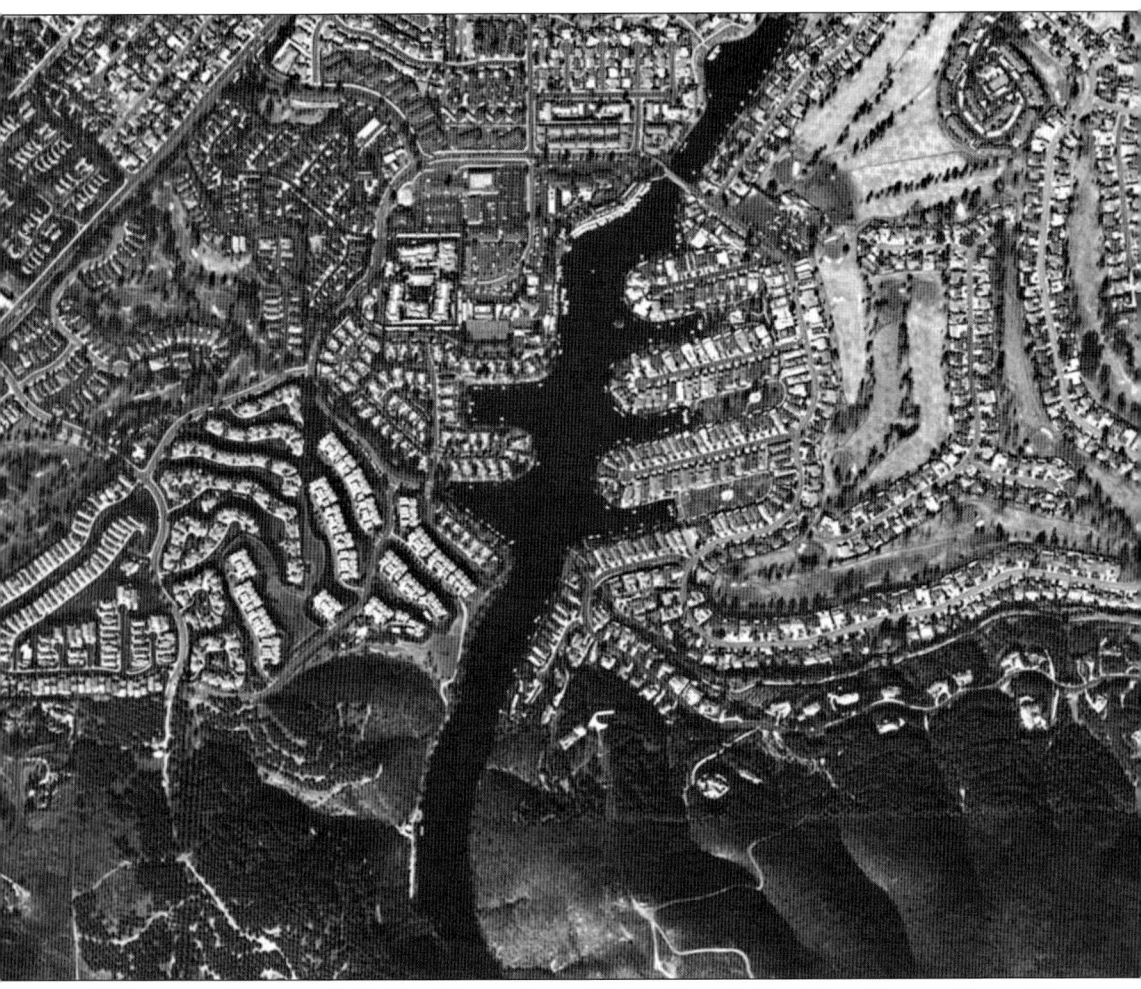
Welcome to the story of Lake San Marcos, located in California's San Diego County. Here, visitors and residents alike experience a unique community. This aerial photograph, taken in the 1990s, shows the two golf courses and nearly 2,500 homes. (Author's collection.)

ON THE COVER: This early photograph of Lake San Marcos shows the lakefront homes, an island where birds gather and nest in the spring, and one of the many sailboats that were commonly on the lake during the day. Shown in the background are the Cerro De Las Posas Hills, which stand to the east and south of the community. The photographer is unidentified, but this image frequently appeared in newsletters and magazines in the area. (*Quail Call*.)

IMAGES
of America
LAKE SAN MARCOS

Jacque Baker

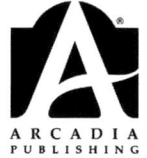

Copyright © 2014 by Jacque Baker
ISBN 978-1-4671-3241-1

Published by Arcadia Publishing
Charleston, South Carolina

Printed in the United States of America

Library of Congress Control Number: 2014936330

For all general information, please contact Arcadia Publishing:
Telephone 843-853-2070
Fax 843-853-0044
E-mail sales@arcadiapublishing.com
For customer service and orders:
Toll-Free 1-888-313-2665

Visit us on the Internet at www.arcadiapublishing.com

This book is dedicated to the people of Lake San Marcos who moved here in the early years to make it the unique community it is today, and to the current residents who continue to volunteer their time to maintain our way of life!

Contents

Acknowledgments		6
Introduction		7
1.	Building Lake San Marcos	9
2.	Early Days	35
3.	Community Development	59
4.	The People	75
The Future of Lake San Marcos		127

Acknowledgments

Fortunately, many people have taken photographs in and around Lake San Marcos (LSM) since it was planned in the early 1960s. Most of these images have appeared in builders' sales brochures or in the monthly community newsletter the *Quail Call*, while some were taken by amateur and professional resident photographers living in the area and watching the building progress. Most of the early photographers are now gone and cannot be located to be recognized for their work, but those I know of will be credited wherever possible. I do know that our residents love sharing their photographs with interested people.

I wish to thank those folks who have given me their early copies of *Quail Call* and other publications that they have saved all these years in hopes that someone would find them useful. One such family was Mr. and Mrs. L.P. Colt. Additionally, early resident Bill Guier gave me a few of his early photographs, many of which were published in the *Quail Call*.

Unless otherwise indicated, all images are courtesy of the *Quail Call*.

I first became interested in preserving our history in 2001 when I purchased a home in Lake San Marcos. While president of the LSM Community Association in 2007 and 2008, I spearheaded an effort with local historians to complete a book about the history of the area. That book, *The Early History of Lake San Marcos*, was well received in the community and provided me with the material to complete this pictorial history to complement it.

I wish to thank Roy and Beverley Haskins, who have been actively involved in preserving the history of not only Lake San Marcos but the city of San Marcos as well. Their guidance with the earlier book gave me the courage and knowledge to not only complete it but to take on this project. I wish to thank the Citizens Development Corporation (CDC) for publishing the early issues of *Quail Call*, where so much about our activities, our people, and our way of life was recorded. Without them, we would not have this book. I also wish to thank Mr. and Mrs. L.P Colt, who provided me with many of the back issues of the *Quail Call*. It is not my place to rewrite the history, but rather to record and preserve it as best as I can. For that reason, I have tried to keep the photograph descriptions as close to the actual captions in the newsletters to capture and preserve the personalities of the people of Lake San Marcos.

I also wish to thank the Lake San Marcos Community Association for suggesting to Arcadia Publishing that I should be interested in this project.

Introduction

Lake San Marcos is located in northern San Diego County ("North County") and is surrounded by the city of San Marcos. Although part of the unincorporated county, it shares city services and a zip code with San Marcos, which incorporated in 1963. Both were once a part of the Los Vallecitos De San Marcos Rancho (the Little Valleys of Saint Mark), an area that was granted on April 22, 1840, to Jose Maria Alvarado by his uncle, the Mexican governor of the region. The name was given by Spanish explorers to commemorate their discovery of the fertile valleys on April 25, 1797, St. Mark's Day.

The early inhabitants were small groups of nomadic Indians living along San Marcos Creek, which originated in the upper Twin Oaks Valley and ran all the way to the ocean. The extensive and interesting history of San Marcos is covered in several books that can be found in the San Marcos Historical Society headquarters at Walnut Grove Park.

The area where Lake San Marcos now stands used to be a cattle ranch with a creek meandering through it. The owners of the land, Mr. and Mrs. George D. Clemson, built a small dam to provide water for irrigation and their cattle. Over the years, they added to the dam until the lake was about 40 acres. The Frazar brothers purchased the land in 1962 and drained and reshaped the lake to build the lakeside community.

Frank Vecchio, of the advertising firm of Hogan and Vecchio in Riverside, California, first designated the quail as the symbol of Lake San Marcos. He visited the area looking for information for his first advertising brochure and saw many quail in the fields. He designed three quails for the brochure. The design was used on many advertising pieces over the years.

The private 80-acre lake is one-and-one-third miles long and contains bass, bluegill, and catfish, offering excellent fishing for residents or guests of the hotel. Privately owned boats belonging to residents must be registered, and fishing licenses are required to fish the lake. The LSM Yacht Club holds several boat parades each year, with residents decorating their pontoon boats with lights and streamers and even costuming themselves before parading in a line around the perimeter of the lake. Residents sit on their patios and lawns to watch from the bridge or beach area. In the late afternoons, one will see pontoon boats cruising the lake, many with residents enjoying happy hour.

The Lake San Marcos Community Association (LSMCA) is made up of volunteers elected from the residents to serve two-year terms. Their purpose is to enhance and investigate community matters and improve the quality of living in Lake San Marcos. The association currently puts out a monthly resident newsletter called the *Quail Call* with information and matters of interest to the community. This newsletter is also available online to interested persons.

The recreational facilities include two pools, tennis courts, and recreation rooms with pool tables, as well as the lake and docks. There is a picnic area in the natural areas at the south end of the lake. The recreational facilities are owned and managed by Citizens Development Corporation, and residents are charged a yearly fee for their use. CDC also owns and operates two golf courses, a hotel, a convention center, and two restaurants in Lake San Marcos. There are more than 25 social clubs and organizations for just about every interest, from golfing, boating, and dancing to card games, gardening, and art. There is a pavilion available for community meetings or for private resident gatherings with reservations.

Armed security patrol is available 24 hours a day to the residents for an annual fee. This area is one of the safest in San Diego County. Although most parts of Lake San Marcos are not age restricted, the area appeals to older families and retirees because of the many clubs, organizations, and activities available.

The area has as many as 347 sunny days a year, due in part to a stable high-pressure system known as the Pacific High lying a few hundred miles west over the Pacific Ocean. This accounts for a range of about 20 degrees between the day's high and the night's low. The uninterrupted Pacific breezes provide nature's air-conditioning, with temperatures seldom reaching above 80 degrees. The Cerro de Las Posas Mountains on the south and the San Marcos Mountains to the north, with an eastern exit, create a wind tunnel that prevents smog from settling in the valley. The few hot days a year are caused by Santa Ana winds from the desert coming from the east.

One
BUILDING LAKE SAN MARCOS

San Marcos Creek meandered through the area, fed by local springs and hillside runoff. In 1927, the Clemson family purchased the land, and in 1946, a dam was built at the south end of the creek, creating a 40-acre lake used for irrigation. In 1962, The Frazar brothers—Don, Bob, and Gordon—bought 1,648 acres from the Clemson and Wells families and made plans to redesign the lake and build a community similar to those they had seen in other areas. In August 1962, the San Diego County Planning Commission approved a tentative Lake San Marcos map.

Citizens Development Corporation was the developer, with Gordon Frazar serving as president, Don Frazar taking charge of home sales, and Bob Frazar managing construction. Before coming to Lake San Marcos, the brothers had built about 6,000 homes in Riverside and San Bernardino Counties. A master plan for the development was designed by a San Bernardino engineering firm, Campbell and Miller. Architects Blurock and Ellerbrock of Corona Del Mar had also been hired to design the community. The best ideas of both firms were consolidated into a master plan. Campbell and Miller won a statewide competition in 1966, and their Lake San Marcos design was honored as "the best planned community in California." In 1967, the National Association of Home Builders convention in Chicago awarded the Lake San Marcos design the title of "Best Planned Lakeside Community in the Nation."

Over the years, the individual blocks of development within Lake San Marcos have resulted in more than 25 homeowners' associations and nearly 2,500 homes.

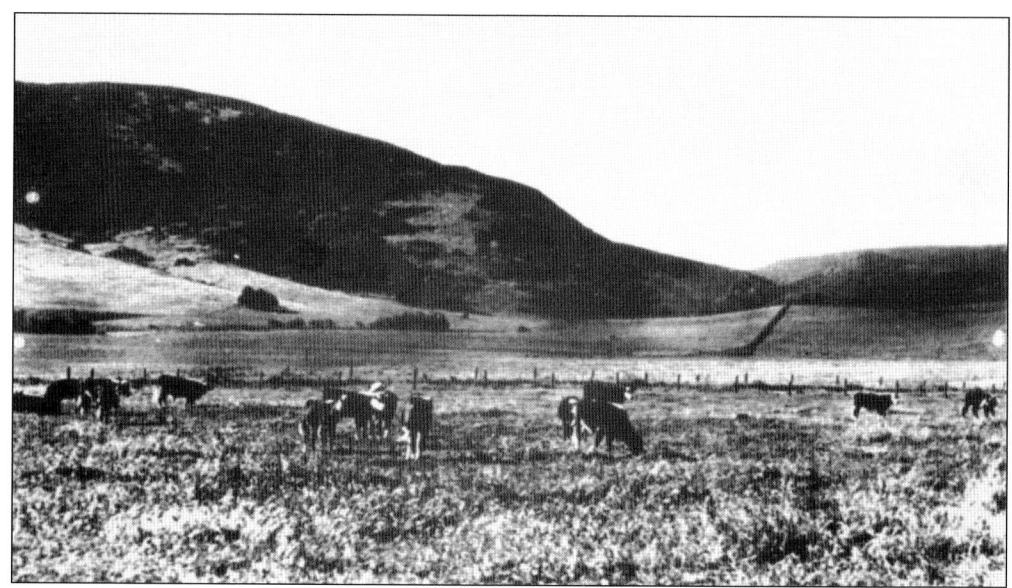

Cows are seen grazing on George Clemson's 1,200-acre ranch in about 1929. The area was a farm and cattle ranch before being sold to the Frazar brothers in 1962. In addition to cattle ranches, San Marcos was home to many egg ranches.

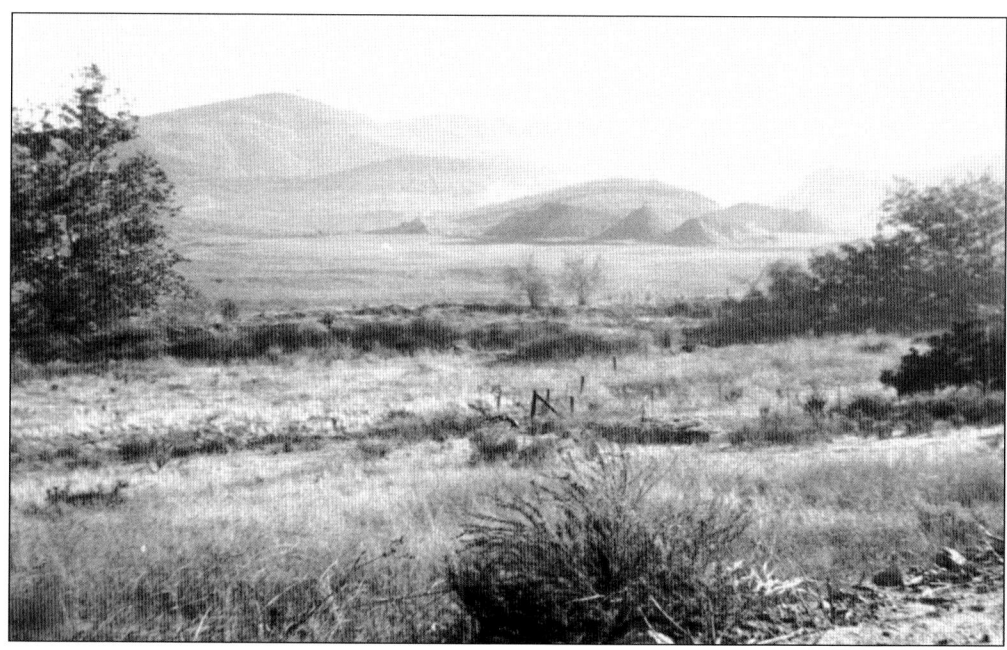

This is an early photograph of the land where Lake San Marcos now sits. The Cerro De Las Posas Mountains are in the background. The lake area is surrounded by the city of San Marcos, although Lake San Marcos is in unincorporated San Diego County. (Author's collection.)

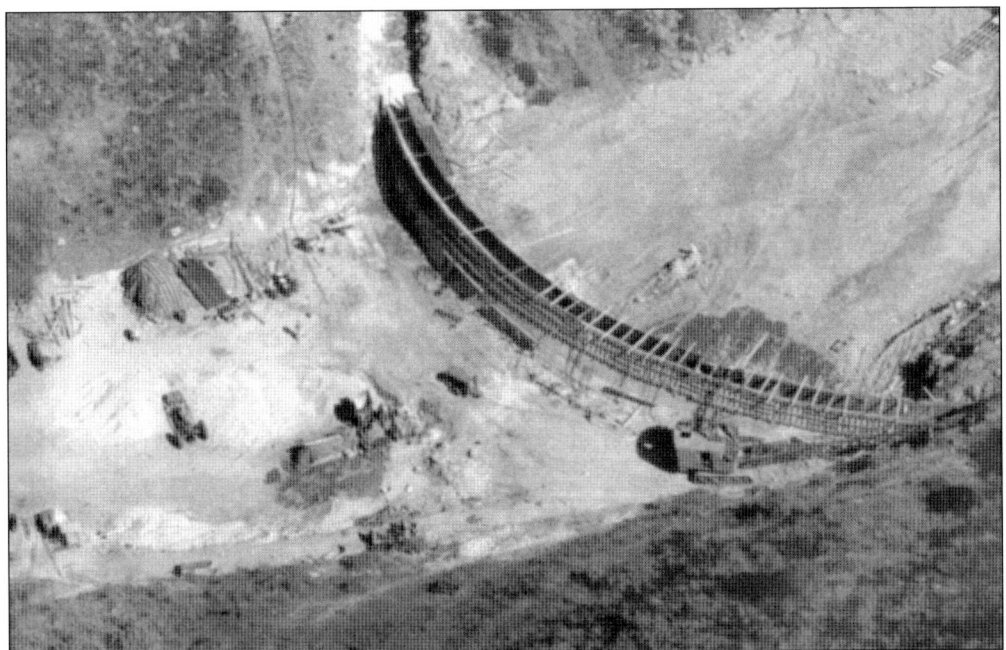
George Clemson and his son-in-law John Wells constructed a concrete dam across San Marcos Creek in 1946, forming a 40-acre pond used to irrigate their crops. The purpose of building a dam across the creek was to have a constant water supply for their farming and cattle ranch. By 1952, the pond was full. (Author's collection.)

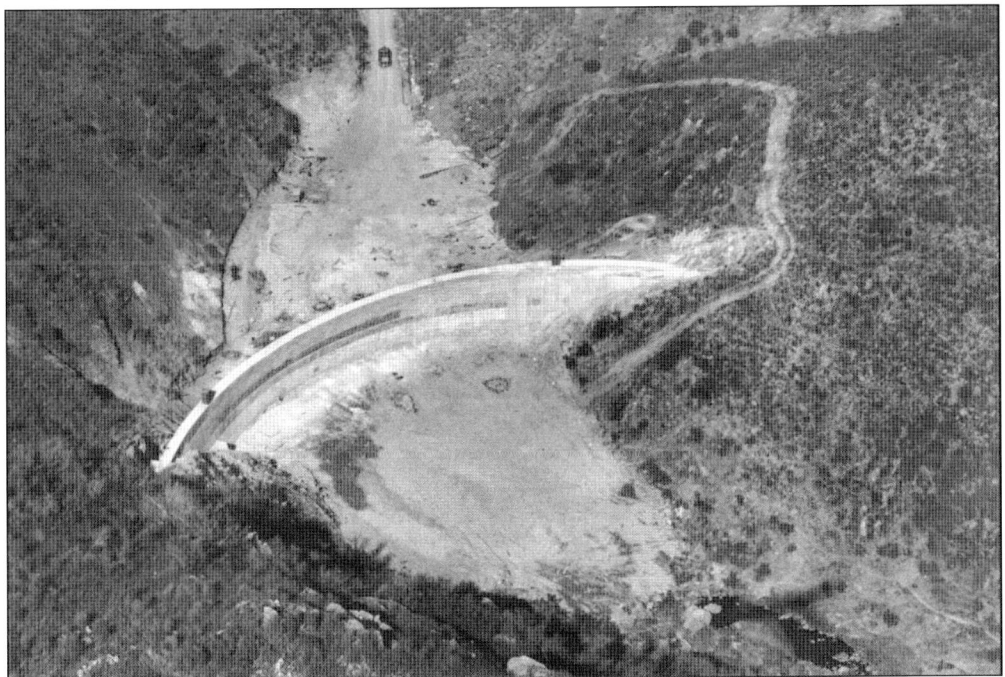
By 1951, the 65-foot spillway was finished, forming the 40-acre pond fed by over 29 square miles of watershed, which included San Marcos Creek, natural springs, and hillside runoff. (Author's collection.)

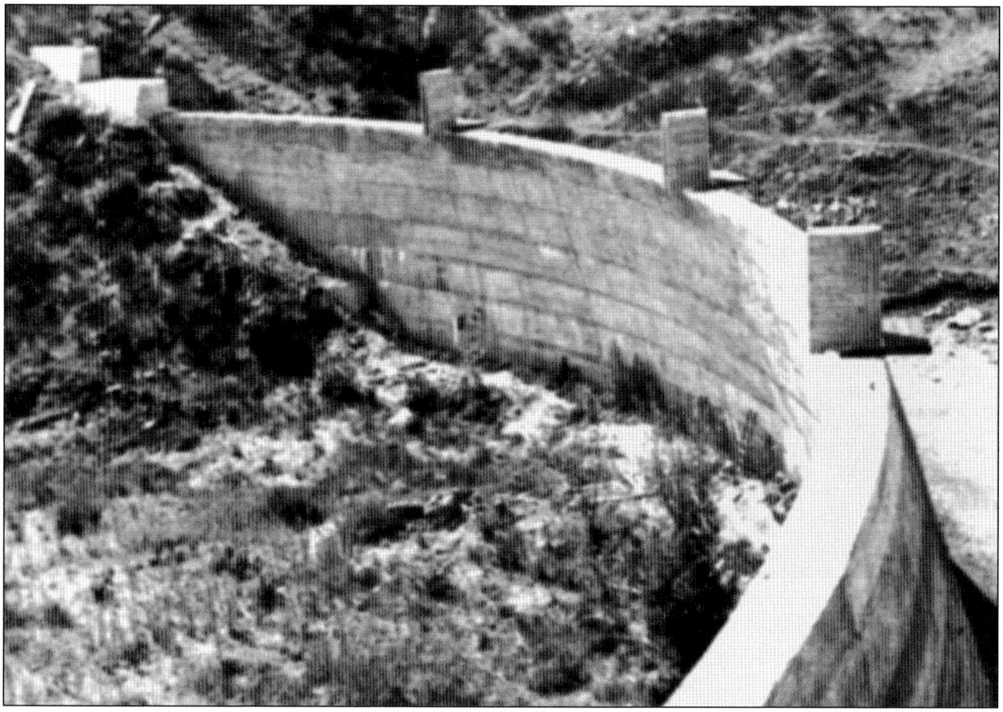

George Clemson completed the dam in 1951. The Clemsons used mostly their own funds to build the dam, with a little help from a government water-conservation program.

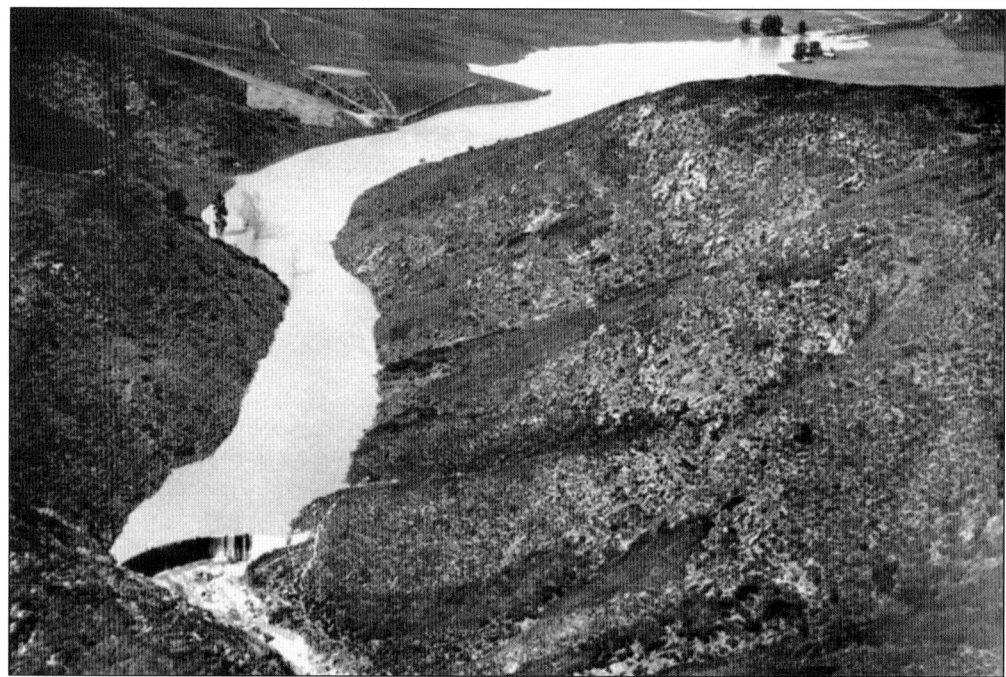

The 40-acre pond was full by 1952 and was used to irrigate the Clemsons' crops and water their cattle since water supply in San Marcos was unreliable. The overflow creek continues all the way to the Pacific. (Author's collection.)

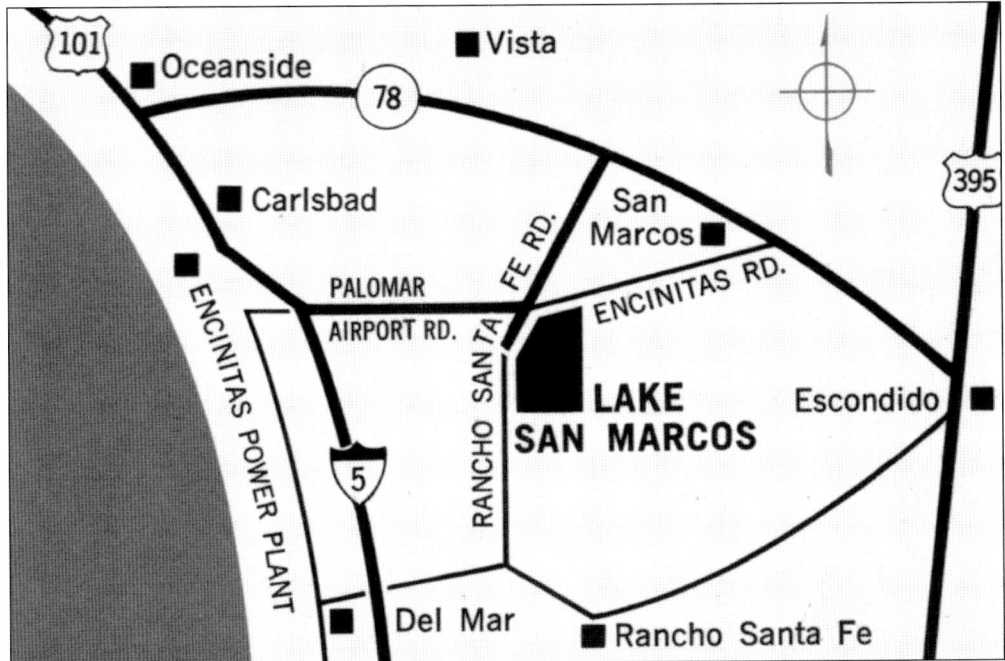

This early map shows the location of Lake San Marcos. Some of the road names have since changed; for instance, Encinitas Road is now San Marcos Boulevard. Lake San Marcos is approximately seven miles from the Pacific Ocean, surrounded entirely by the city of San Marcos. (Author's collection.)

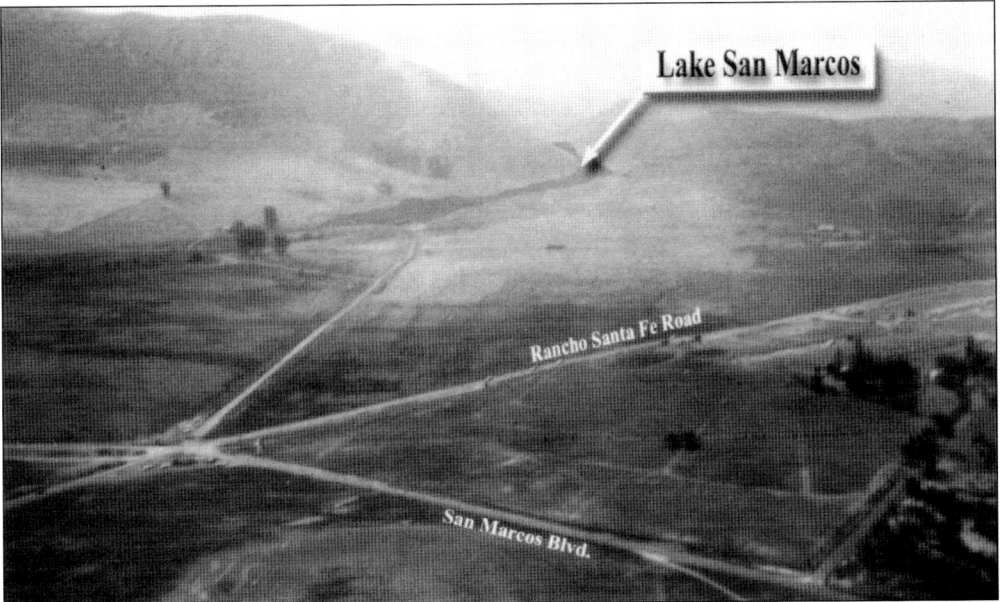

This 1953 photograph shows dirt roads as well as Encinitas Road (now San Marcos Boulevard) and Rancho Santa Fe Road. In the distance is the Clemson Wells irrigation lake. The area to the right of the intersection was originally the town of Barham, now largely a condo area above Albertson's Market and directly across Rancho Santa Fe Road from the main entrance into Lake San Marcos. (Author's collection.)

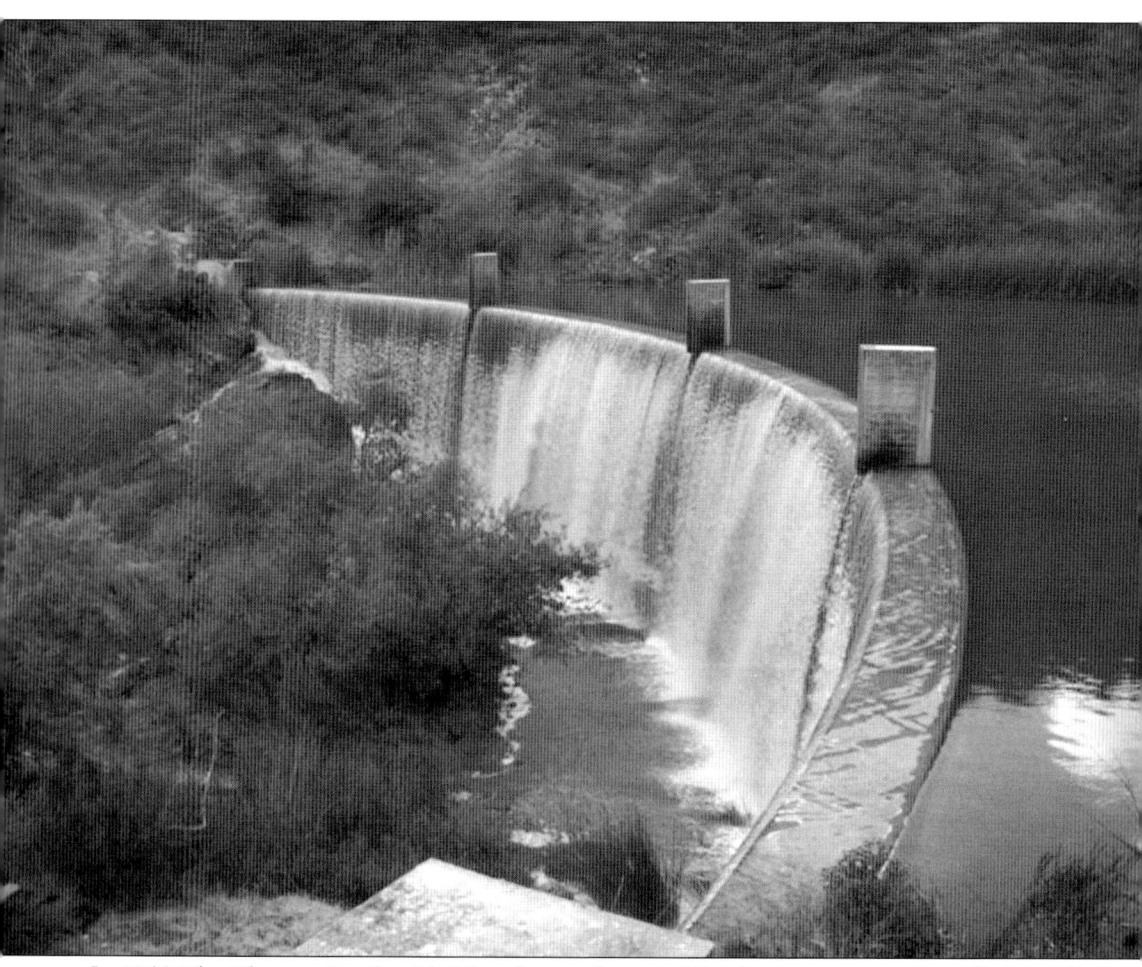
In 1956, The Clemson family added four feet to the top of the dam, increasing the spillway to 69 feet. (Author's collection.)

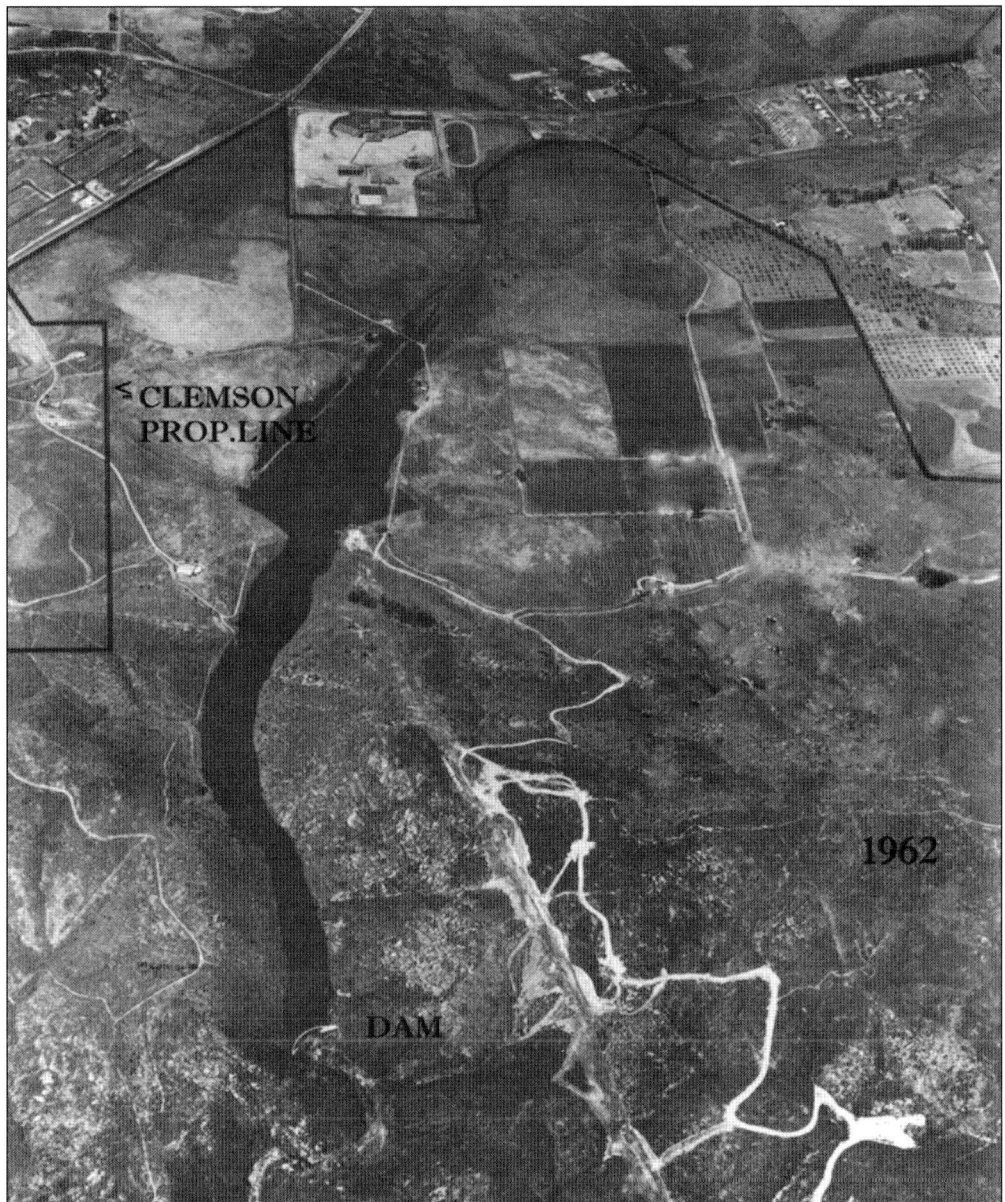

This 1962 aerial photograph shows the Clemson-Wells property lines, San Marcos High School under construction, and, at far-right center, the Wells farmhouse. (Author's collection.)

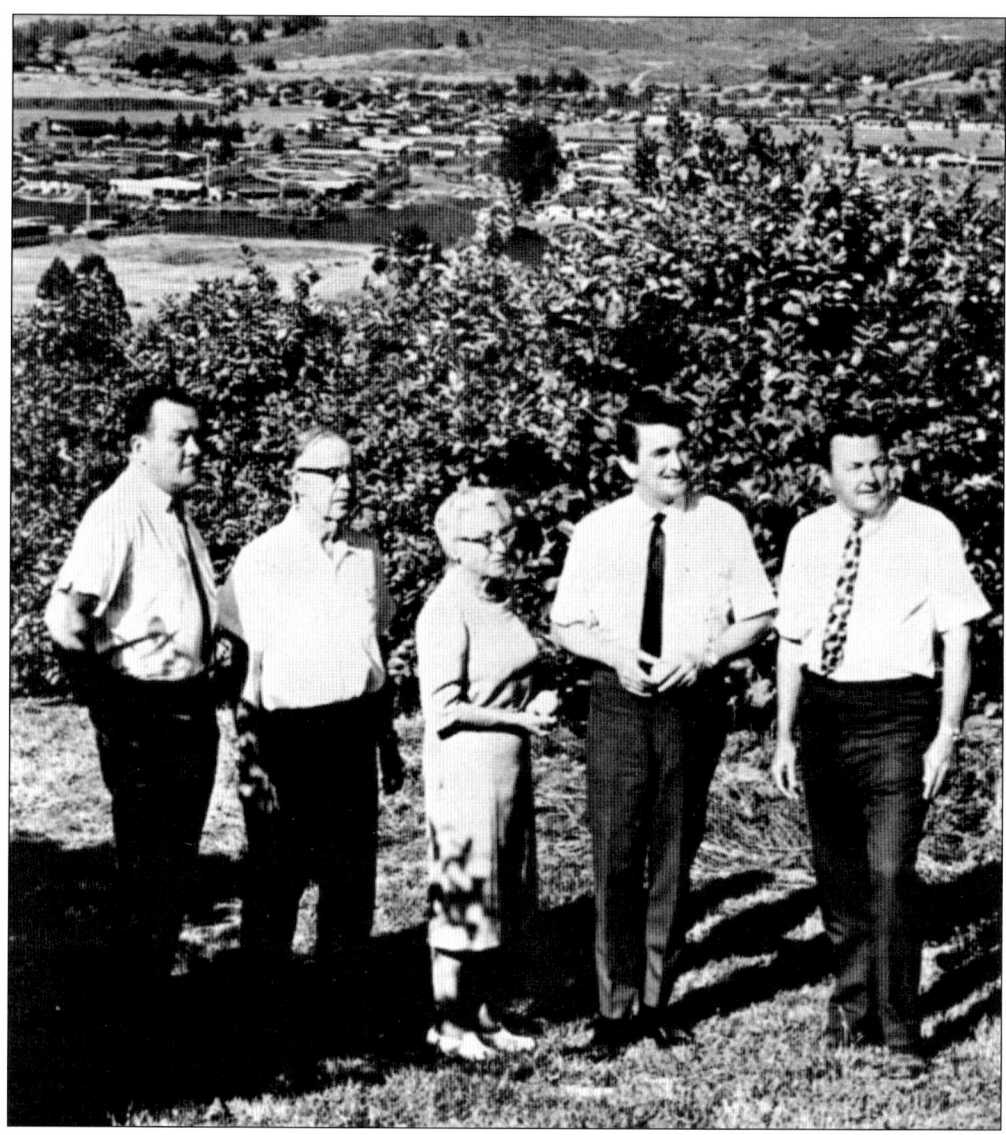
The Frazar brothers purchased the land from Mr. and Mrs. George Clemson in 1962. Standing on a knoll in Lake San Marcos are, from left to right, Gordon Frazar, Mr. and Mrs. George Clemson, Don Frazar, and Bob Frazar. After purchasing the land from the Clemson and Wells families, the Frazars formed Citizens Development Corporation. Needing to find workers and places for them to sleep and eat, they completed the Quail's Inn Motel and Restaurant first. Ground was broken on August 23, 1962, the same day the tentative Lake San Marcos map was approved by the San Diego Planning Commission. Escrow closed on September 18, 1962. They made plans to redesign the lake and build a lakeside community similar to those they had seen in other areas. The Frazars insisted on underground utilities and no antennas.

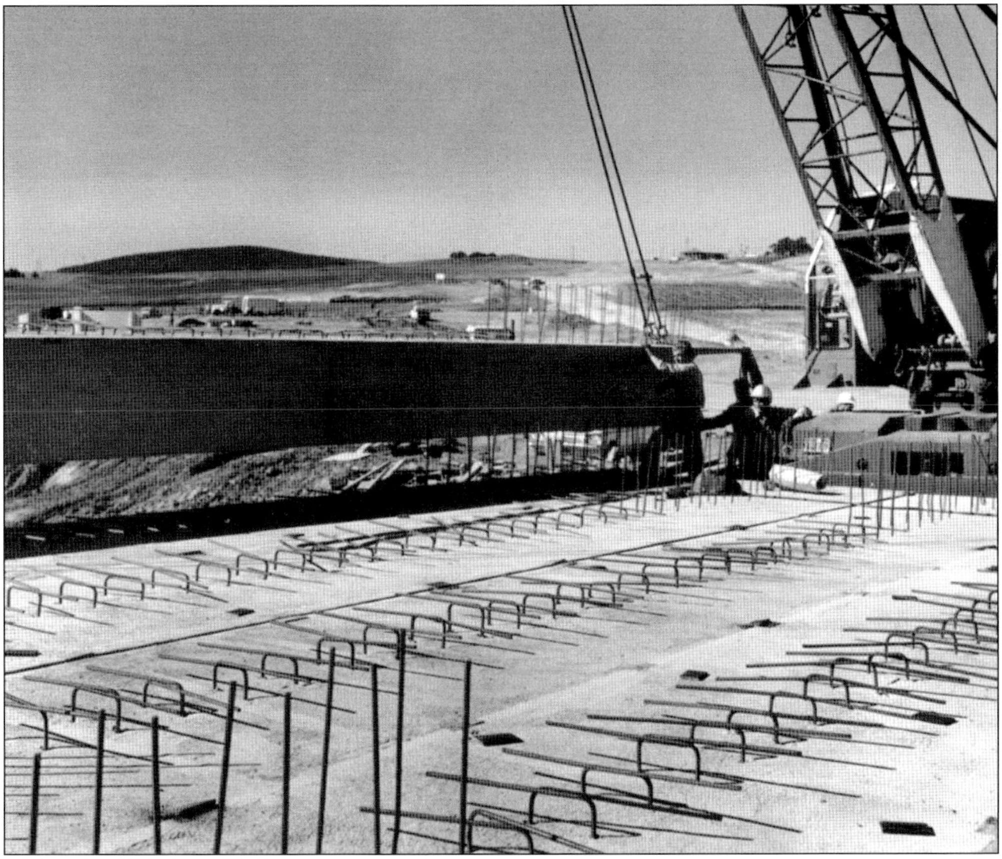

This photograph shows the ongoing construction of the bridge in 1963. After reshaping the land and lake, the brothers decided to construct a bridge across the water. The bridge is completely owned and maintained by Citizens Development Corporation in order to reduce county control of access and maintenance. (Author's collection.)

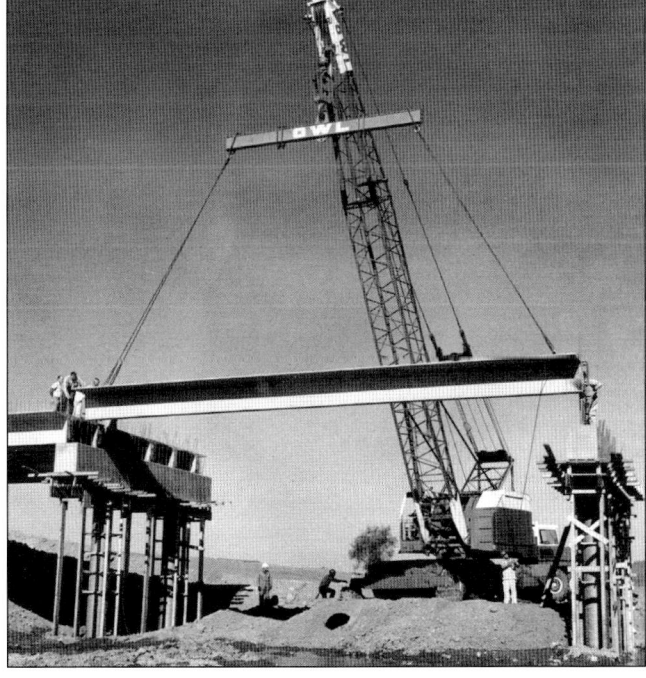

Here is another photograph showing the construction of the concrete bridge connecting the east and west sides of Lake San Marcos. Both sides of the lake were developed, eventually boasting more than 2,500 homes. (Author's collection.)

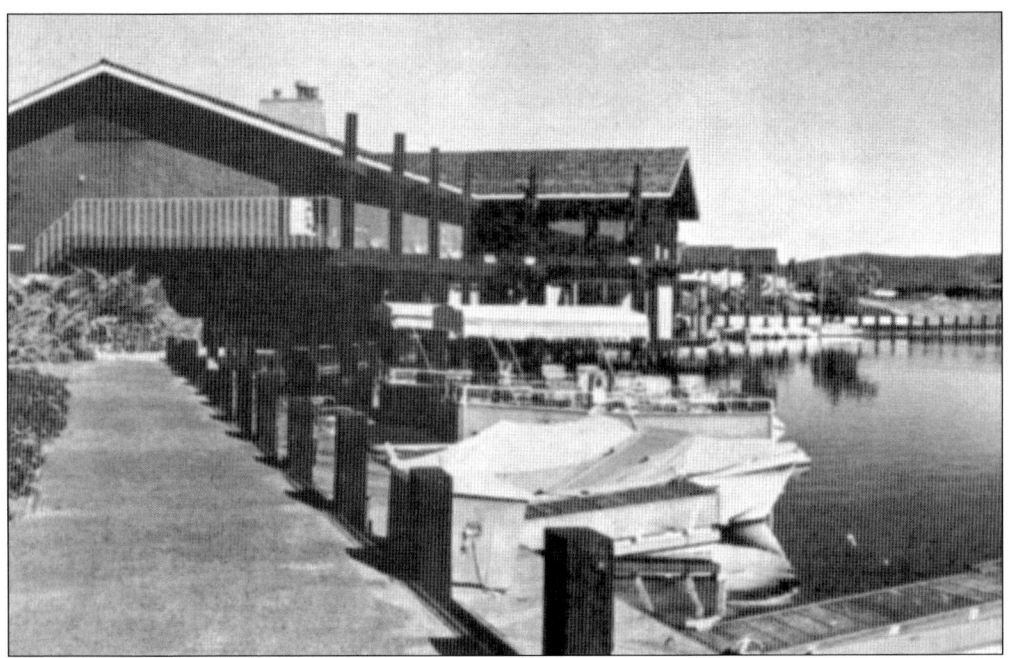

Seen here are the beginnings of the Quail's Inn Dinner House in December 1962. This bulkhead extends from the information center to the recreation center. Here, the lake was eight feet deep; it deepened to between 10 and 12 feet.

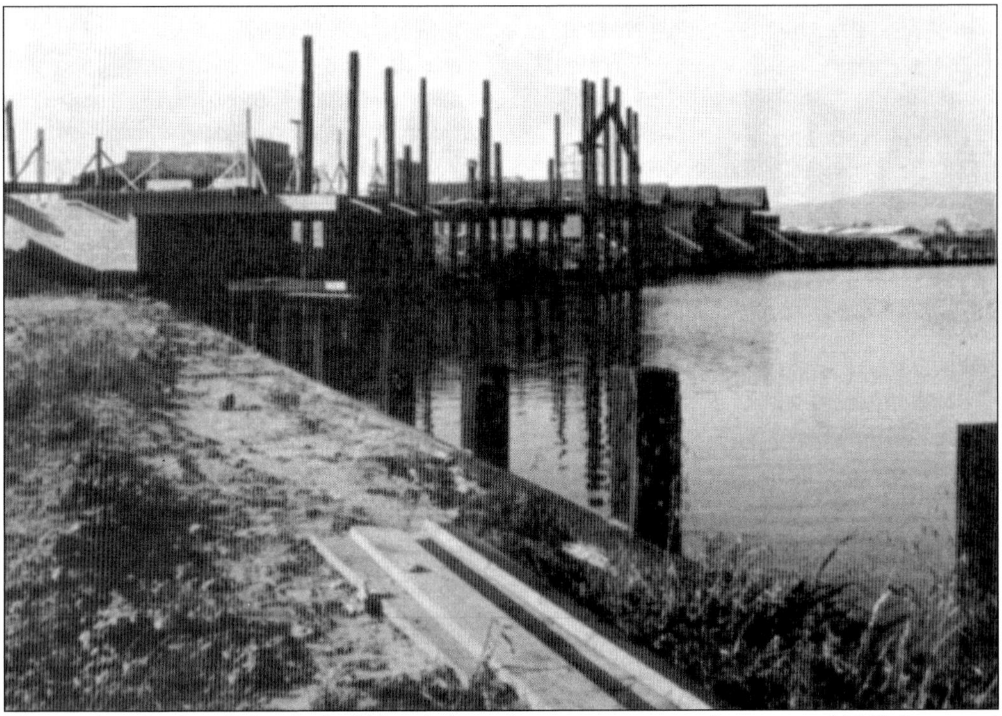

This is what the Quail's Inn looked like while under construction in the spring of 1963. It opened for business on July 15, 1963. Over the years, it has changed names several times, and is now being remodeled. It is planned to reopen in 2015.

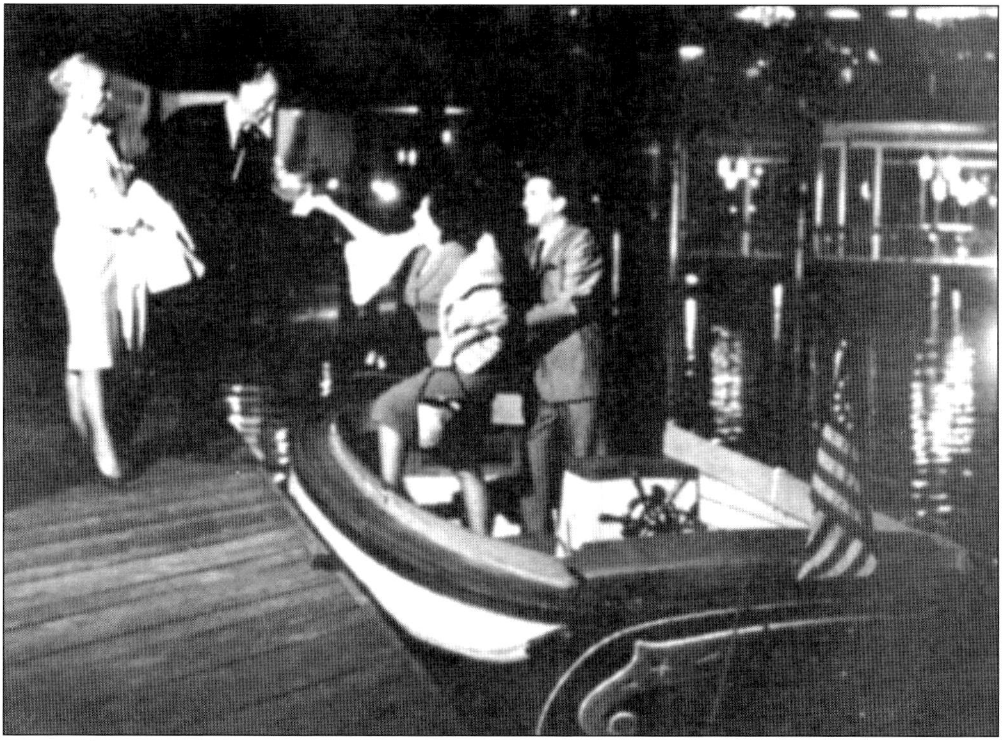

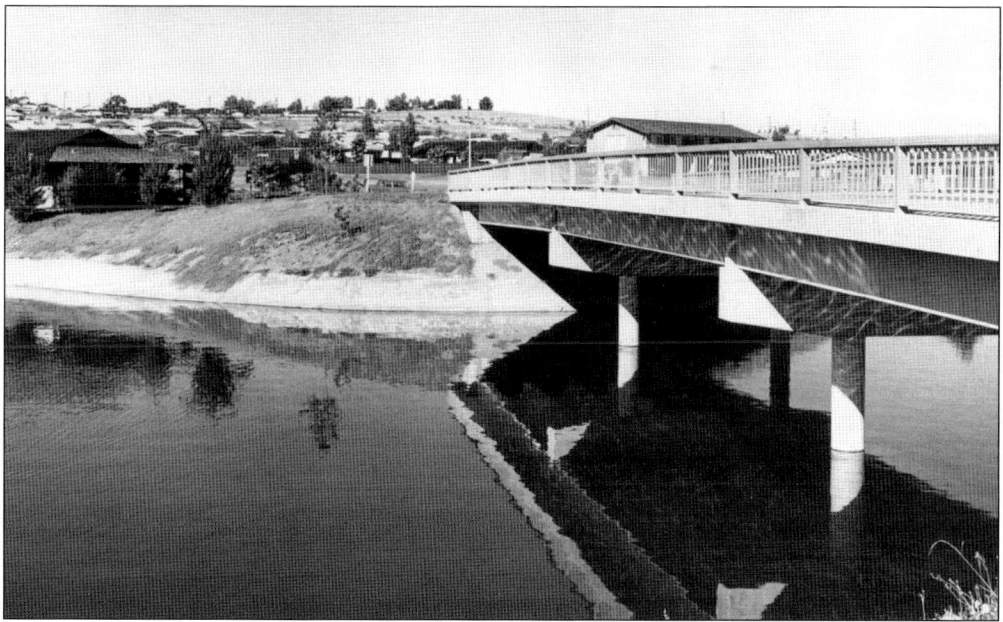

Don and Dorothy Frazar arrived by boat for opening night at the Quail's Inn on July 15, 1963. The dinner house was accessible by automobile or boat, with docks outside its doors. For years, residents loved docking their boats and going in for lunch or dinner.

This is the completed concrete bridge across Lake San Marcos in 1963. The CDC built this bridge with its own funds to maintain control and access. The bridge is still a focal point of the area where residents can watch the boat parades, observe ducks and swans, and see some gorgeous sunsets.

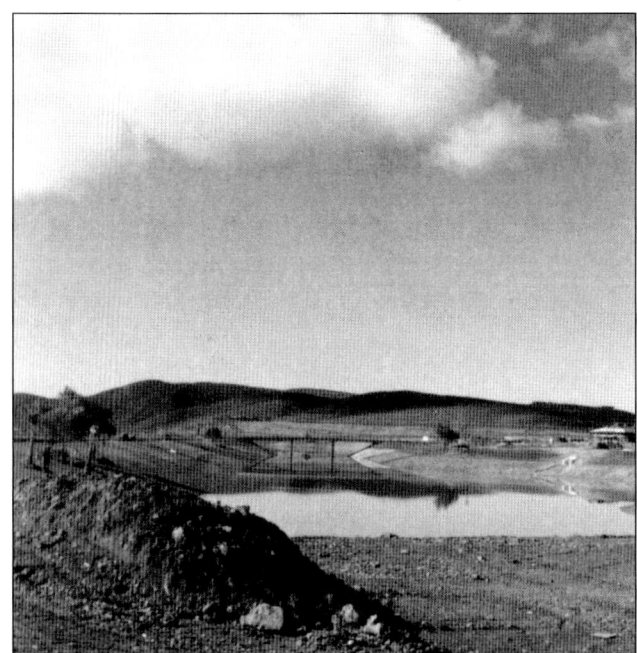

This view of the finished bridge and the surrounding area dates to around 1963. The Quail's Inn Motel is in the distance. The view is to the south before the lake was full. (Author's collection.)

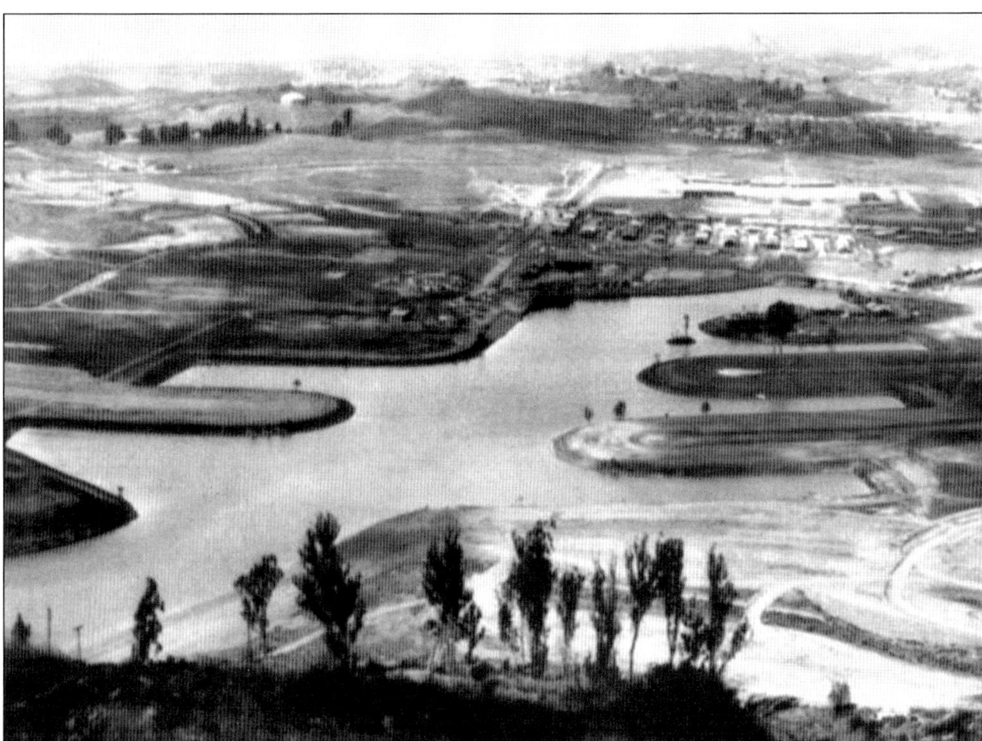

This 1963 aerial photograph was taken looking north and shows the reshaped lake and bridge in the distance. The Frazars dredged the pond, making it wider and deeper, and created numerous inlets. On the right side were the malls, which were greenbelts with the lake at one end. On the left side was the land where Sunrise Pointe Homes was to be built. (Author's collection.)

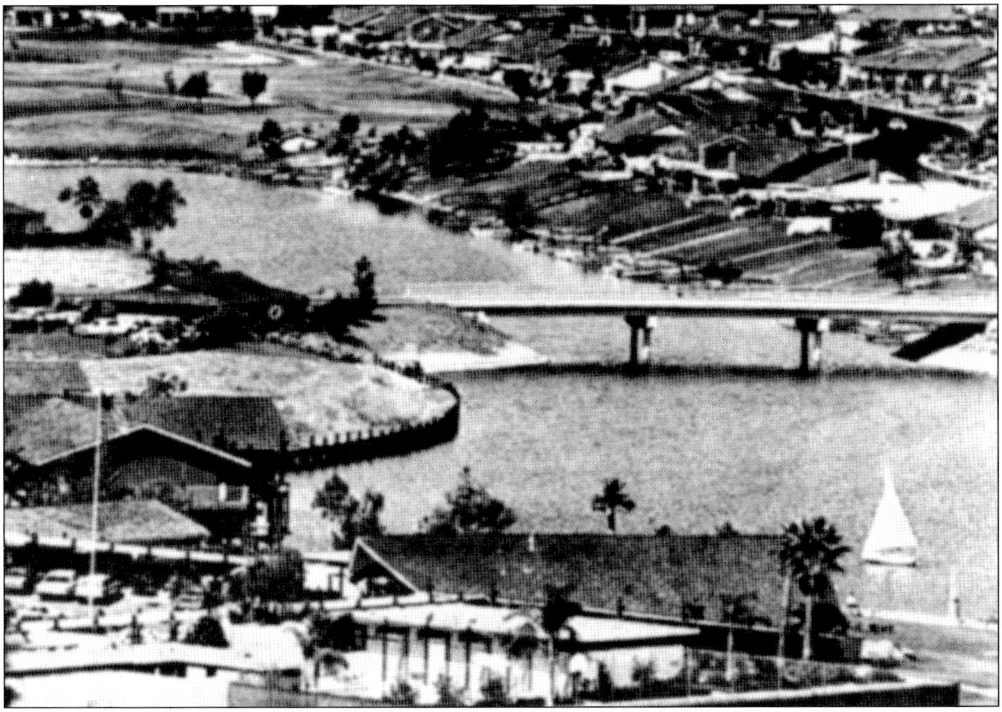

Here, the north end of the lake is seen from a fence post in George D. Clemson's front yard. This was the starting area for the earliest construction of homes. The date of the photograph is unknown.

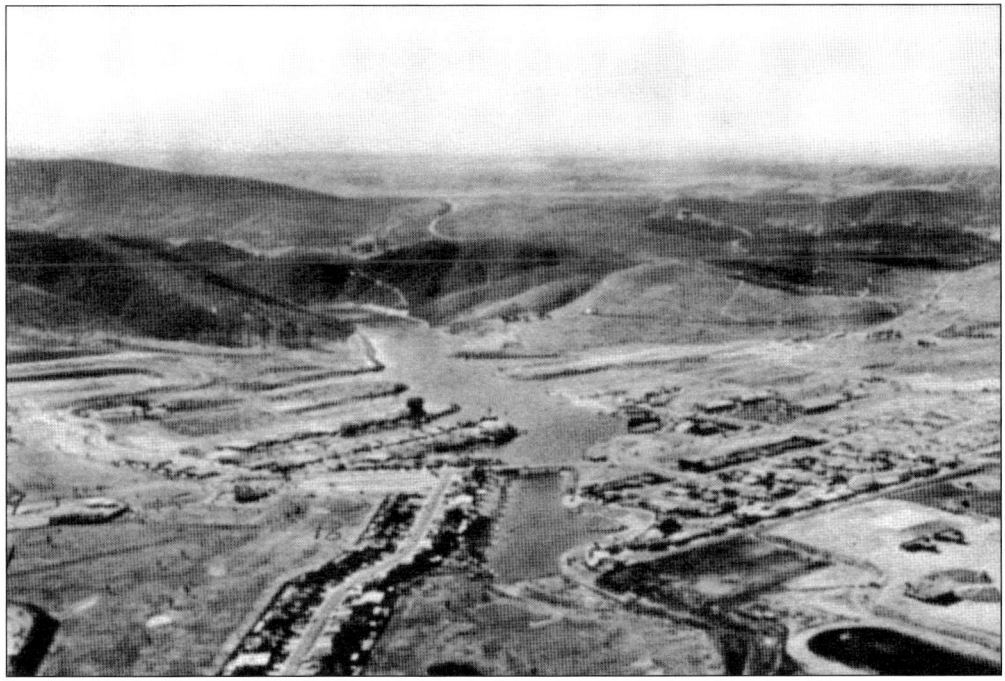

This is Lake San Marcos around 1963, looking southwest with the Pacific on the horizon. It is easy to see why coastal breezes reach the area so readily and keep the temperature mild year-round. Nearby mountains create a wind tunnel, preventing smog from settling in the valley.

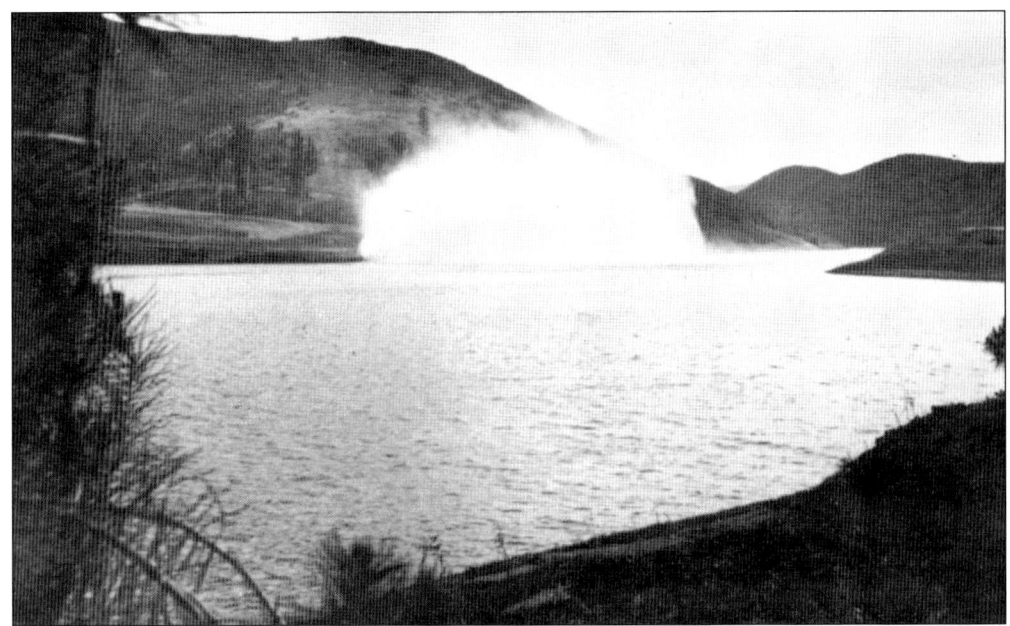

The aqueduct carrying water from the Colorado River was owned by the San Diego County Water Authority and was about six feet in diameter. It went under the lake near the recreation center. Additional water could be purchased to feed the lake from this line if there was ever such a need. The main water supply came from 29 square miles of watershed drain, which included about half a dozen wells and three springs. When full, the level of the lake is 494 feet above sea level. It was 1.3 miles long and 54 feet deep at the dam in 1965. Since then, much sediment has flowed into the lake from San Marcos Creek, and the depths are much less in many areas. For six days in 1963, a plume of water 100 feet high and 200 feet long spouted from a 12-inch valve attached to the San Diego Aqueduct, filling the lake.

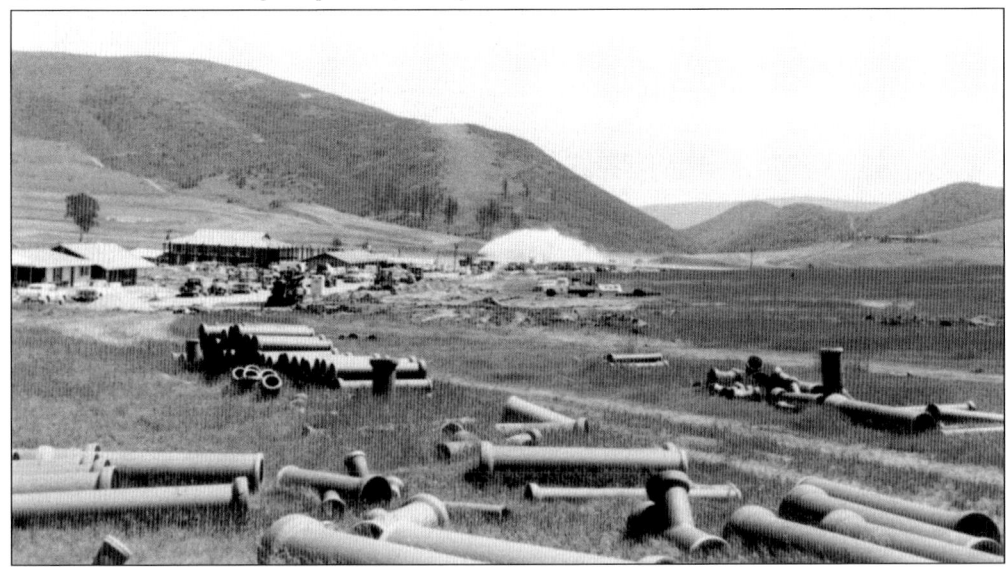

These photographs document early construction in the building of a shopping center in 1963. On the hill at center is the path of the aqueduct. The lighted beacon eventually was located at the top of that path. (Author's collection.)

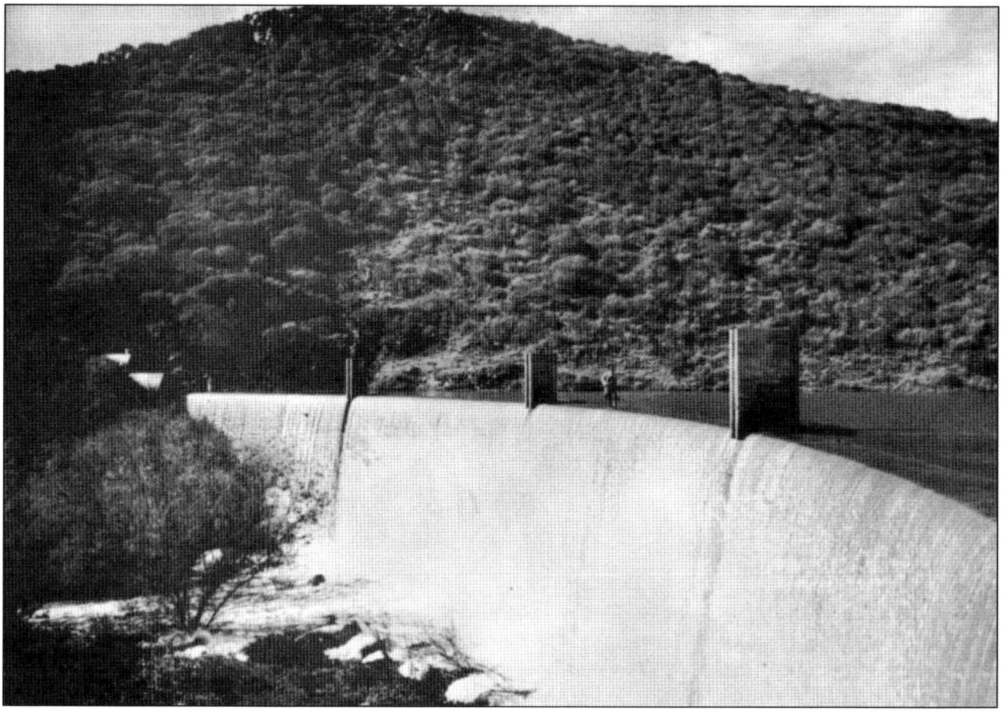

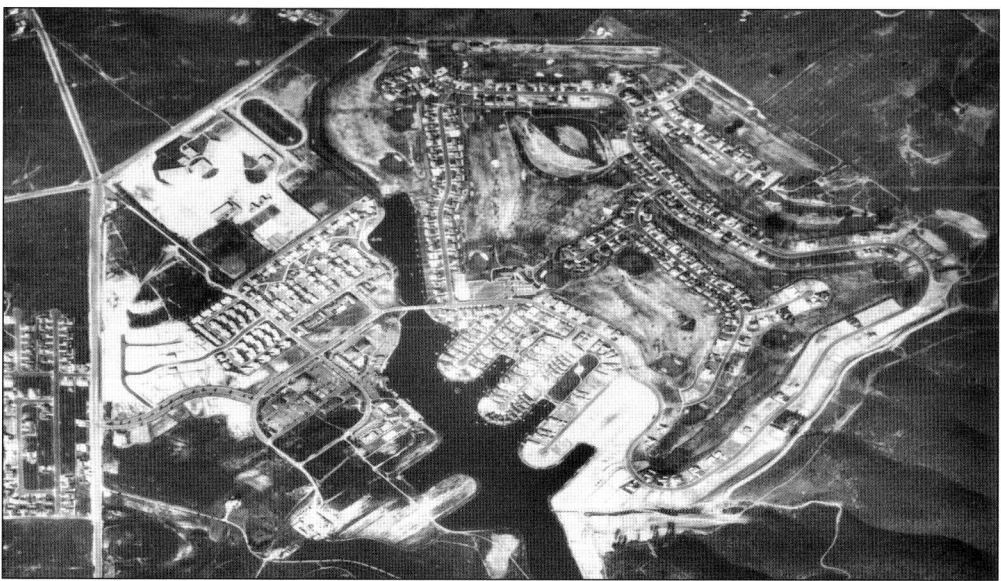

The dam was full following unusually heavy rains in November 1965. The water level was almost 32 inches below the top of the dam on November 1, and by November 23, it was overflowing by between 12 and 14 inches. November rains totaled 6.91 inches that year.

This aerial shot of Lake San Marcos was taken about 1964. San Marcos High School (under construction) is in the upper left. The LSM Country Club and Golf Course can be seen as well, with many homes already built around it. Below San Marcos High School, the first homes built at Sun Park are visible. (Author's collection.)

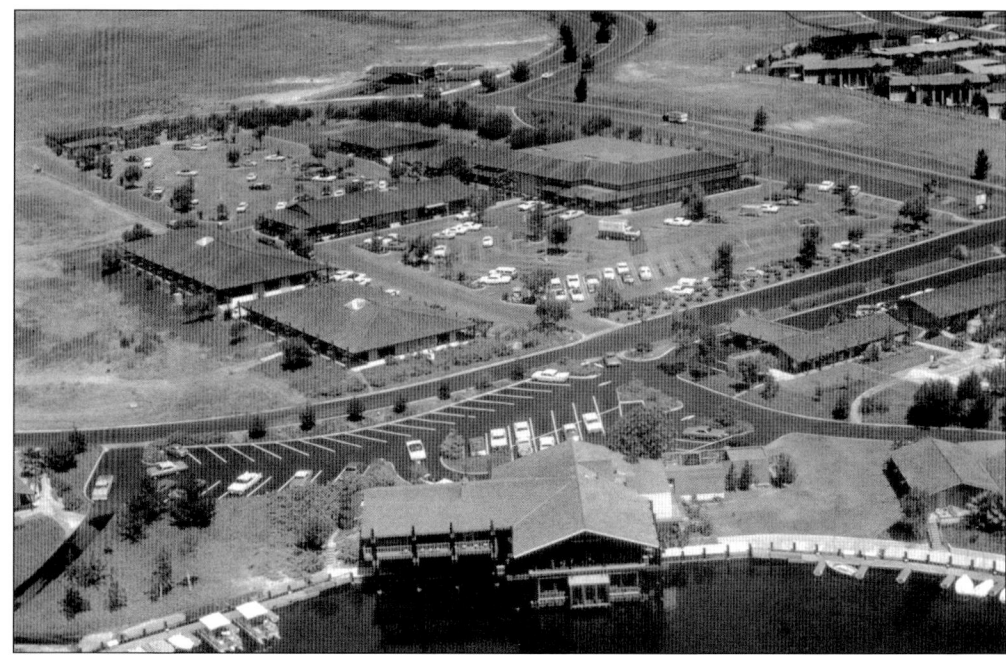
The Quail's Inn Restaurant and the shopping center are visible in this aerial view from 1964. The shopping center opened on August 23, 1964, with 23 merchants and services available to the new community. Harry Deuel was charged with leasing the center. The first homes sold in 1963 for $30,000. (Author's collection.)

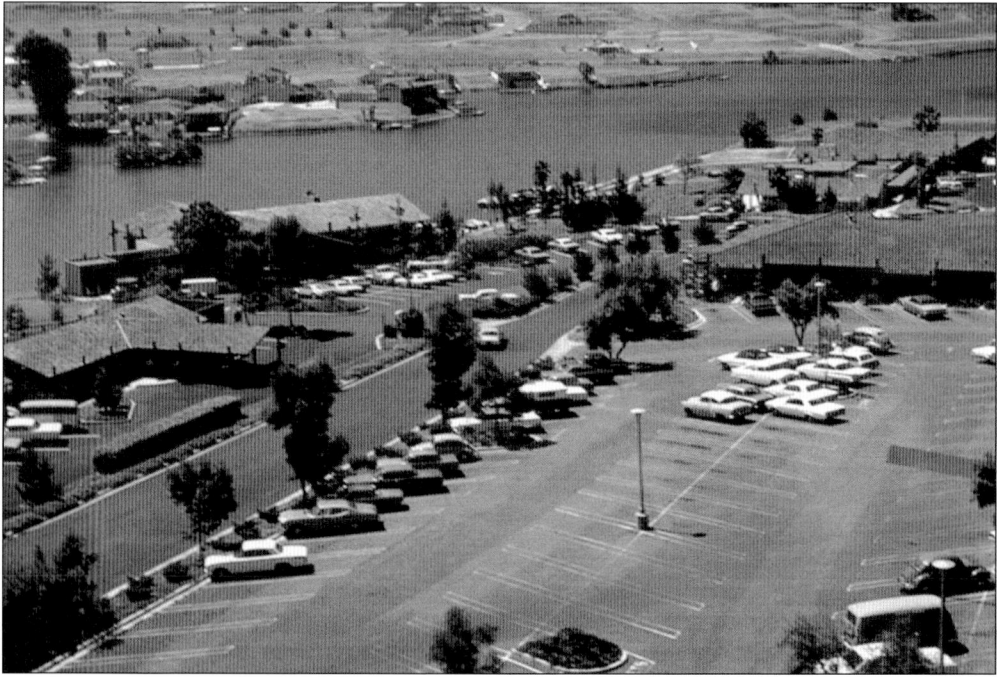
This aerial view of the shopping center's adjacent parking lot was taken sometime in 1965, also capturing the lake and the Quail's Inn Hotel and Restaurant. The shopping center opened in 1964 with 23 merchants and shops. (Author's collection.)

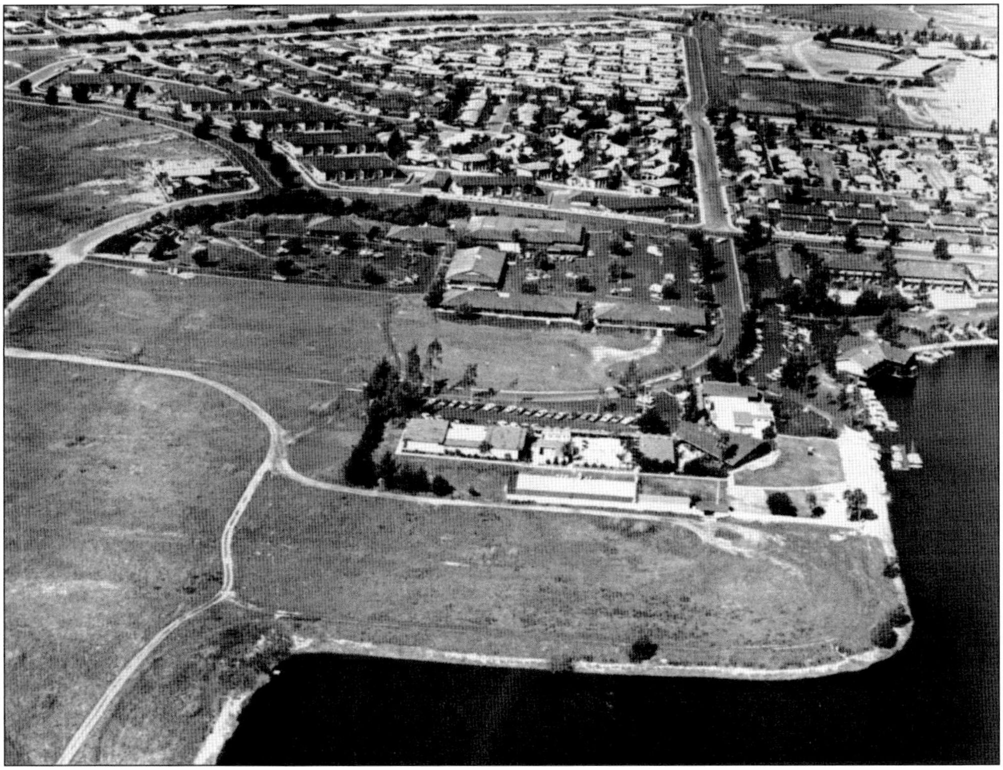

This is another 1965 aerial view of the community, showing the Quail's Inn Hotel, the shopping center, and the recreation areas. San Marcos High School is in the upper right, and most of Sun Park is visible below it. (Author's collection.)

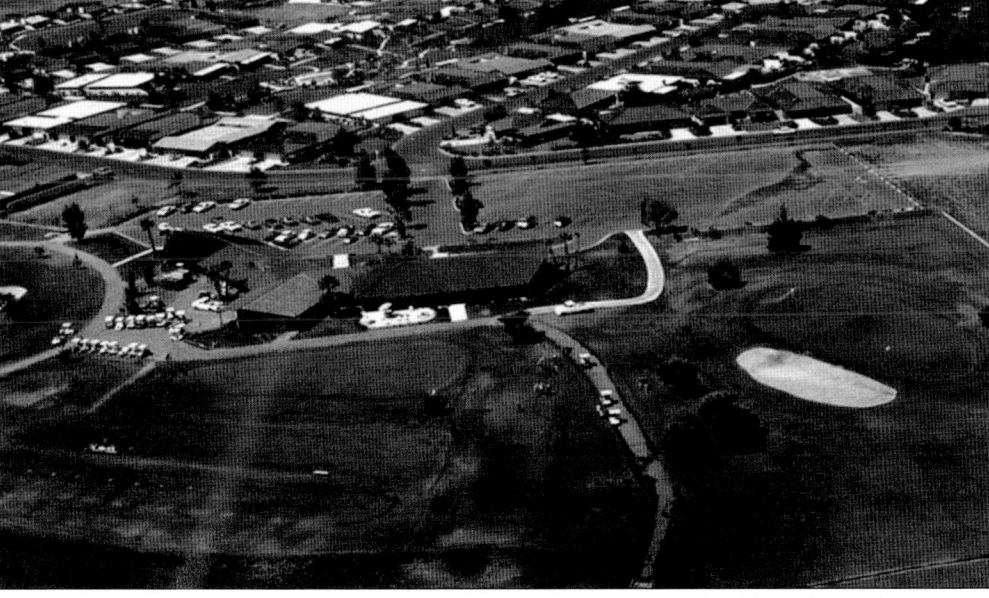

The Lake San Marcos Country Club is seen here on the east side of the lake. The golf course was designed in the earliest stages of LSM development to maximize the number of homes around it. (Author's collection.)

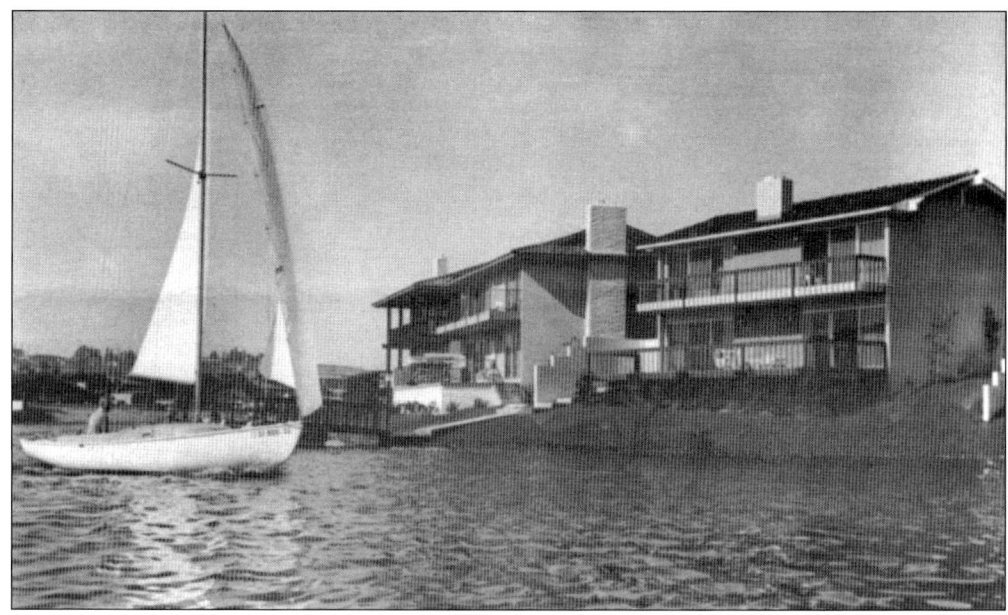

Three new two-story homes were built at the end of La Linda Drive. They were the only two-story homes constructed at the lake. Their first owners were Mr. and Mrs. Stuart Babcock, Mr. and Mrs. Edward J. Piggott Jr., and Mr. and Mrs. Robert Frazar. Two of the homes were furnished as model homes.

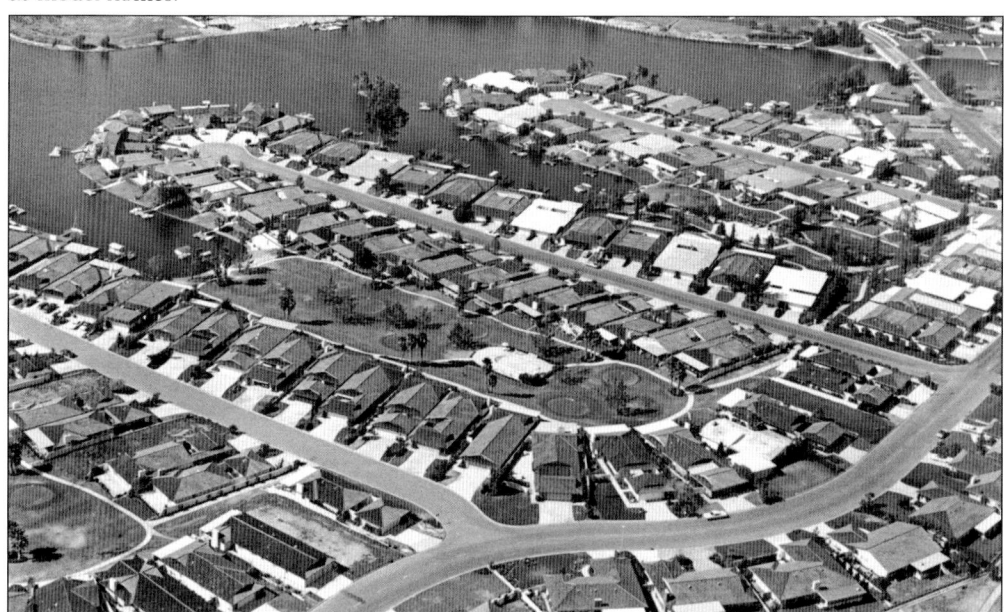

This photograph taken in 1965 captured the areas known as Malls 1, 2, 3, and 4. A mall in Lake San Marcos is a greenbelt surrounded by homes backing up to it. In the middle of the greenbelt is a pool, with docks at the end for boats of mall homeowners. Each mall has a home owner's association with fees to maintain the common area. Mall 4 is partially visible at lower left, Mall 3 is in the center, Mall 2 is just above it, and Mall 1 is the smallest, located just on the east side of the bridge. The malls were originally managed by CDC but in later years were turned over to the residents to organize and establish their own homeowners' associations. (Author's collection.)

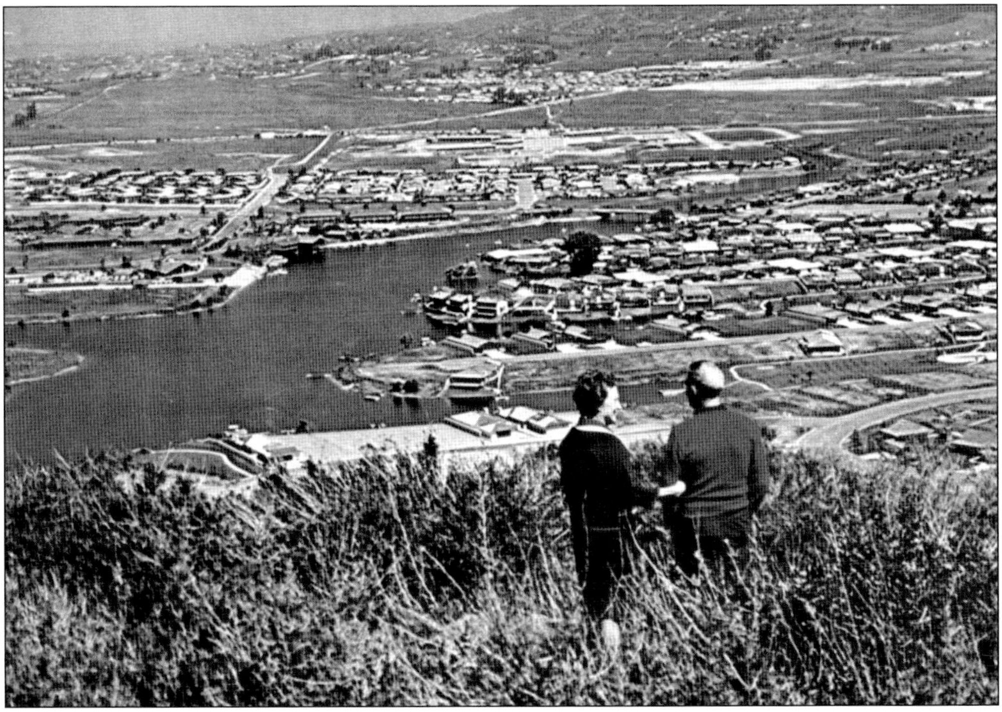

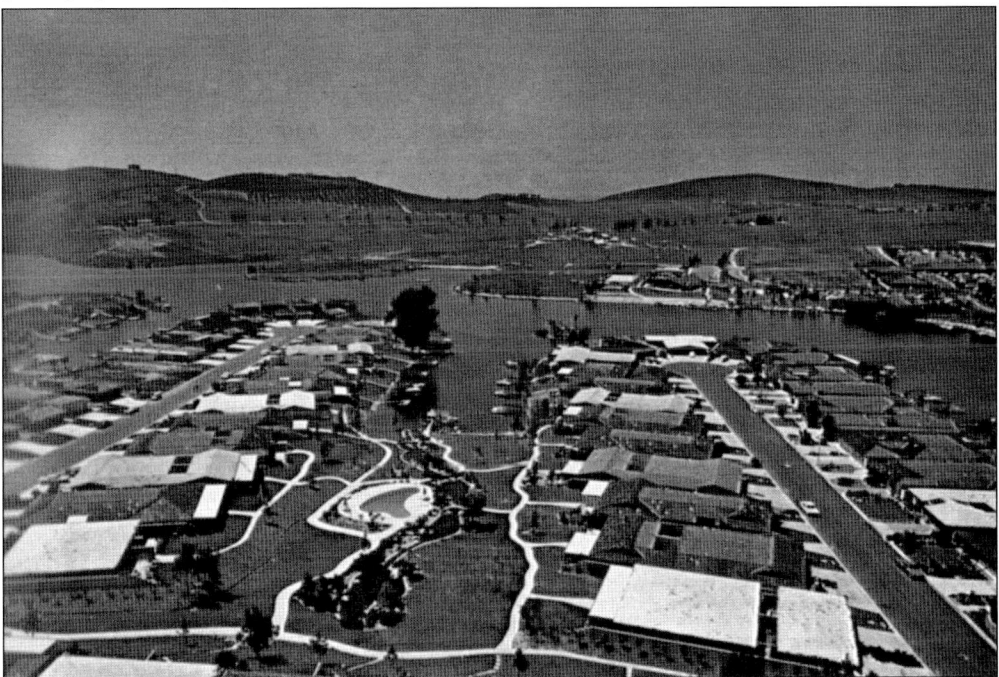

Residents Bill and Amy Arnoldy take in the views of the lake and malls from the hillside. This photograph is looking north.

This view of Mall 2 shows the pool and landscaping, with the lake and docks at the end. Each of the four malls eventually developed its own homeowners' association managed by the residents who lived around it.

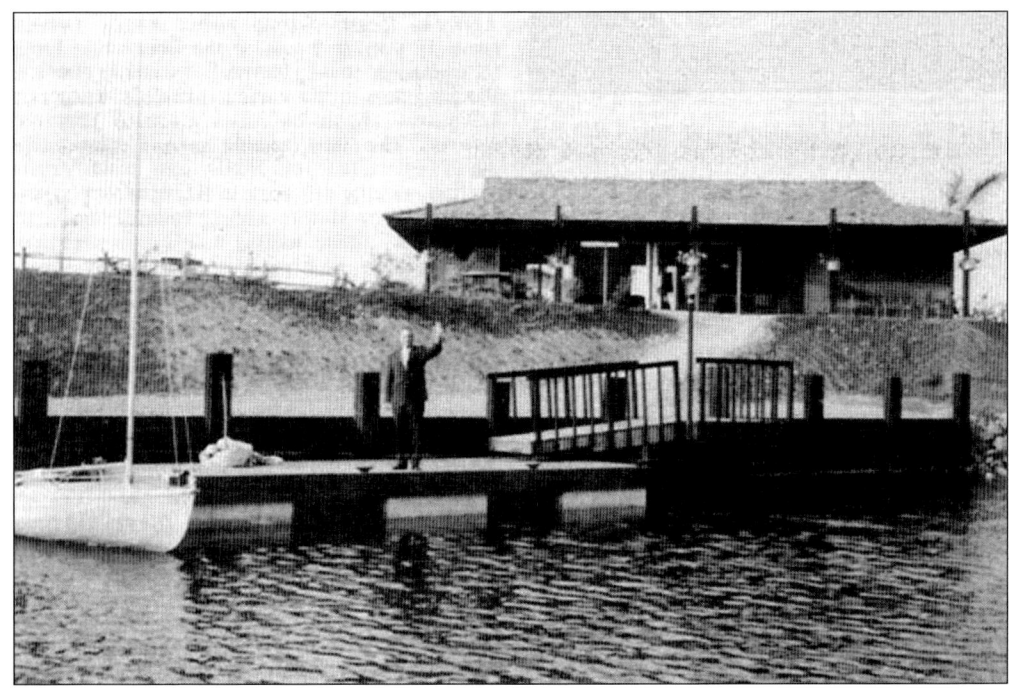
Potential new buyers were given a boat tour of the lake. This photograph shows the new information center, with Bill Corbin waving to prospective buyers.

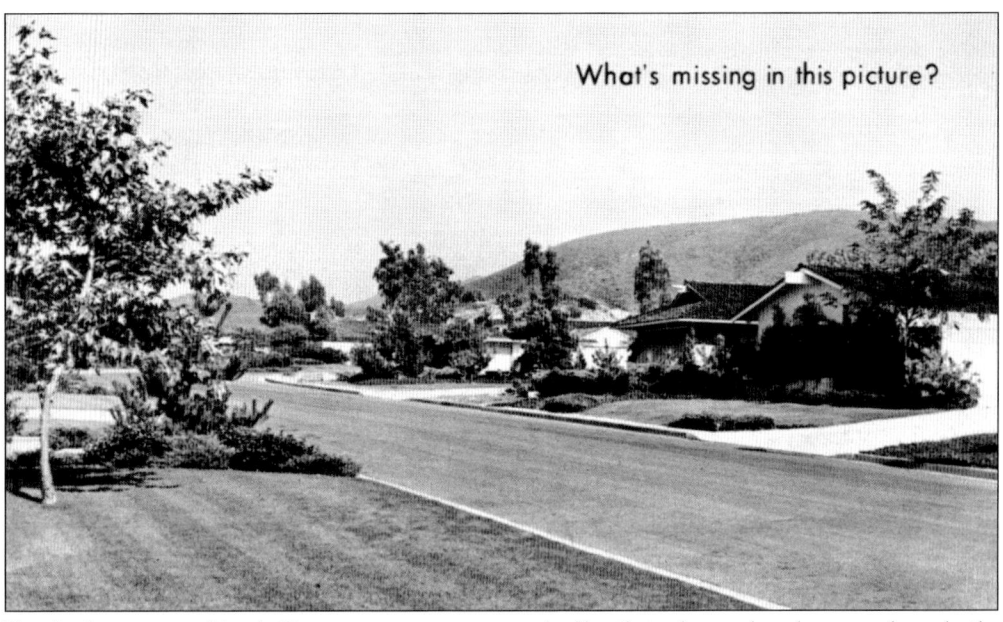
For the first time in North County, a community with all utilities located underground was built. The Frazar brothers were determined to maintain the area's pristine beauty and did not want telephone lines and electric poles littering the landscape. (Author's collection.)

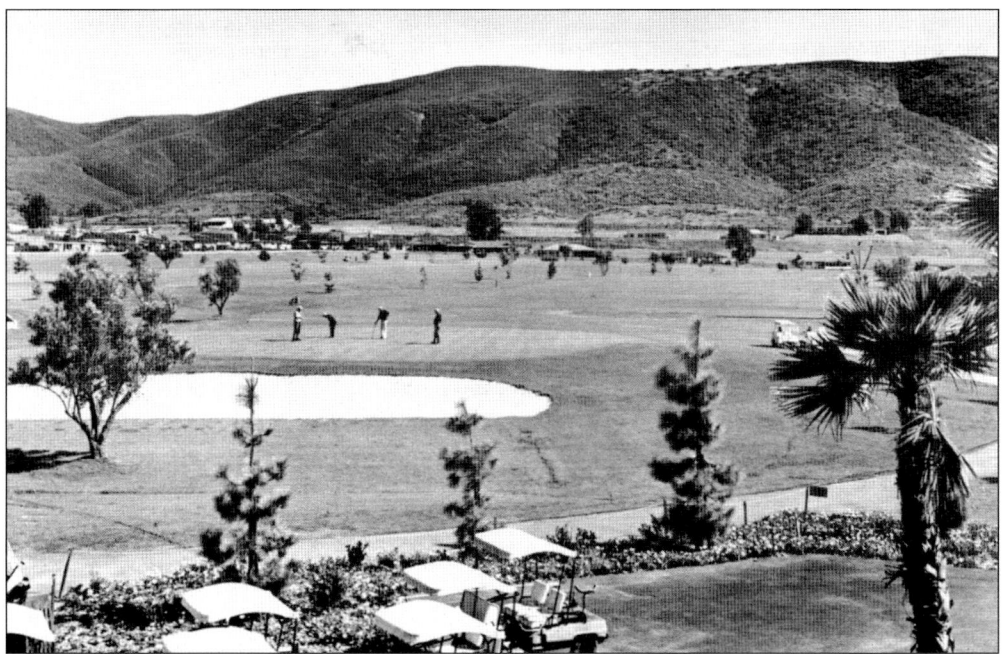

About 400 homes line the LSM Country Club, making for beautiful backyard living. The country club golf course was located on the east side of the dam and was laid out to maximize the views of the homes that would be built around it.

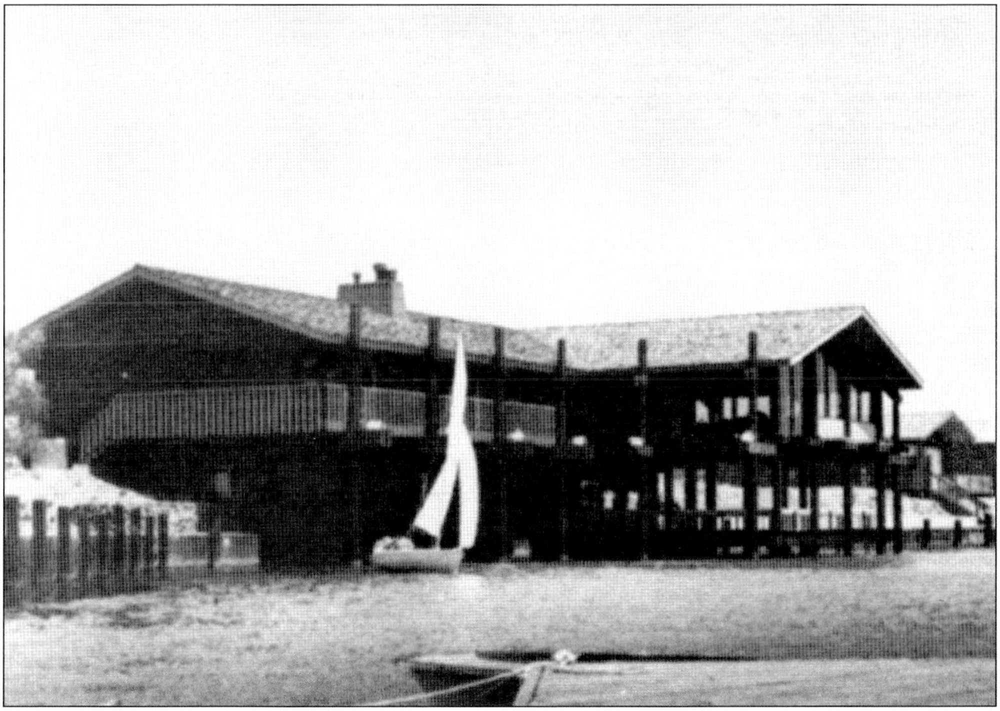

This photograph shows the completed Quail's Inn Restaurant (also named Reuben's Restaurant for a short time in the 1960s). The dinner house was opened on July 15, 1963, and was a favorite restaurant for north San Diego for many years. (Author's collection.)

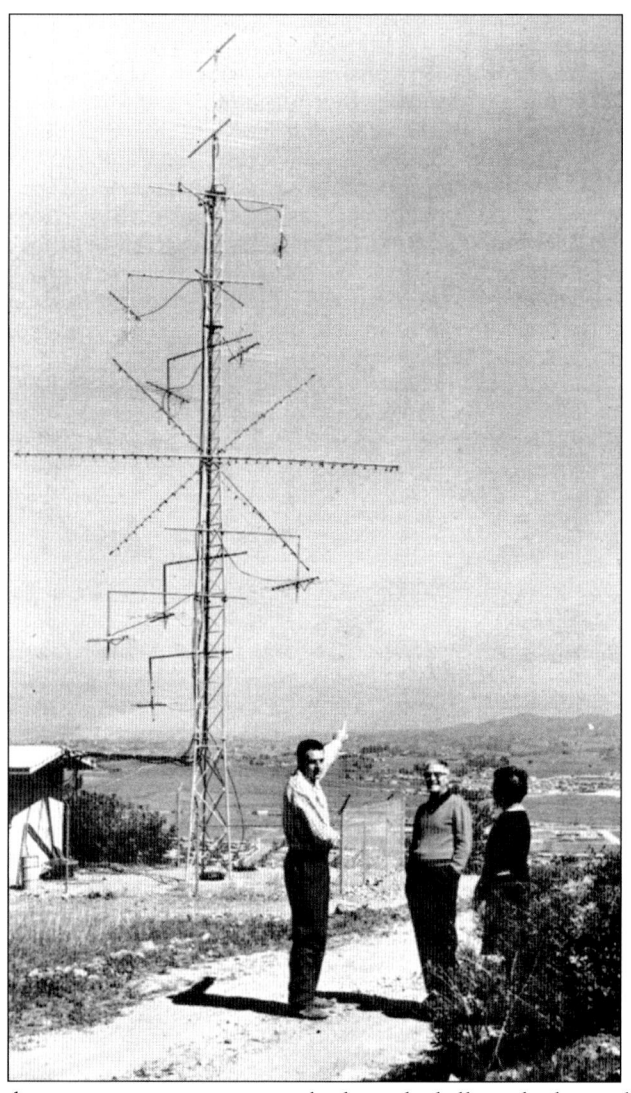

In 1963, a cable and communications tower was built on the hill overlooking what would become Lake San Marcos. The builder of the community, Citizens Development Corporation, owned the land and wanted to provide cable television to the newly planned community. They hired Bob Layton, owner of Cable Tronic Systems, to build and maintain the tower and provide cable service to the residents. During Christmas 1963, he built a cross arm and strung Christmas lights up the tower to celebrate the season and promote the fledgling community. The lights—15-watt bulbs—were easily seen for miles. The response from the community was overwhelming, and the newspapers picked up the story. Soon, the story had made the Associated Press newswires, bringing publicity that led to the cross becoming part of the growing system of landmarks used by pilots to navigate across North County. So Layton kept it up, occasionally replacing light bulbs as they burned out. During the early 1980s, the cable company was purchased by Daniels Cablevision, which continued to maintain the cross. Occasionally, lights would go out and take a week or more to repair, never going unnoticed by the public. Residents in the area considered it a landmark and had strong feelings about keeping it lit year round. According to Layton, the master antenna picked up the signal of Los Angeles and San Diego stations. Lake San Marcos had its own television cable tower built on a hill overlooking the community. (Author's collection.)

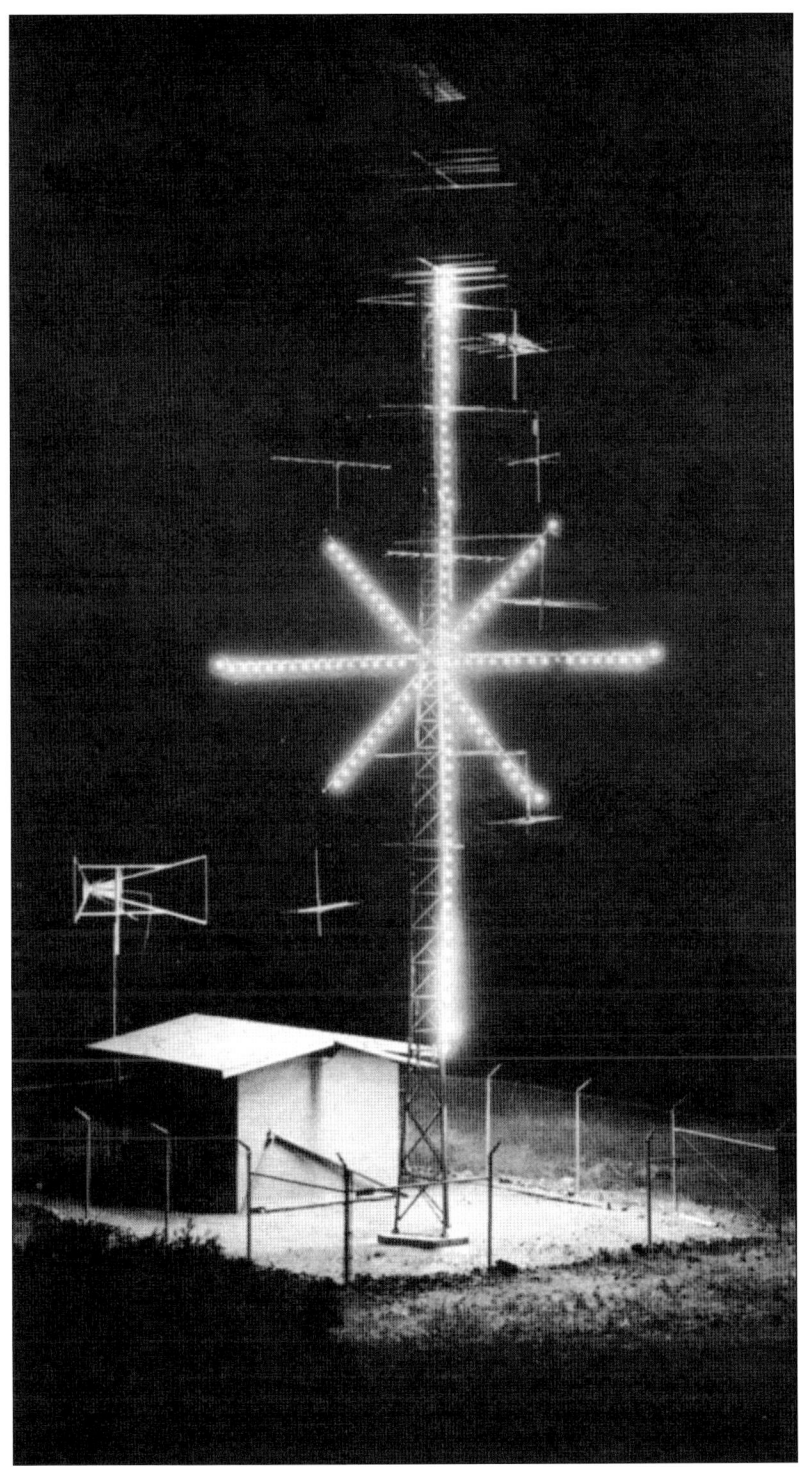

The television antenna on the southern hill, decorated with lights for Christmas, was so well liked that the "star on the hill" became a North County landmark that designates Lake San Marcos. It still shines over the community today and turns into a star at Christmastime. (Author's collection.)

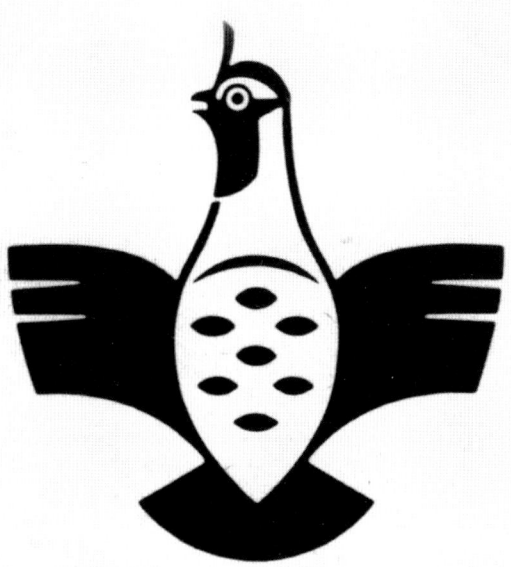

The quail became the logo of Lake San Marcos when Frank Vecchio, an artist with the Hogan and Vecchio advertising agency in Riverside, visited the area. As Vecchio walked through the fields, quail flushed up by the hundreds. After returning to the agency, he created a rough cover for the brochure with the caption, "We're rustling the brush in North San Diego County." He depicted three stylized quails flying up out of the grass. (Author's collection.)

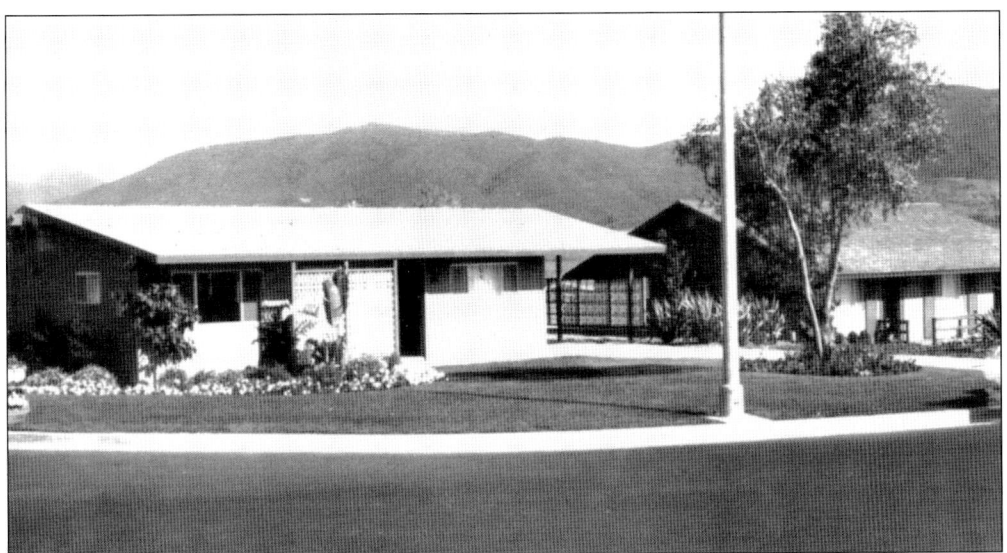

In 1964, Sun Park was the first home development completed and available for sale. This lakeside community of single-story homes was designated a senior community and was a mix of duplex and single-family homes. For recreation, there were a pool, shuffleboard courts, and a clubhouse with pool table, ping-pong table, and full kitchen for entertaining. To become a resident of Sun Park, one had to make an application to become a member and be interviewed and accepted before purchasing a home. The first home built in the development was on the corner of La Bonita and La Casita Drives and was a model home later purchased by Grace C. Warfel from the San Francisco area. Warfel saw the advertisement for Lake San Marcos in the *Los Angeles Times* and bought the model home fully furnished in 1964. The house and furnishings were well cared for and were kept mostly in their original state until being sold in 2005. Most of the homes in the development had two bedrooms with a carport. All the utility lines were buried. (Author's collection.)

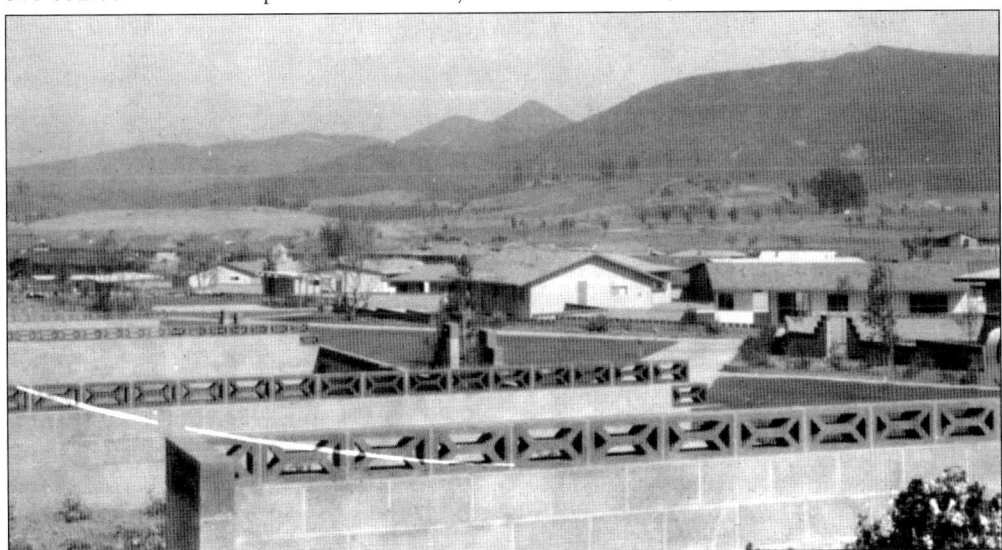

Lots in Sun Park were separated by block walls. Behind most of the lots was a sidewalk that led to the pool and lake so that residents did not have to drive or walk on the roads. Views of the mountains were in the distance. Sun Park is still one of the few age-restricted complexes in Lake San Marcos today. (Author's collection.)

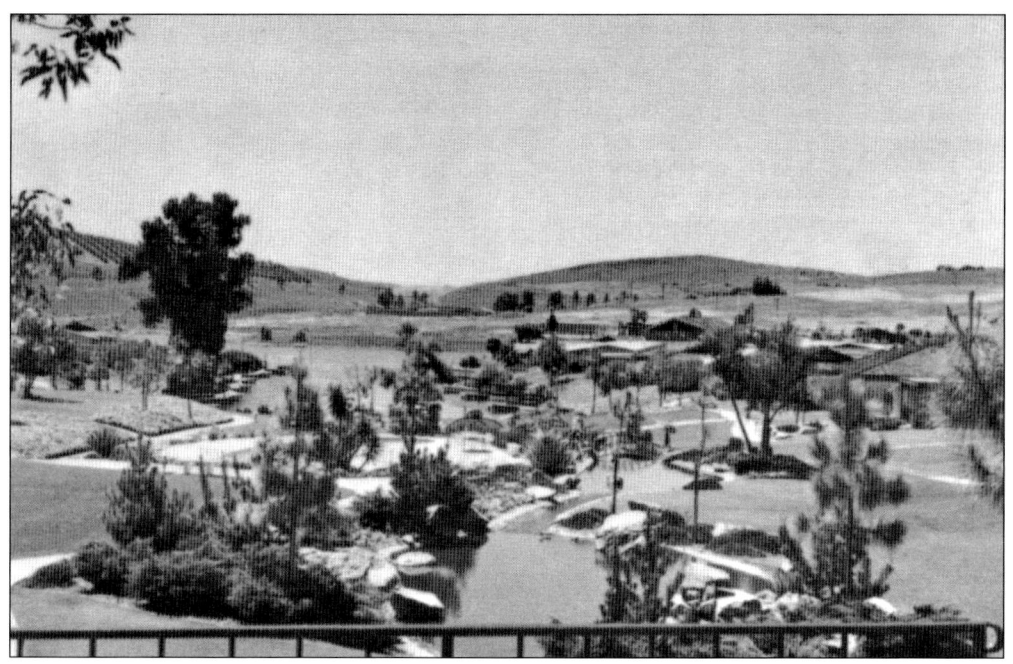

This is a concept drawing of a Lake San Marcos mall. Each mall had a homeowners' association to maintain the common areas. (Author's collection.)

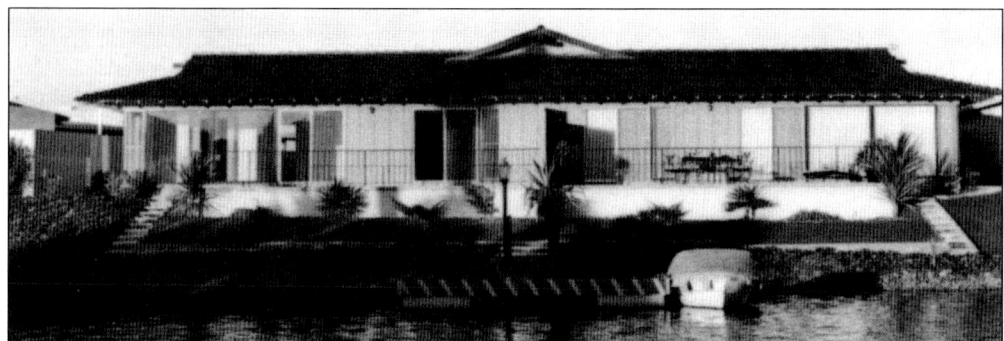

Shown is one pair of the lakefront cottage twin homes at the end of La Habra and La Linda Drives. The homes shared a dock, with both having stairs leading from their patios, and were separated by a block wall between them. Most of the homes on Malls 1 and 2 were twin homes. (Author's collection.)

Two

Early Days

Early life at Lake San Marcos was active and social. The area appealed to retirees because of the climate, the golf courses, and the many social clubs and organizations. The Frazar brothers advertised the community nationwide, and a number of the first residents came from the East Coast or even Hollywood. Jim Murray of the *Los Angeles Times* described Lake San Marcos as "a picturesque man-made finger lake, a little over a mile long, in a valley of the Dons where the Frazar brothers . . . have built a self-contained community seven miles from the sea, 1,500 acres of green hills and gold meadows."

Bill Kennedy, "Mr. L.A." of the *Los Angeles Times*, described watching a group of small boys fishing from the shores of Lake San Marcos: "Instead of the poles and bent pins, the young fishermen were employing a technique new to me. They spread out a towel, sprinkled with a few potato chips, just below the water level and the blue gills leaped into it by the dozens." Kennedy goes on to write about Don Frazar, a former two-time Marine combat pilot, saying, "He and his brothers put Lake San Marcos resort area together as a personal campaign to combat ulcers. The emphasis is on quiet and serenity and this has to be one of the few places within the easy reach of Angelenos where it has been achieved. They constructed the place with such deliberate thought that, if I were Howard Hughes, I would buy it for my very own and put a large sign in low-key lighting, which would read: 'please Do Not Disturb Middle Aged Man Smiling.' "

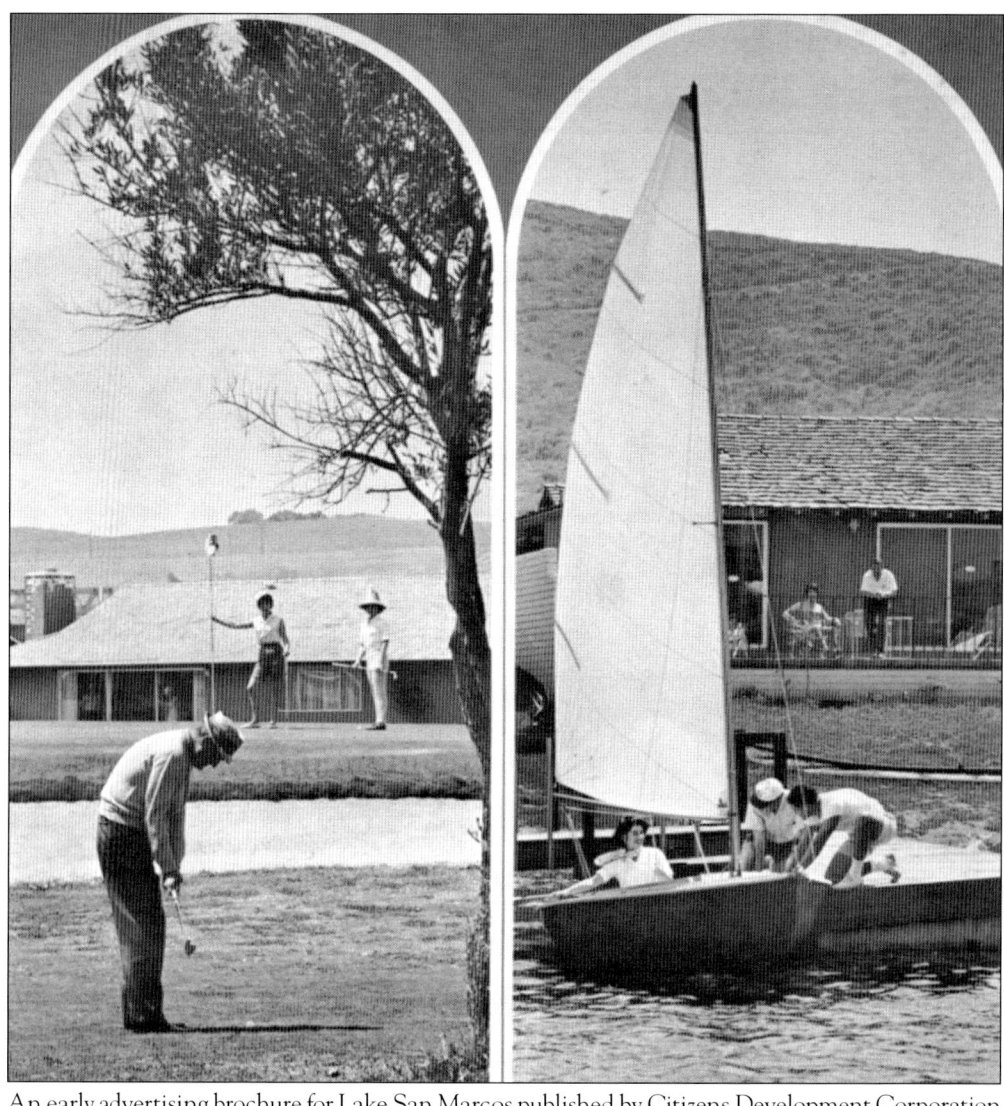

An early advertising brochure for Lake San Marcos published by Citizens Development Corporation is pictured here. The resort was advertised in many newspapers in the United States, including the *Los Angeles Times*. Many of the first homebuyers and visitors came from Los Angeles, Hollywood, and the East Coast. (Author's collection.)

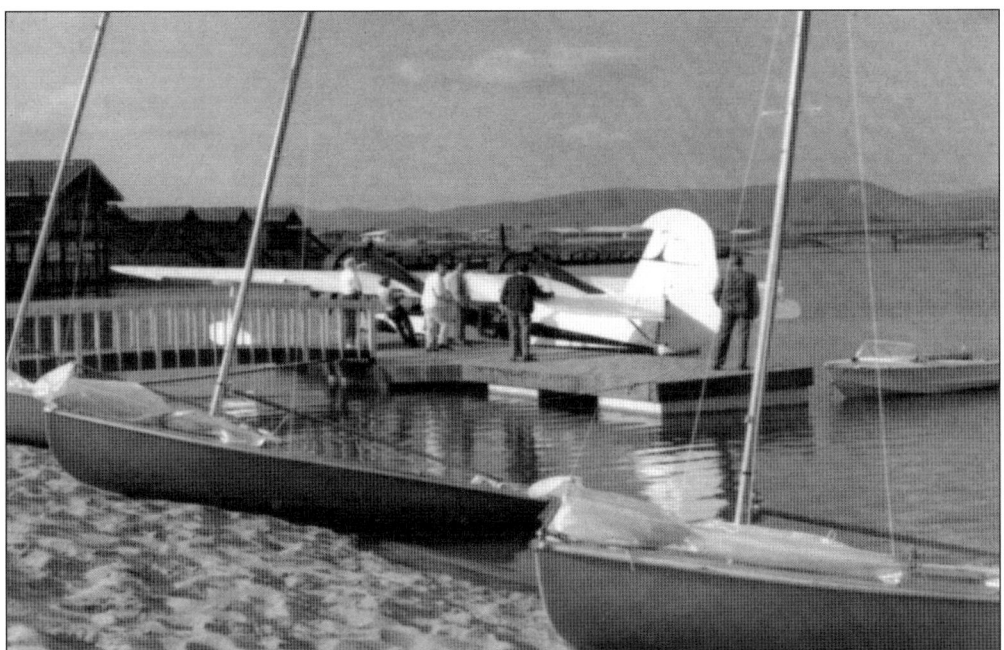

Citizens Development Corporation flew dignitaries in from the Los Angeles area to promote their new development. The planes landed on the lake and taxied up to the docks at the Quail's Inn. The Frazar brothers were excellent at advertising and marketing Lake San Marcos. (Author's collection.)

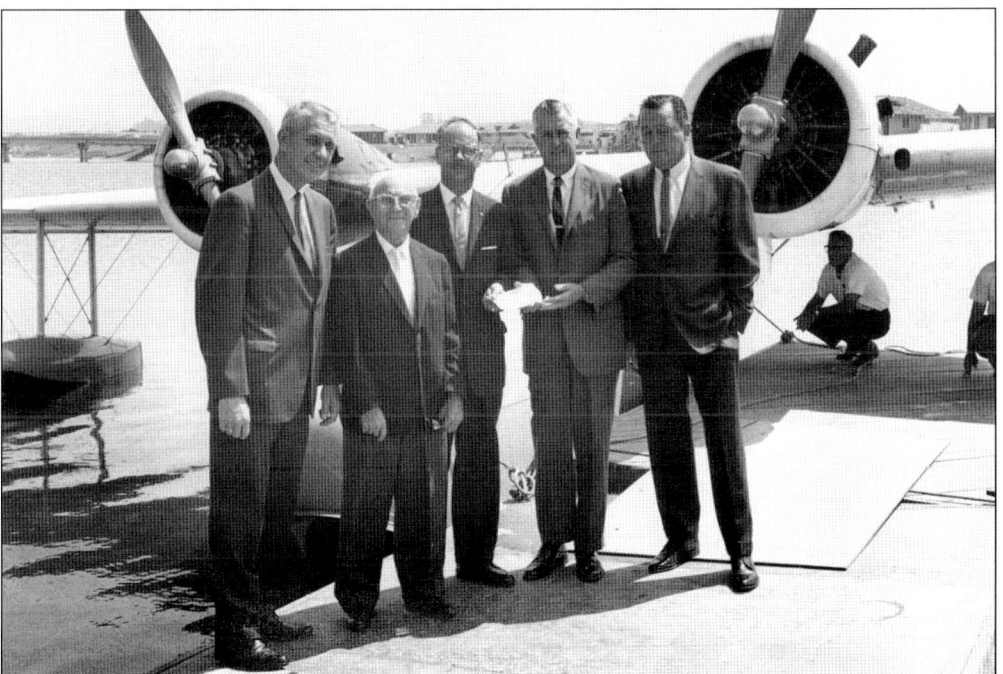

Gordon Frazar (far right) and dignitaries were flown into Lake San Marcos on a hydroplane. One of the keys to the Frazars' success was that they built most of the development's amenities before they started selling homes.

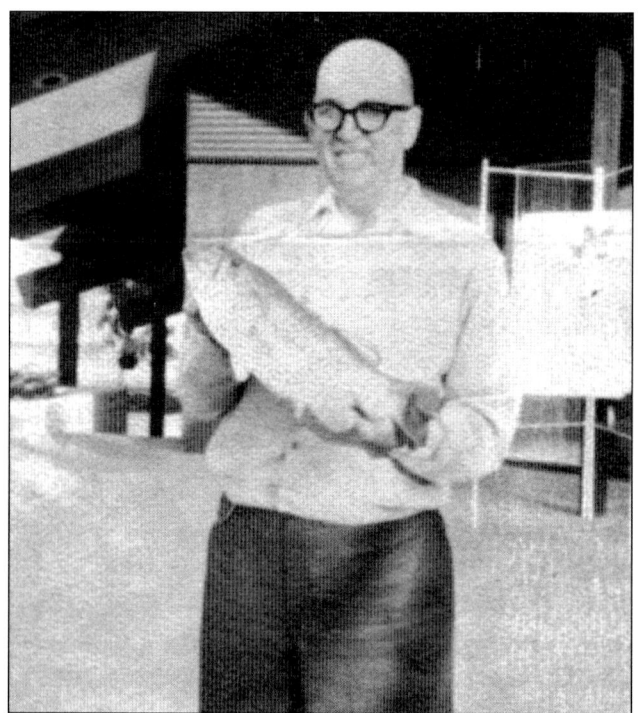

John Wyatt caught this 18-inch long, 4.5-pound bass while fishing off of his dock. He was trying to perfect a cast that would permit him to sit in a chair on his porch, therefore saving his energy for the golf course. A Massachusetts native, Wyatt moved to California in 1948 and was active in LSM Kiwanis and the coordinating council, also serving as commodore of the yacht club.

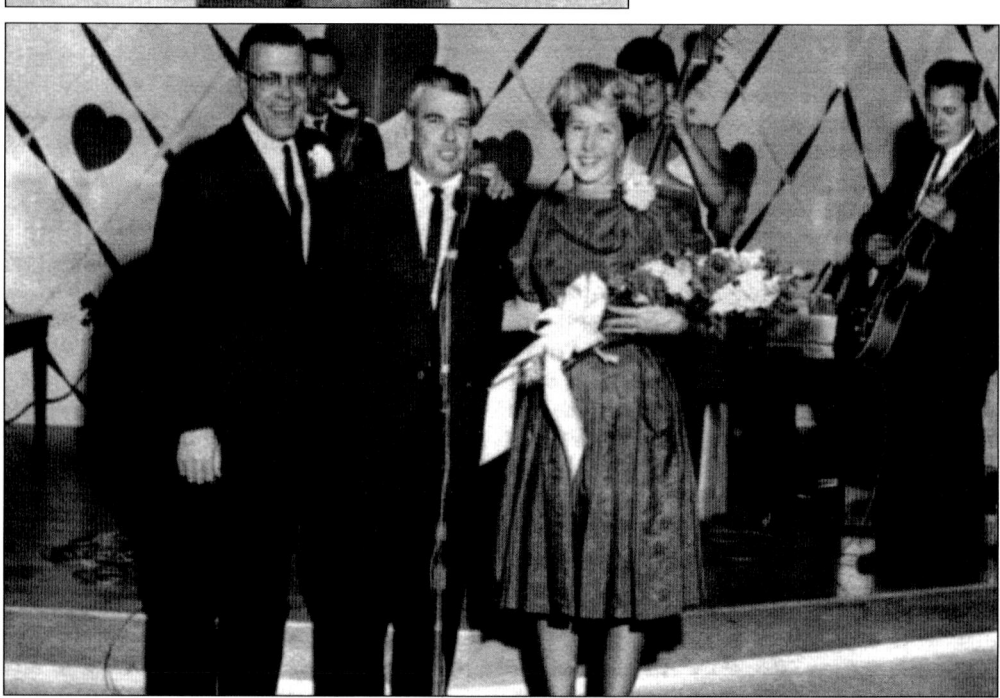

Mr. and Mrs. Robert Christy were elected sweethearts of the second annual Valentines Ball, held at the Recreation Lodge. They are shown here with Bob Dawson, recreation director, standing between them. The sweethearts were also invited to be guests at all Recreation Lodge dances for the remainder of the year. The Recreation Lodge held monthly dances for the residents, and they were very popular for many years.

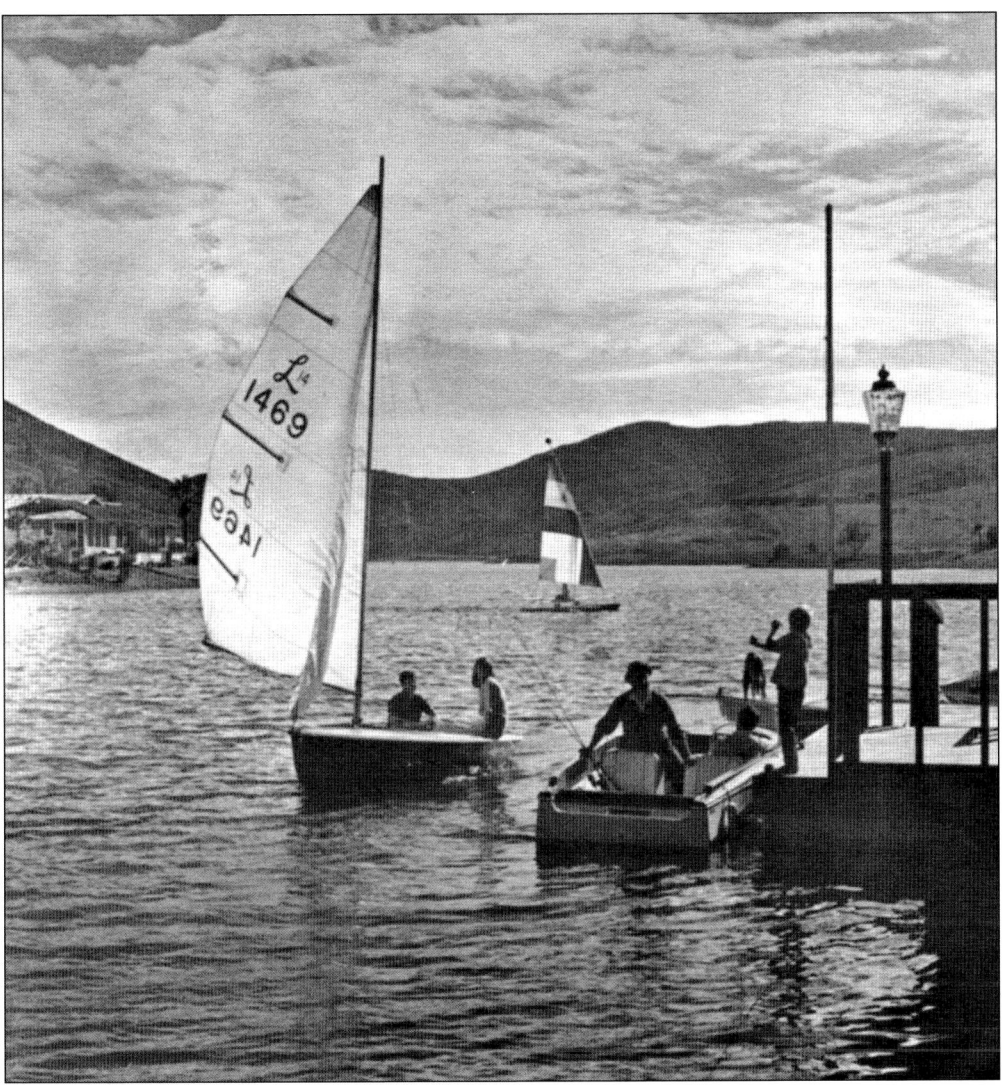
The 1965 Huck Finn Day fishing derby was sponsored by the San Marcos Little League. The day resulted in many bluegill and catfish being caught by more than 520 youngsters. In all, 1,958 fish were caught: 1,325 bluegill, 625 catfish, and 8 bass. The largest single catch of the day was 63 fish. The youngest prizewinner was four-year-old Cary Craig of Vista, California.

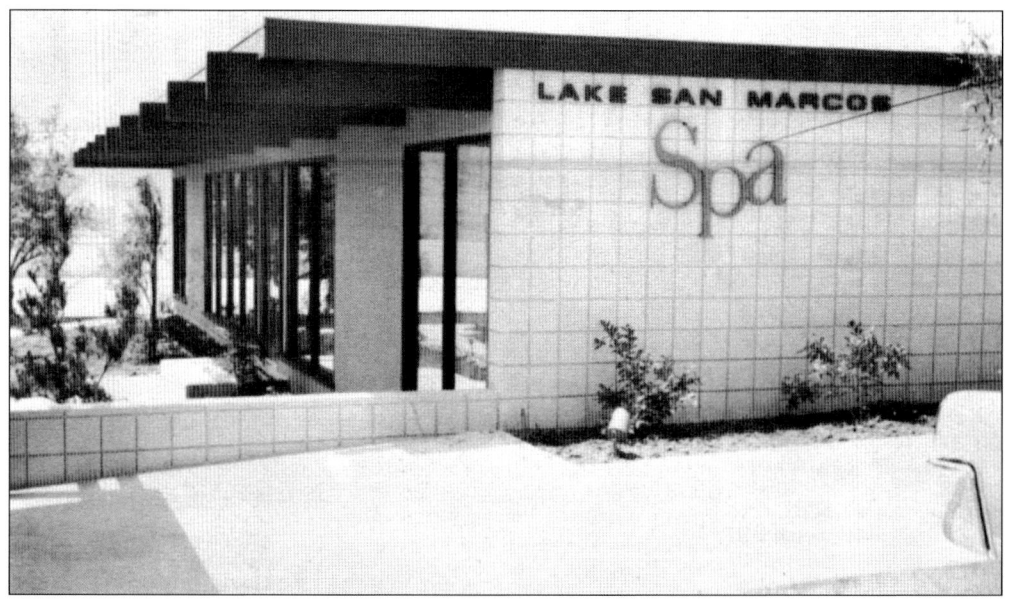

The Lake San Marcos Spa officially opened on June 3, 1965, after its "coming out" participation in the Country Friends Summertime Festival. Many celebrities attended, including Carroll Righter, the internationally famous astrologer. The festival was a very ambitious charitable and social event for the area and was attended by many people. In July, the spa began offering "Figure Improvement and Body Conditioning" programs for men and women on Monday and Thursday evenings; these included use of the sauna, hydrotherapy, and exercise pools.

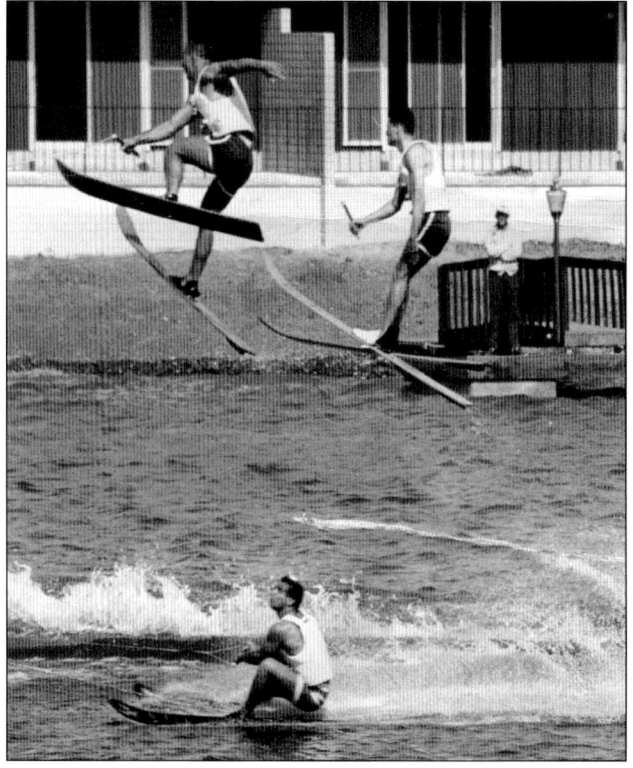

An action photograph from the LSM Invitational Water Skiing Tournament is seen here. Larry Panacho (1963–1964 national overall champion) cut under two jumpers in the dangerous crisscross jump. He went on to participate in the June 19 Lake San Marcos Invitational Water Ski Tournament. Those one-day events were popular with the residents and brought many new people to this area. Water sports were important to the lakeside community, and the yacht club is active to this day.

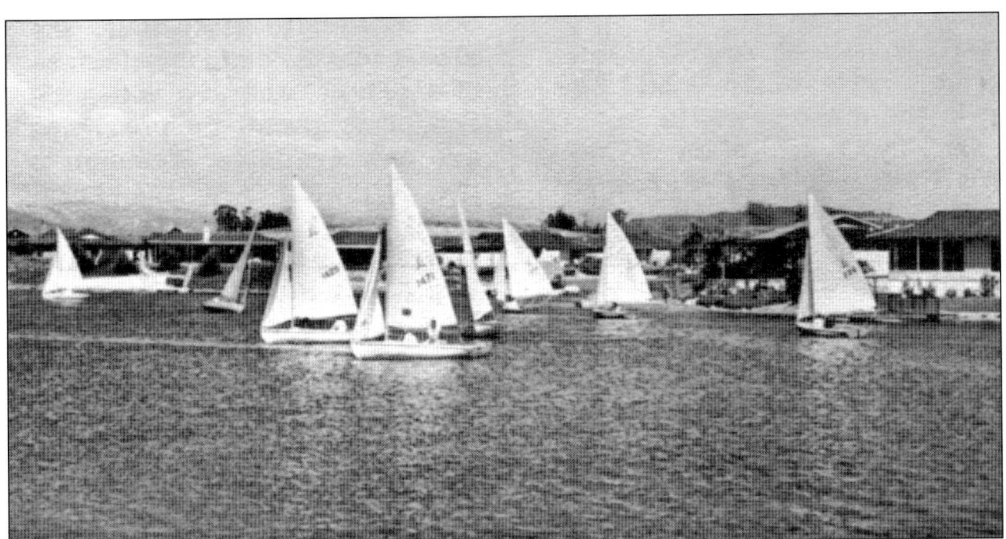

There were 22 boats that participated in the second annual Lido 14 Regatta at Lake San Marcos. Yacht clubs represented included Oceanside, Lake Arrowhead, King Harbor, Lido Isle, and Mission Bay. First place in the Class A races was won by Ed McKenzie from Alamitas. Five teams participated, each sailing in three races. Juniors between the ages of 12 and 18 were encouraged to learn to sail, and classes were held each summer without charge.

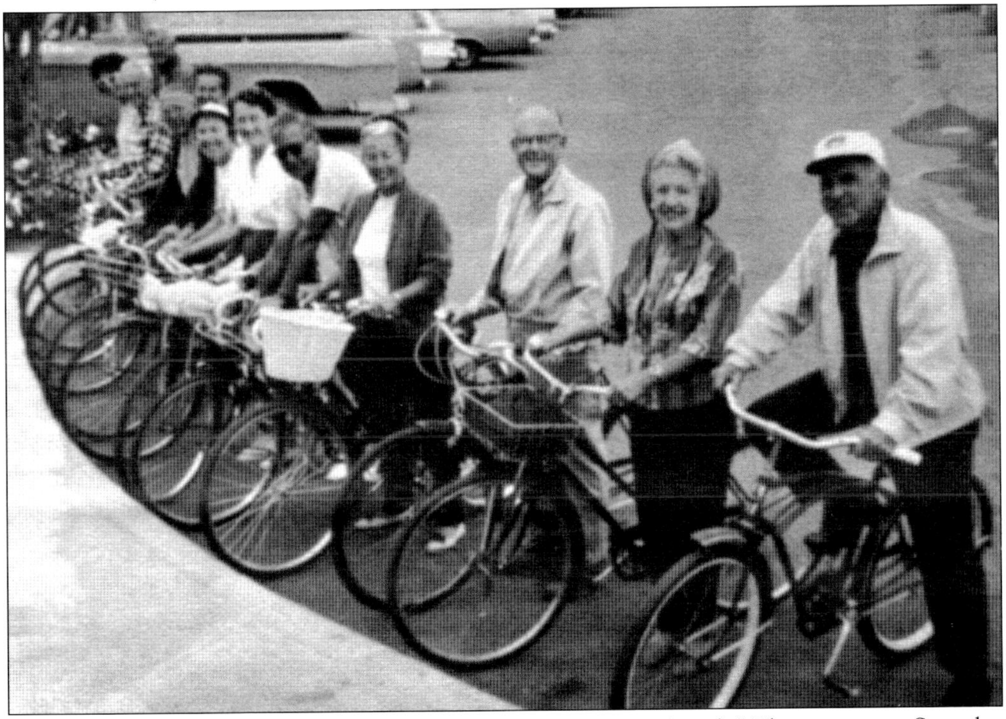

The Lake San Marcos Bicycle Club called themselves "Heaven's Angels." They met every Saturday morning and rode for about an hour and a half. Purely a social club, they rode for fun, exercise, and good fellowship. Many rides took them down back roads and through country scenery. Marion Griffiths first mentioned the idea of starting a bicycle club in 1965, and it was opened to everyone at the lake, including beginners. The club was active in Lake San Marcos for many years.

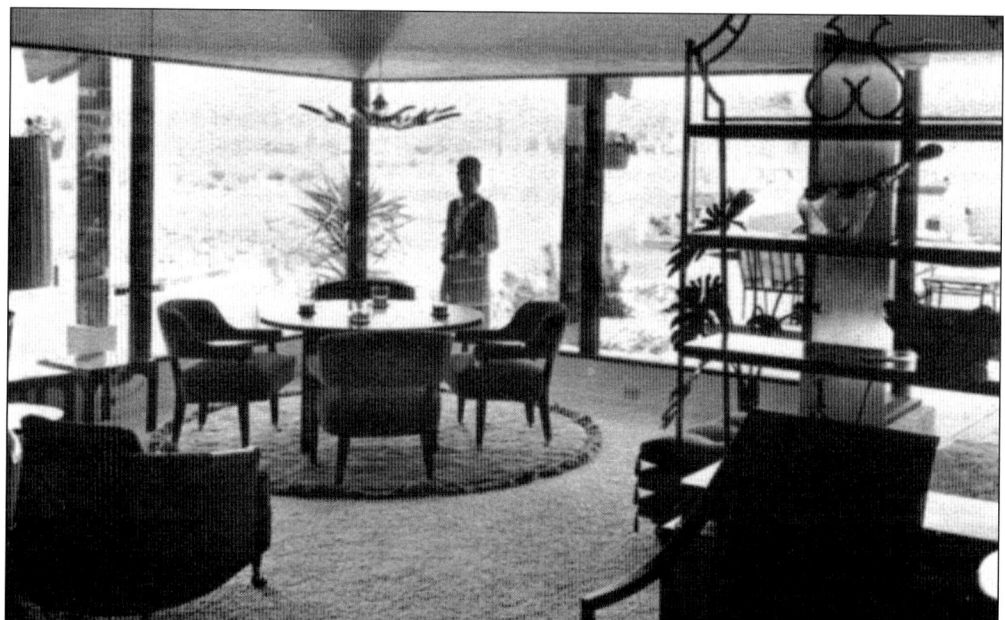

Jessica Furst arranged an attractive display in Tom Furst's decorator studio in the LSM Shopping Center. Her husband, Tom, was one of the finest decorators in the area, and Furst Interiors was a popular shop in the center.

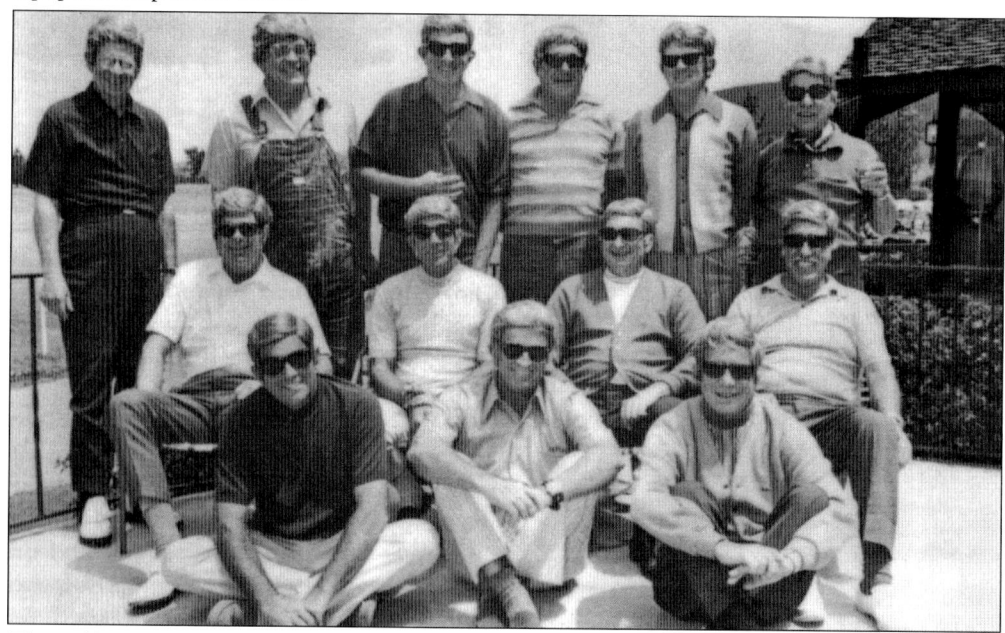

The golfing group pictured here, sometimes known as the "Flying Divots of Lake San Marcos," gathered for a formal portrait in the newest disguise of wigs and sunglasses. The story of their "dome doilies" and golf antics was picked up by a news service covering some 600 papers nationally. Obviously, they would do anything for attention. Pictured from left to right are (first row) Wes Stevens, Don Sharp, and Bob Wilson; (second row) Don Heffer, Bob Steven, Hall Grisamer, and Mike Graziano; (third row) Art Benton, Neil Montank, Bill Ream, Gordon Frazar, Jack Vanderbeck, and Val Browne.

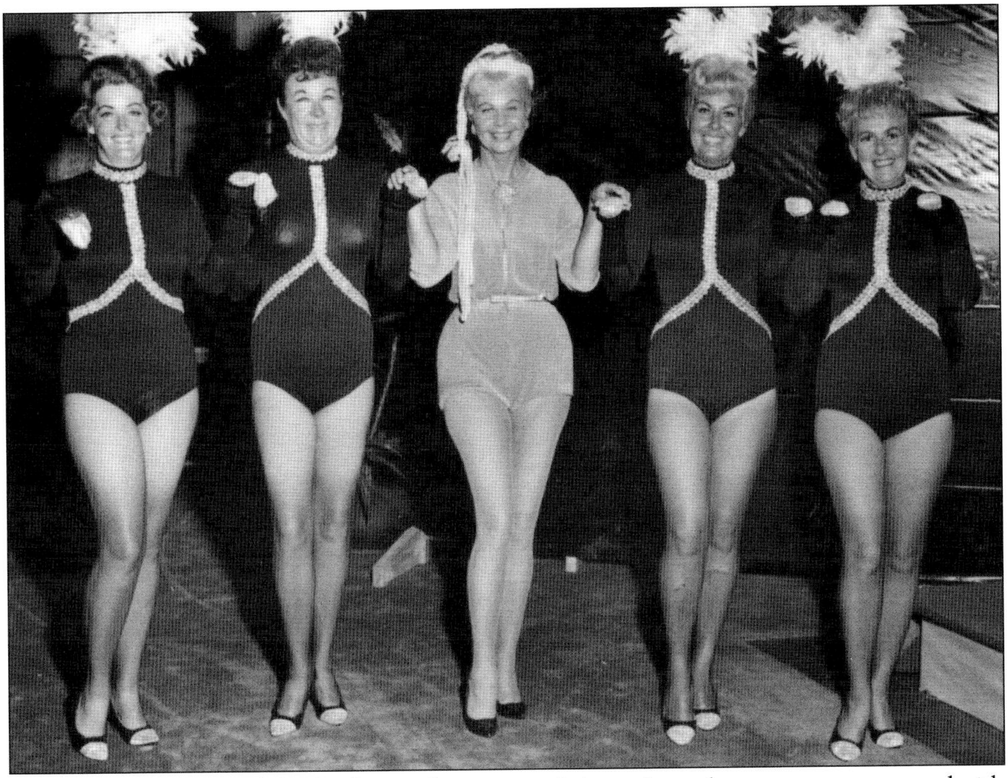

The LSM women's golf club's third annual invitational circus-themed tournament was staged with 106 guests from 45 Southern California and Arizona golf clubs. The golf gala included a dinner show under the big top produced by Eddie Ream. Pictured from left to right are Grace Meyer, Eddie Ream, Anolyn Arden, Irene Garnjobst, and Dorothy Faulkner.

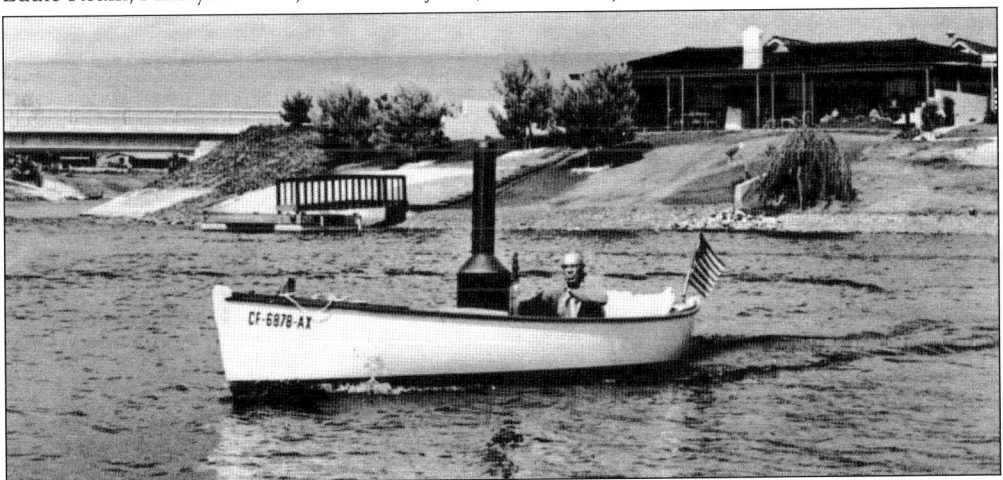

The newest addition to the Lake San Marcos fleet was a 16-foot steamboat with Stuart Babcock at the helm. Stu's grandfather invented the Babcock boiler, an item any resident with an industrial background was bound to remember. Castings for the boiler and engine were produced in England to Babcock's designs. The hull was made in Costa Mesa. It was fired with butane and developed a working head of steam in three minutes. The engine developed 900 revolutions per minute and was directly connected with the drive. The boat traveled at about six knots and could stop on a dime.

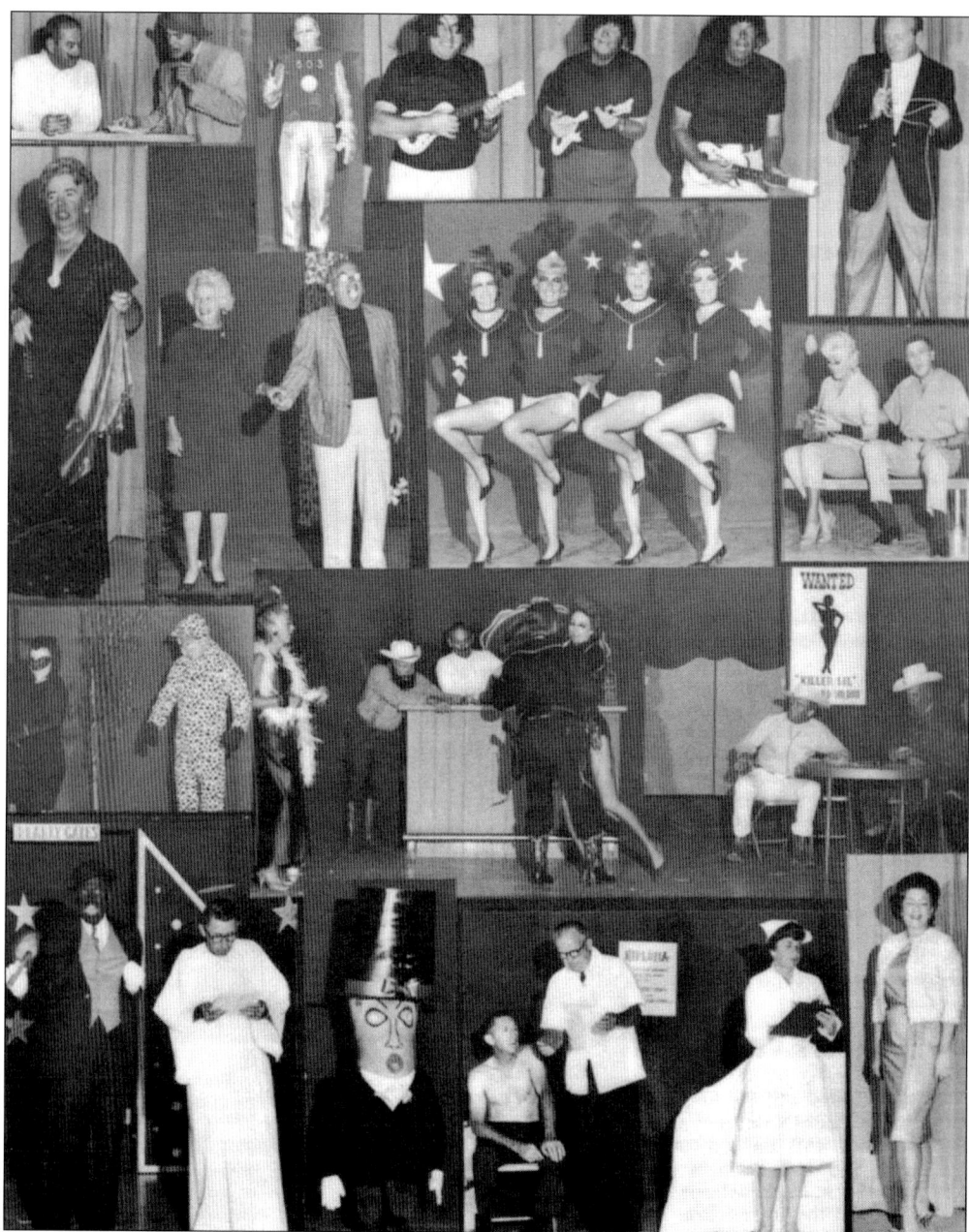

Eddie and Bill Ream spent nearly two months planning, preparing, and spearheading a theater show with the Blackouts, a group of women's golf club members who performed skits. Everyone had a great time, and it was a job well done. The Blackouts inspired the formation of a theater group.

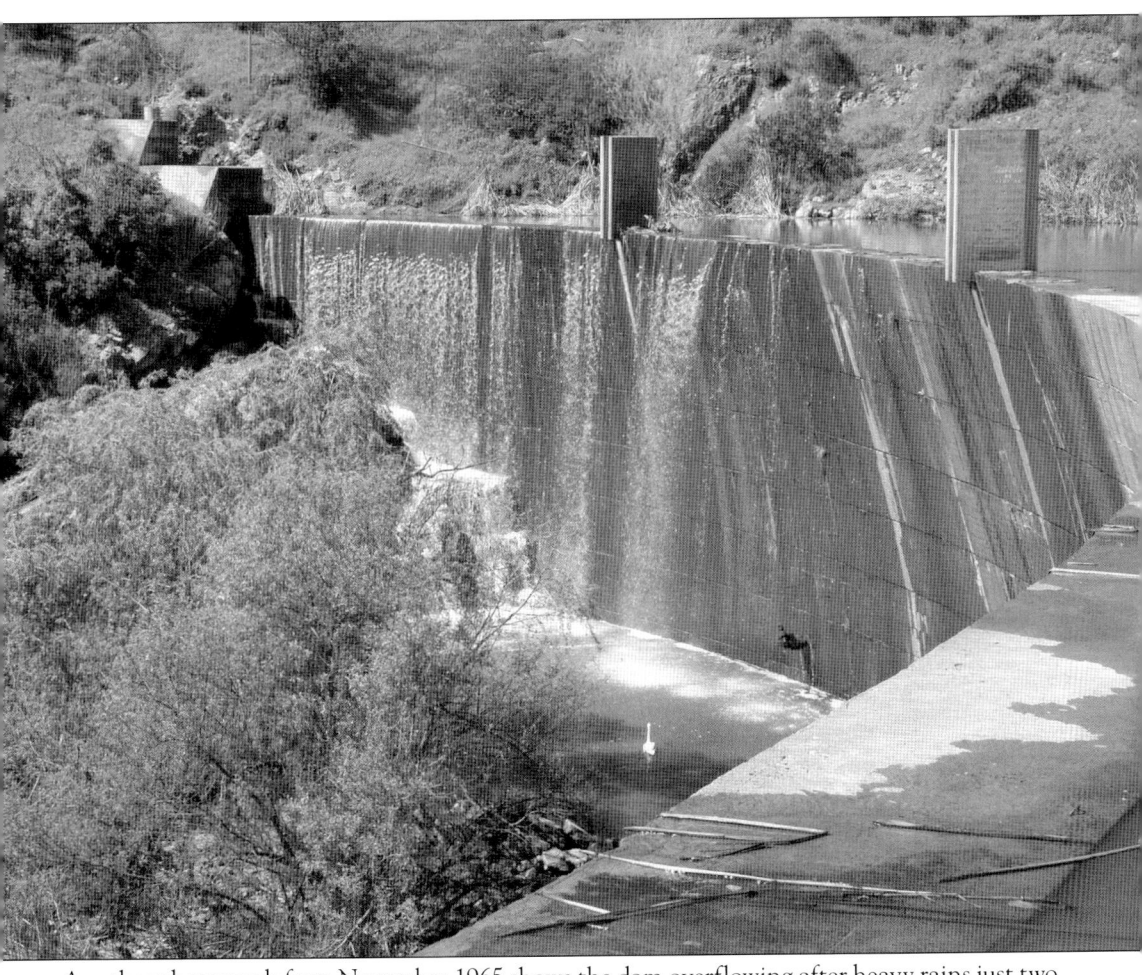
Another photograph from November 1965 shows the dam overflowing after heavy rains just two years after the dam was completed and the lake began filling.

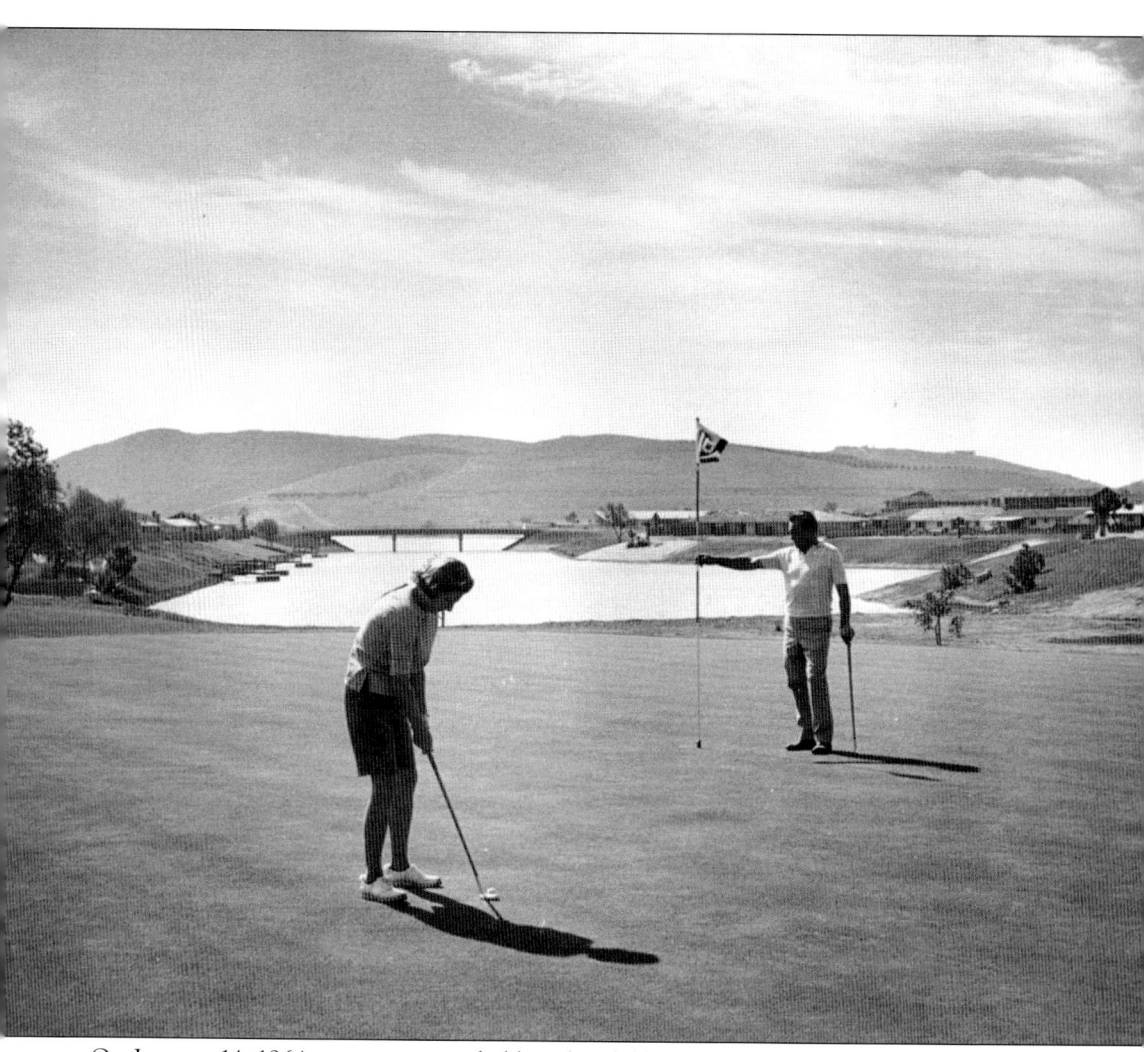

On January 14, 1964, a meeting was held at the clubhouse to form the women's golf club. The following officers were chosen from the townspeople who attended: Ruth Hipacher, president; Marie Hall, tournament chairman; Thea Wilson, handicap chairman; Alice Wilson, treasurer; Eddie Ream, secretary. Here, Vivian Frazar demonstrates her putting skill as her husband, Gordon, looks on. Life at the lake was always centered on golf-related activities and the "nineteenth hole" at the country club. The newly constructed bridge can be seen in the distance, with Sun Park and the Quail's Inn Motel to the right. (Author's collection.)

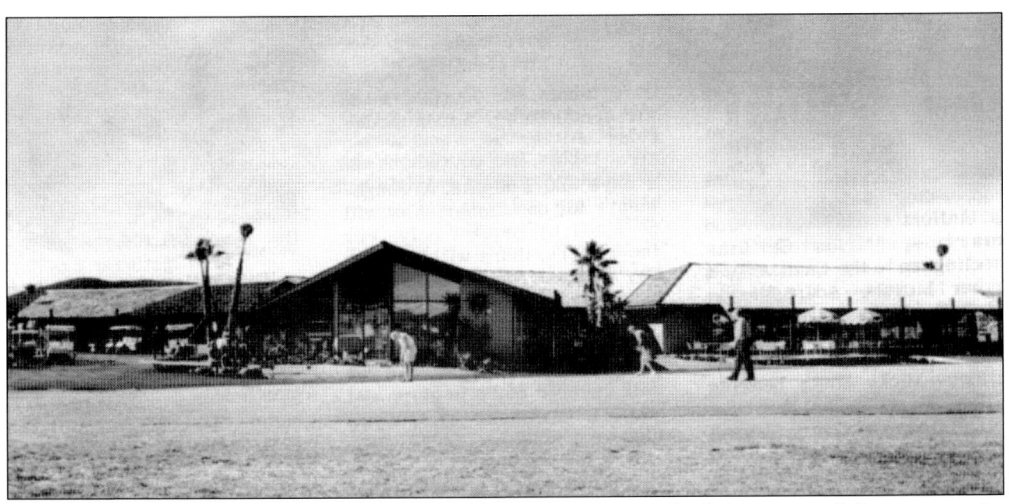

The recently completed new cart shed and locker rooms were in the left wing, and the new trophy room for dining was in the right wing at the Lake San Marcos Country Club. Nongolfers were welcome to participate in the social activities sponsored by some of the social clubs.

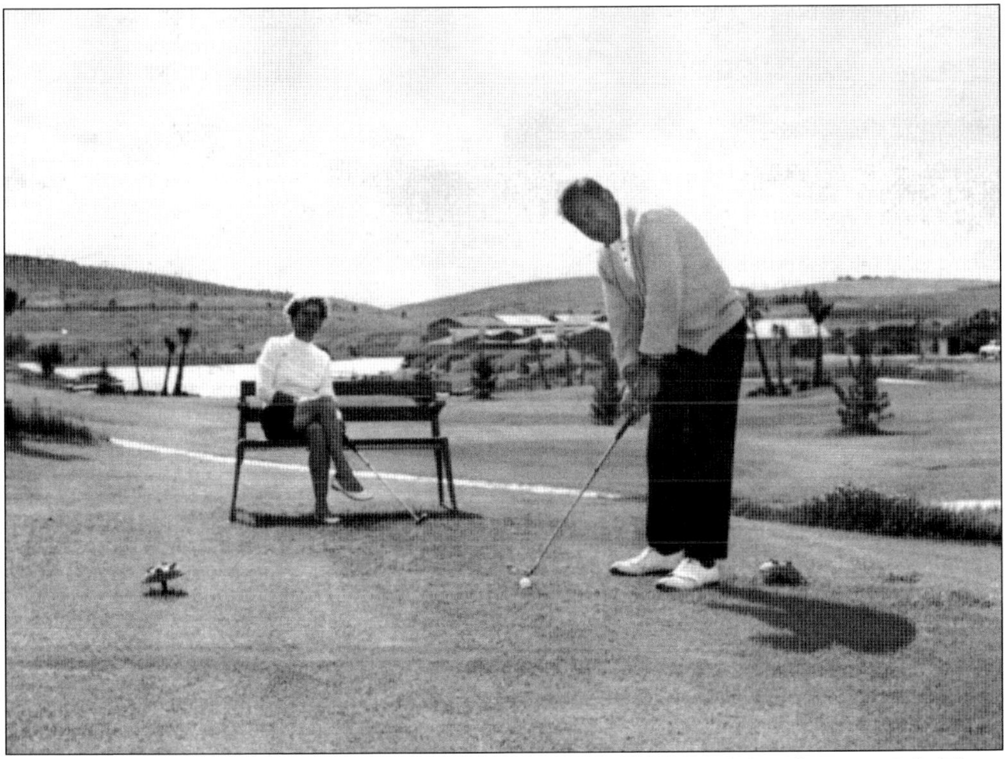

The first players on the new par-three golf course on Mall 3 were Phil and Marie Hall. These two new residents, who already had a near-perfect short game, no doubt became unbeatable. Phil was the first president of the men's golf club at Lake San Marcos, and Marie was famous for her straight-line game. This exclusive course was planted with the same kind of grass used on the greens of the 18-hole course at the country club.

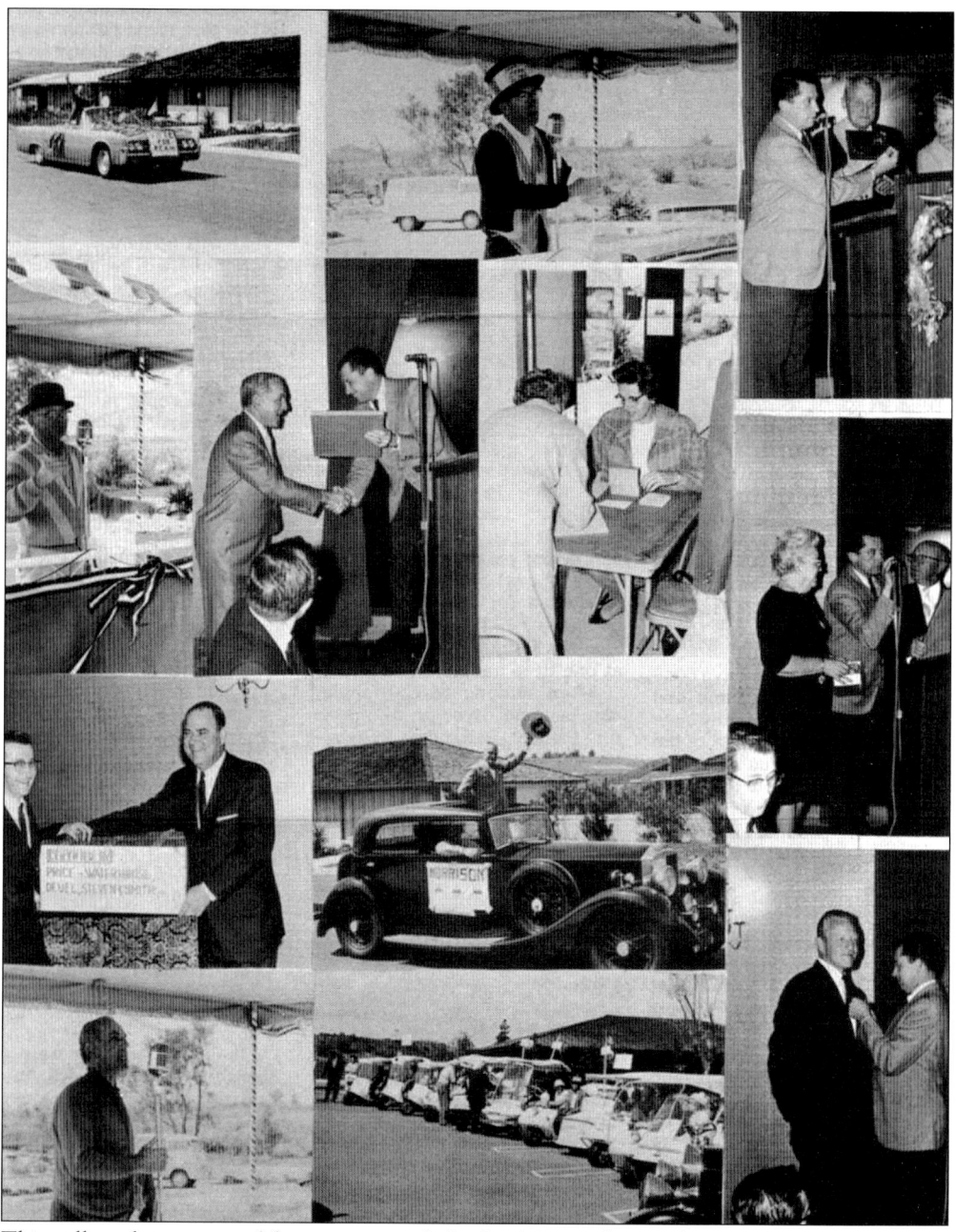

This collage shows some of the activities in Lake San Marcos during the month of February 1966. Several images capture the campaign for the first election for honorary mayor.

Walter Warren and his wife, Edith, lived on La Habra Drive. Walter was one of the world's greatest marksmen, having mastered all of the world competitions in sport shooting from 1930 to 1938. He also won the Gran Prix Monaco in 1933, the French trapshooting championships in Paris three times, and the championships of Italy three times.

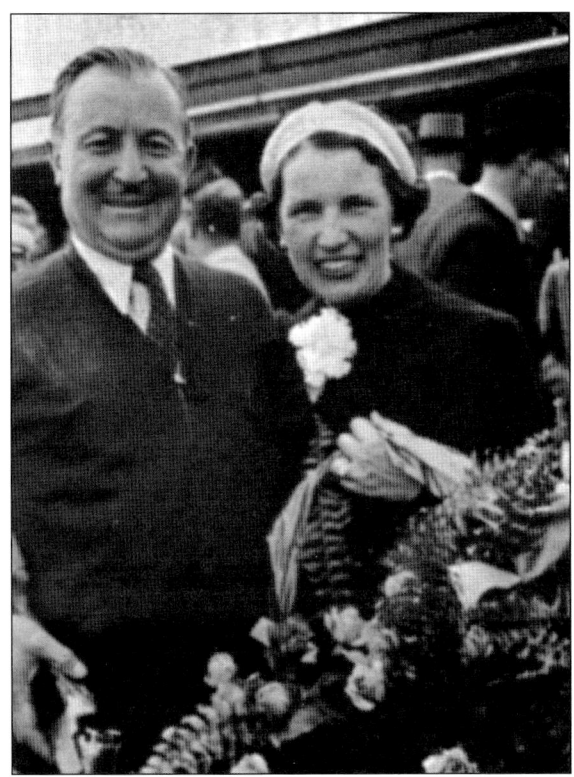

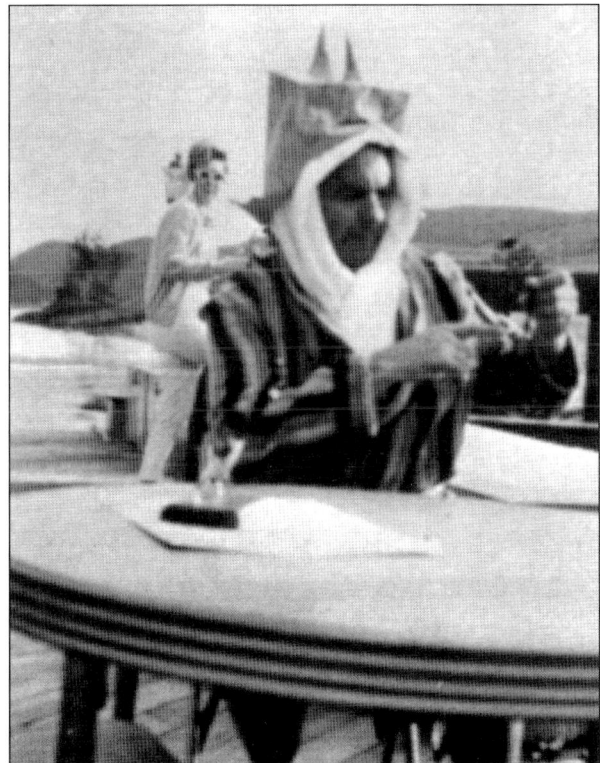

Sir Hutch Sabiston, knight of the Quail Table (as dubbed by the Canoe Club), remained the uncontested canoe jousting champion of Lake San Marcos. Evidently, he was the only contestant on hand for the signing of the jousting agreement and the joust.

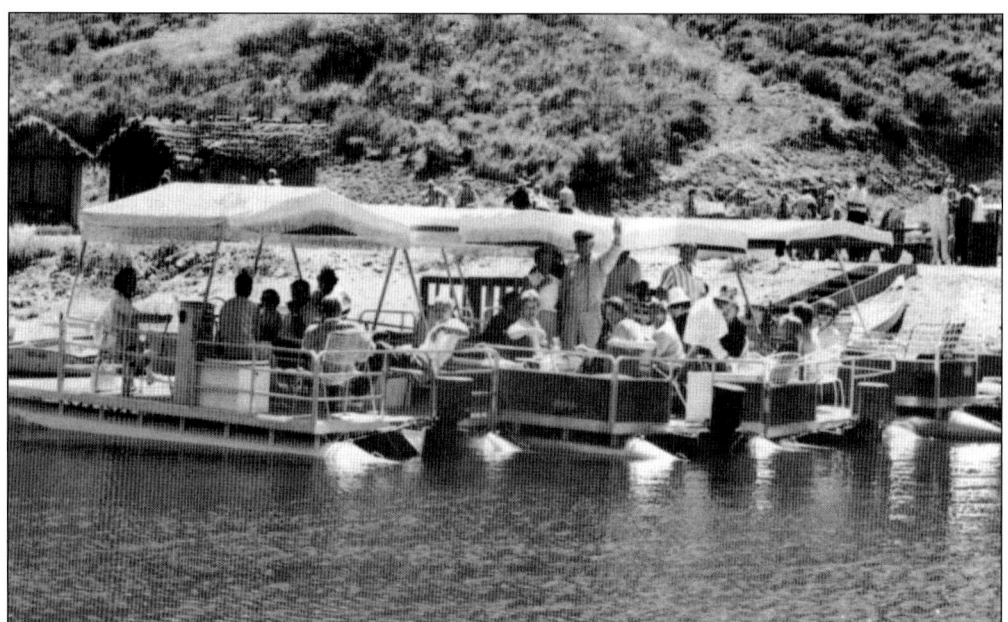

Residents enjoyed the Lake San Marcos Yacht Club picnic and their pontoon patio boats. Commodore D.J. Wyatt and wife Tensie were hosts of the afternoon, with members enjoying boat hopping as well as good food. Margaret Lindh was credited for introducing the pontoon patio to Lake San Marcos. All boat owners were eligible for yacht club membership and were invited to attend the monthly picnics.

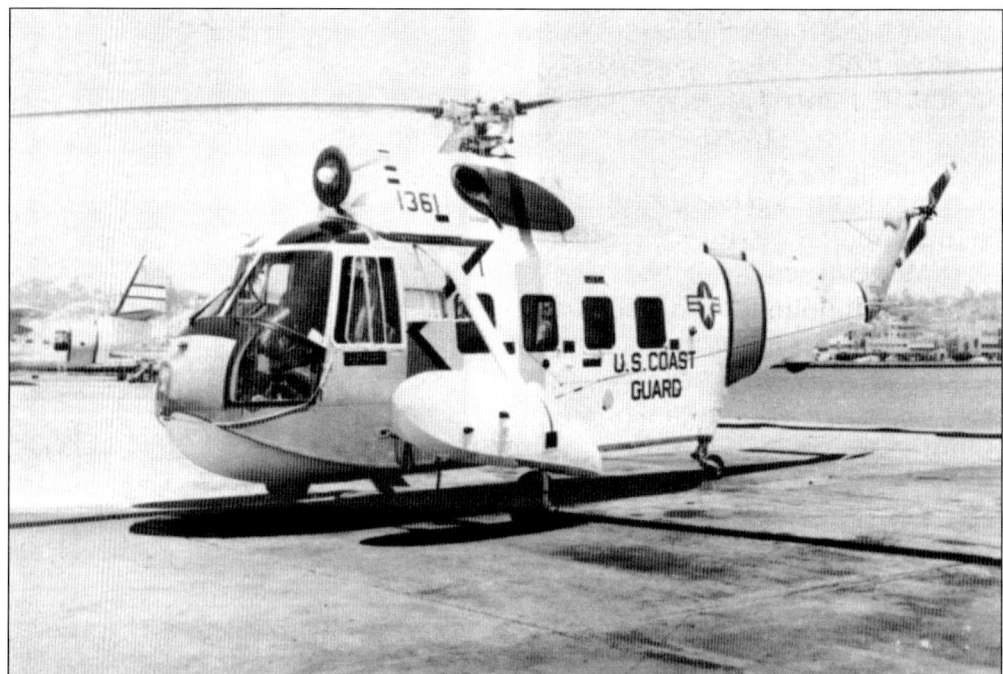

A demonstration of air-sea rescue operations took place in May 1966. A 7,600-pound Sikorsky jet-powered amphibious helicopter under the command of Capt. W.E. Rast of the US Coast Guard, demonstrated direct water recovery from the waters of Lake San Marcos.

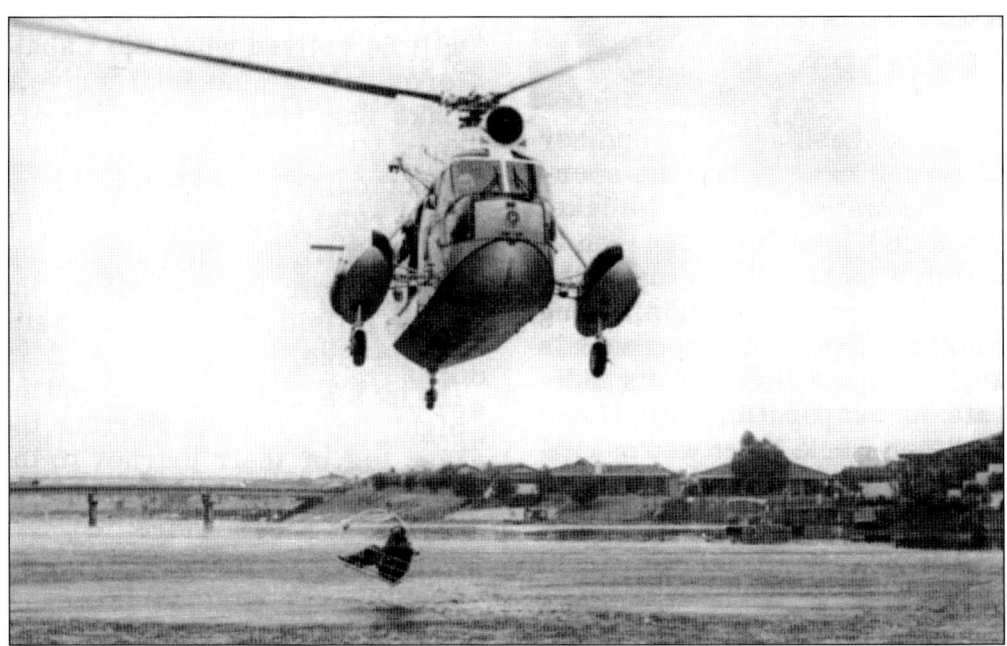

The Coast Guard helicopter crew under the command of Capt. W.E. Rast put on a display at the lake. Two staged rescues were made: one from the air, pictured here, and a second when the amphibious craft landed on the lake. Lake San Marcos honorary mayor Adm. Don Morrison made this demonstration possible.

This photograph was taken during the 1965 Lake San Marcos Open Water Ski Tournament, which included kite flying, barefoot skiing, and trick jumping, and also featured pyramids of skiers. The 1966 tournament took place on July 16 and 17 with about 80 contestants. On July 24, there was a water ski exhibition that included spectacular water-ski acts hosted by the Carlsbad Boat & Ski Club.

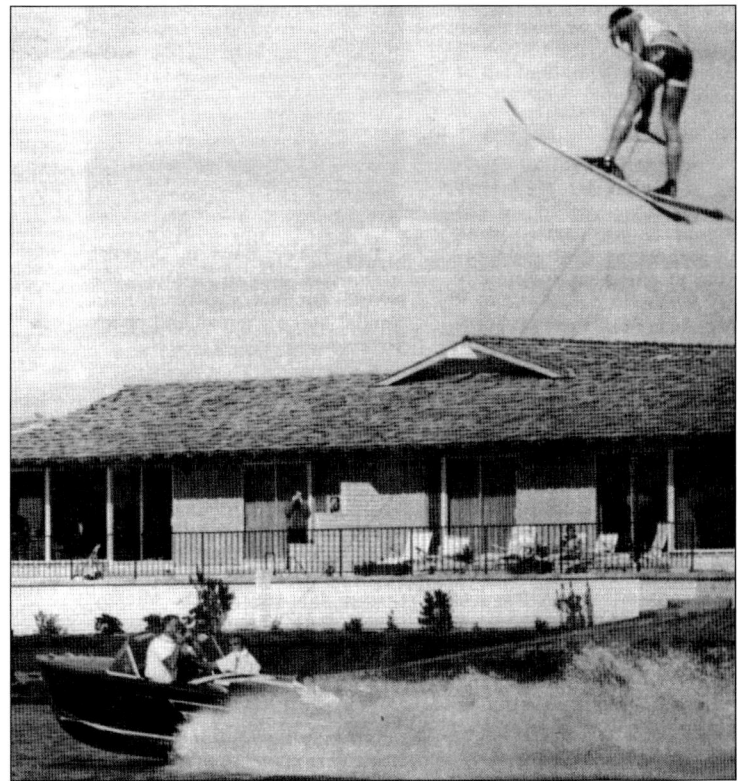

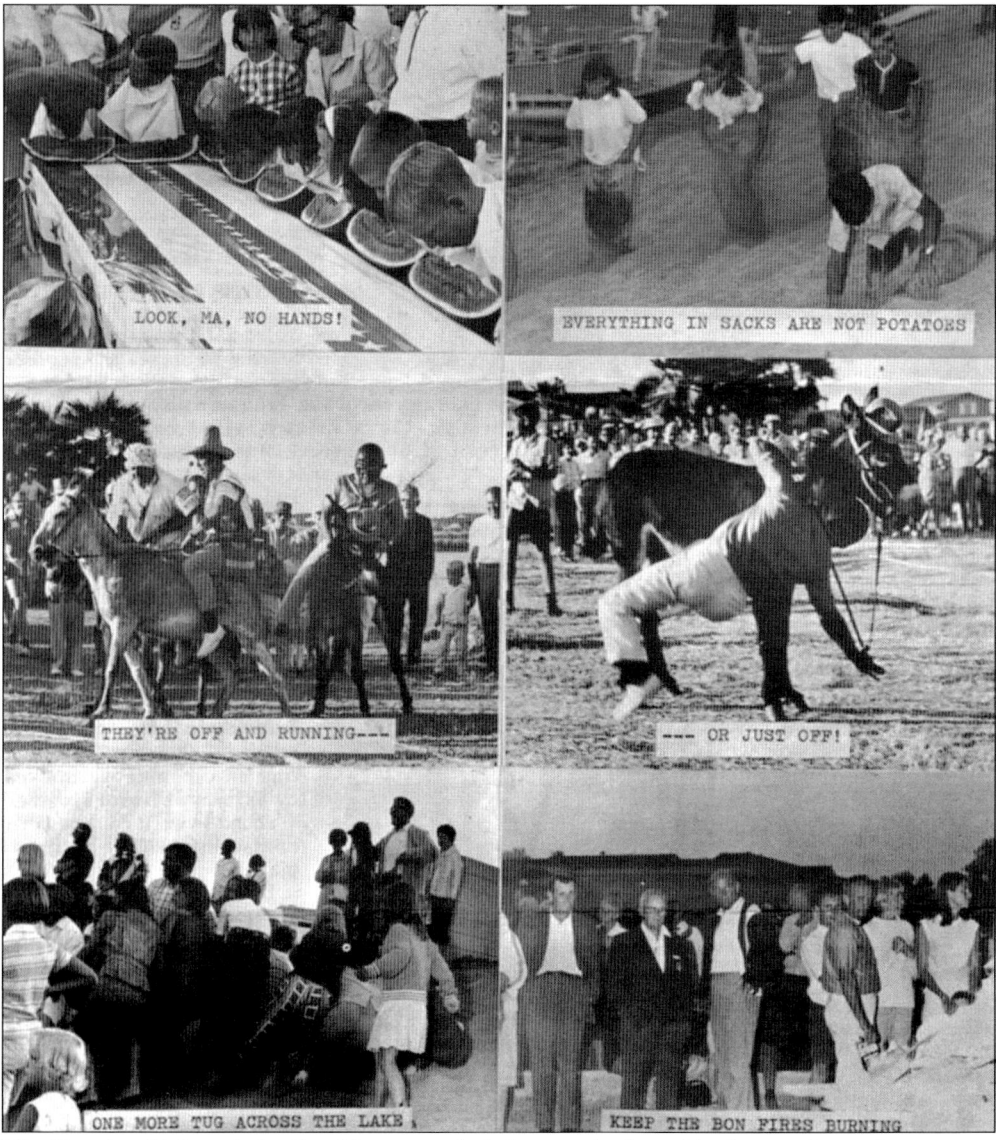

The Fourth of July at Lake San Marcos included picnic baskets, blankets, cider and peanuts, a watermelon-eating contest, sack races in the sand, a tug-of-war across the lake, donkey riding, a big bonfire after dark, and a parade of red, white, and blue decorated boats. Fourth of July activities at the lake were always popular, and everyone had a great time. This yearly celebration remains just as popular today and is attended by residents and their families, as well as by people from all over San Diego County.

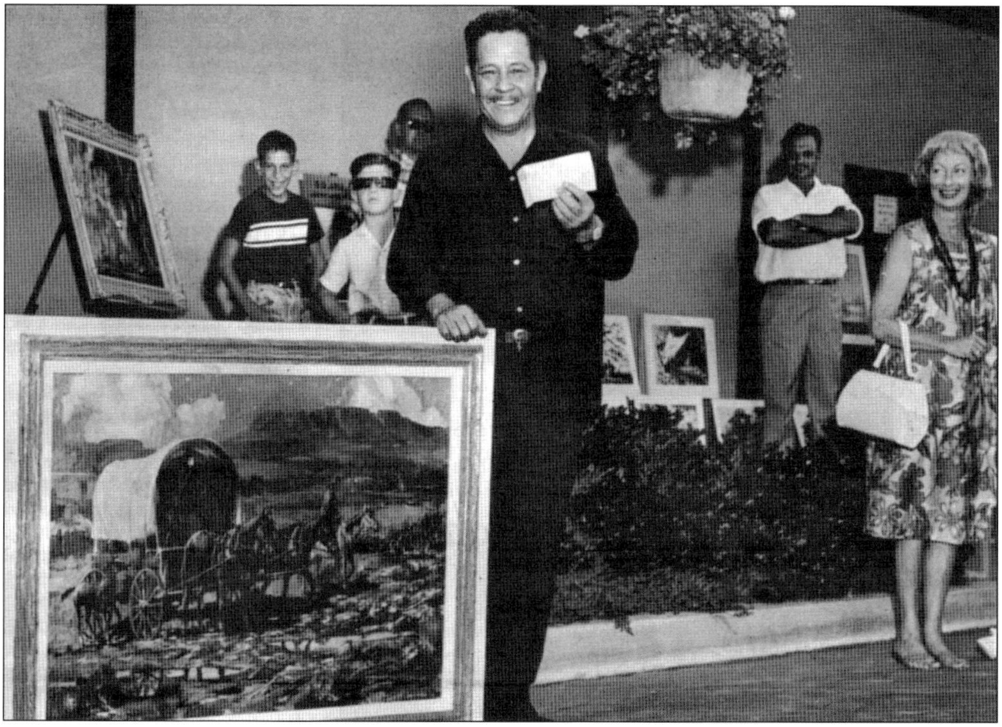

The second annual Lake San Marcos Invitational Art Exhibit was attended by thousands, many of whom claimed it was the most exciting art show they had ever seen. There were 50 professional artists present with their paintings. A $1,000 prize for oil paintings went to *Late Journey* by M.A. Gomez. Gomez was one of the finest artists of the Southwest, and some of his paintings hung in the Grand Central Art Gallery in New York, as well as in the Saks Denver Art Gallery, Taos Art Gallery, Gainsborough Gallery in Canada, O'Brien's Gallery in Scottsdale, the Saddleback Gallery in Santa Ana, and the Lake San Marcos Gallery.

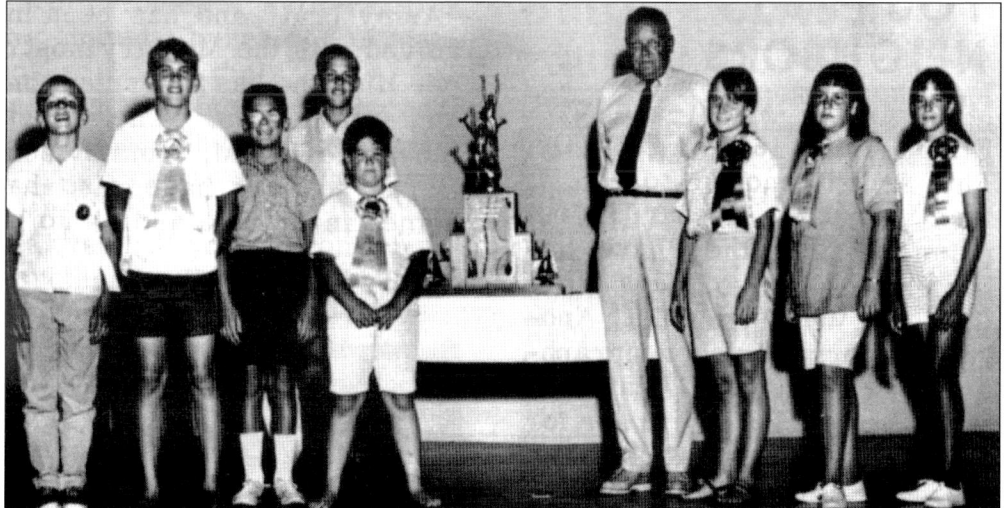

Max Smith is pictured with several members of his sailing class who proudly flaunt their trophy and ribbons. From left to right are Kent Cutter, Chris Cutter, Greg Hanssen, Nelson Cutter (rear), Gary Snavely, Smith, Tina Steven, Sue Snavely, and Gay Gadbois.

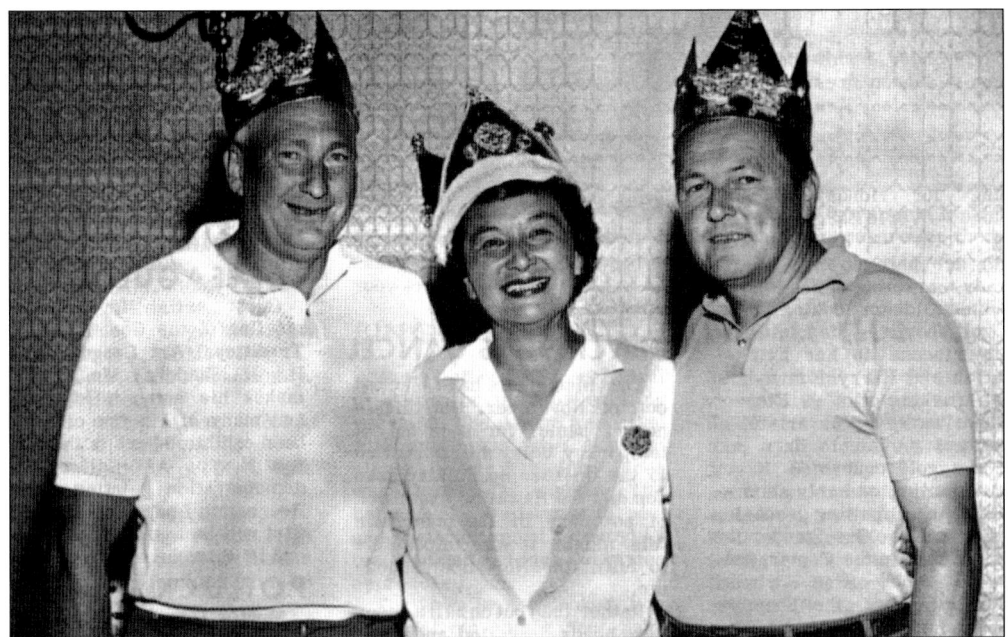

The annual Queen's Tournament sponsored by the Women's Club resulted in the crowning of the new queen, Sherrie Hanssen, and her two prince consorts, Hal Grisamer (left) and Bob Frazar (right). This year's tournament had 85 entries made up of teams of one lady, one low-handicap man, and one high-handicap man.

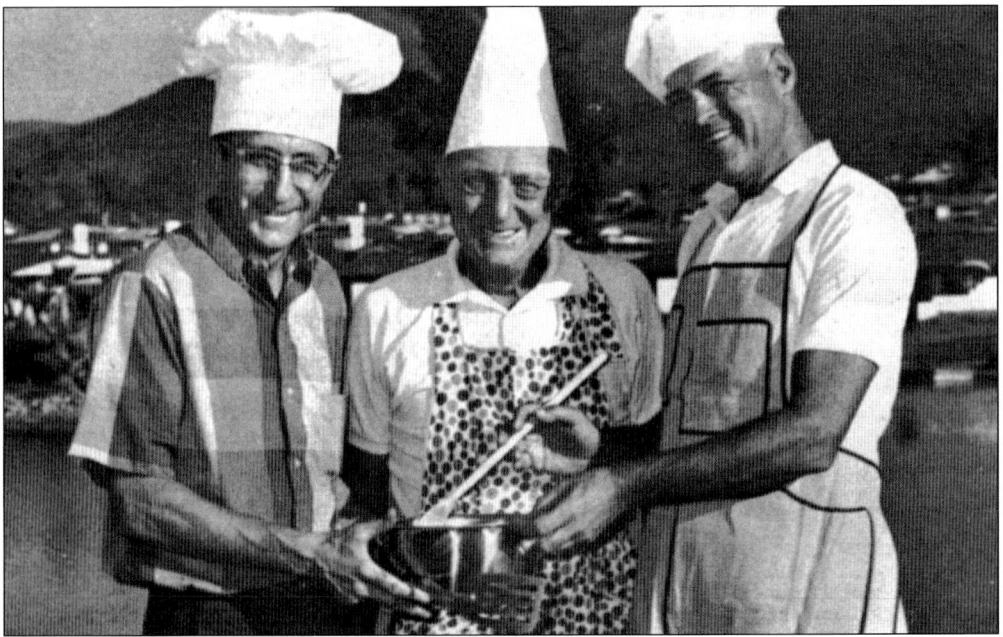

From left to right, Kiwanians Norm Bucher (mayor of San Marcos), Don Morrison (president of the LSM Coordinating Council), and Frank Brence prepared pancake batter for the Pancake Jamboree. This yearly fundraising event was sponsored by the LSM Kiwanis and continues today. Proceeds from the annual event were donated to underprivileged and disabled children in the San Marcos area.

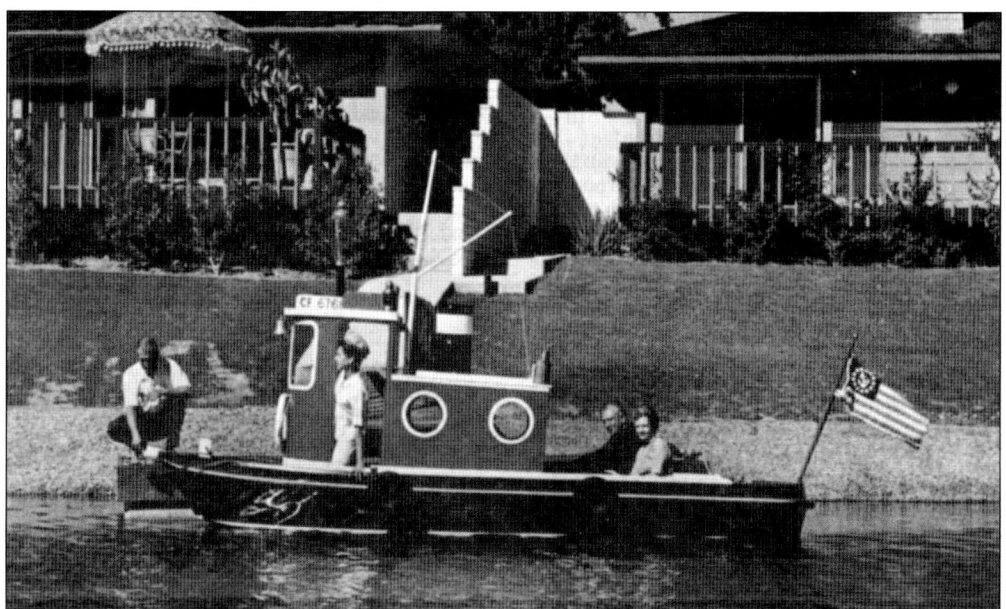

This 16-foot steamboat was called the *Whistling Teakettle*. Owned by Ed Merritt and moored at his dock, it appeared in many boat parades in Newport Harbor before being moved to LSM. It had kerosene lights and a steam whistle. Here, Woody Bynum helps to cast off lines for Kay Merritt, while Jane Bynum and Harry Deuel ride in the back. Ed Merritt was president and art director of his own advertising agency in Hollywood, which specialized in advertising campaigns for motion pictures released by Disney, MGM, and Universal Studios.

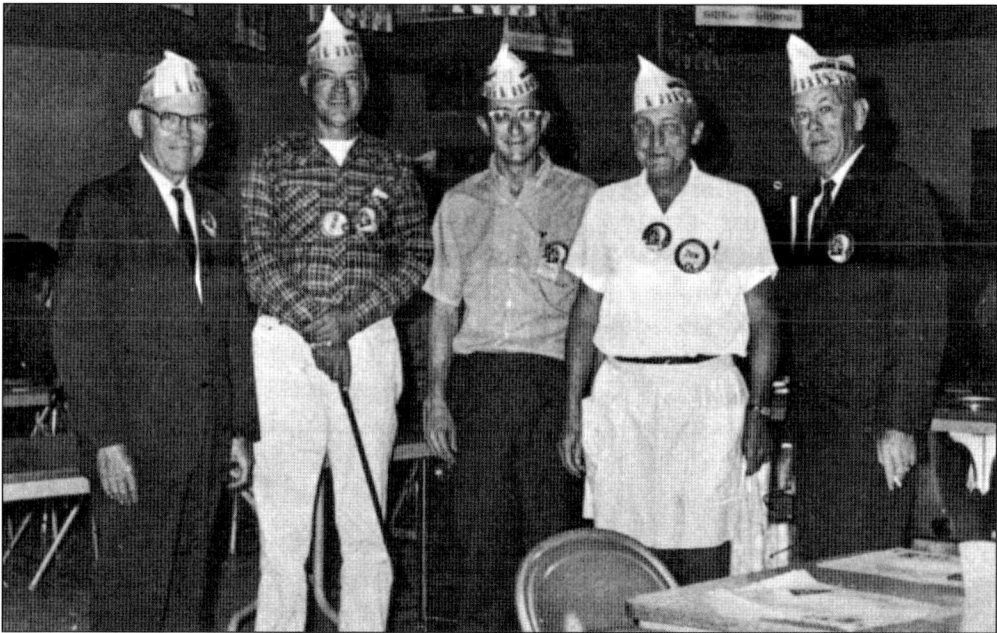

The Kiwanis Jamboree crew included, from left to right, Junius Oldham, Frank Brence, Norman Bucher, Don Morrison, and "Doc" Taylor. They, along with 43 other Kiwanis members, worked in shifts to cook and serve 850 breakfasts at the San Marcos High School cafeteria. The net proceeds benefitted the Kiwanis fund for underprivileged children in the San Marcos area.

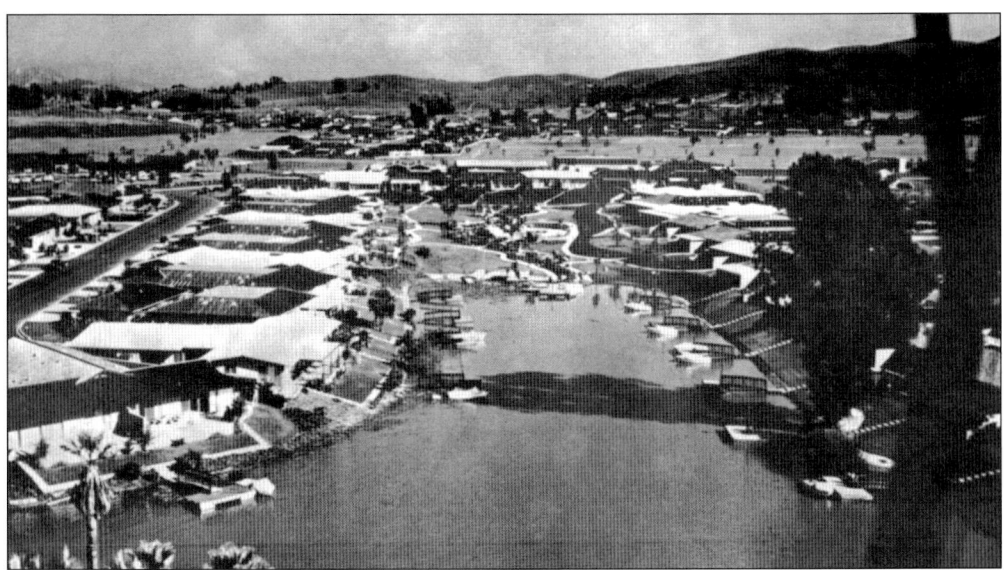

This photograph was taken by Art Brune on December 8, 1966, just minutes before a tragic plane crash that left him seriously injured and took the life of the pilot. The plane was on a photographic mission and was en route to Palomar Airport when it struck a power line. Brune was the lone survivor. He remembered crawling on his hands and knees with two broken arms and a broken collarbone to recover scattered films he had taken on the flight. Art and his wife, Millie, moved to Lake San Marcos from Newport Beach in 1950 and were frequently seen on the lake in the *Millie B*, the beautiful 14-foot inboard boat he built himself.

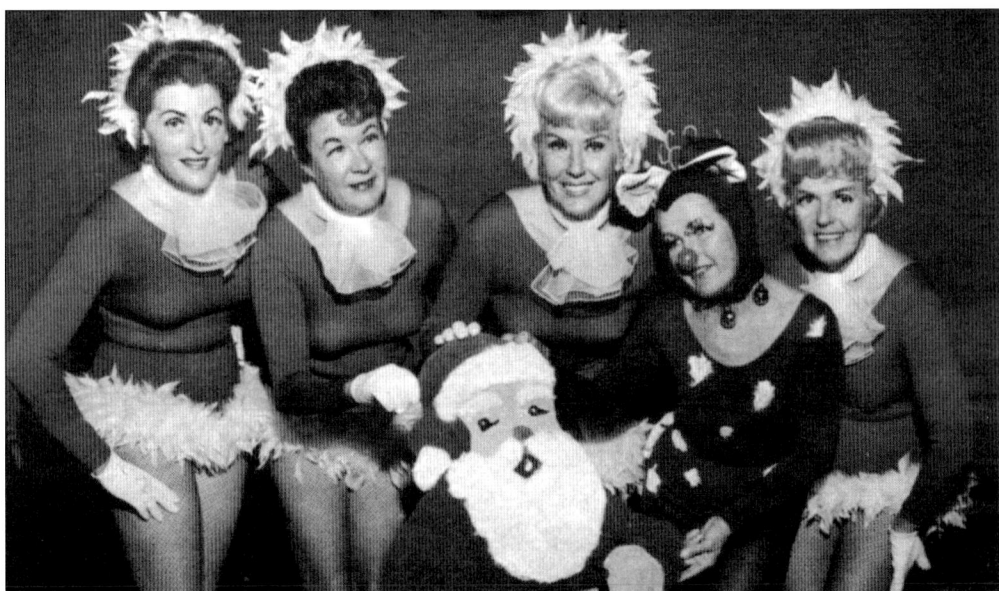

The Sleigh Belles were the featured entertainers at both the Ladies' Golf Club luncheon and the Men's President's Cup dinner held in the Trophy Room. Pictured from left to right are Dorothy Faulkner, Irene Garjobst, Eddie Ream, Marcie Chace, and Grace Meyer. The Sleigh Belles were members of the bicycle club who toured the streets of Lake San Marcos at Christmas on their bikes, stopping at various homes to serenade the residents with Christmas carols by candlelight. Afterward, they got together for refreshments and more songs at one of the members' homes.

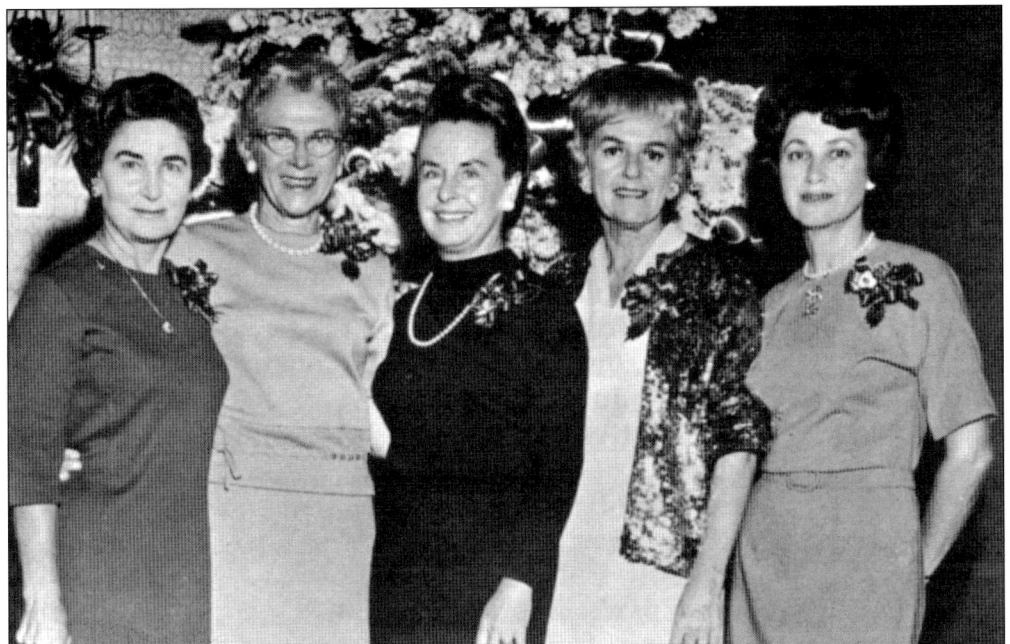

The women's golf club newly installed officers for 1967 were, from left to right, Olive Taylor, Minnie Harn, Ruth Sharp, Grace Meyer, and Vee Skaff. The annual Christmas and installation luncheon was attended by 150 members, and the tables were beautifully decorated with red topiary trees. The men's and women's golf clubs are still two of the most active clubs in Lake San Marcos.

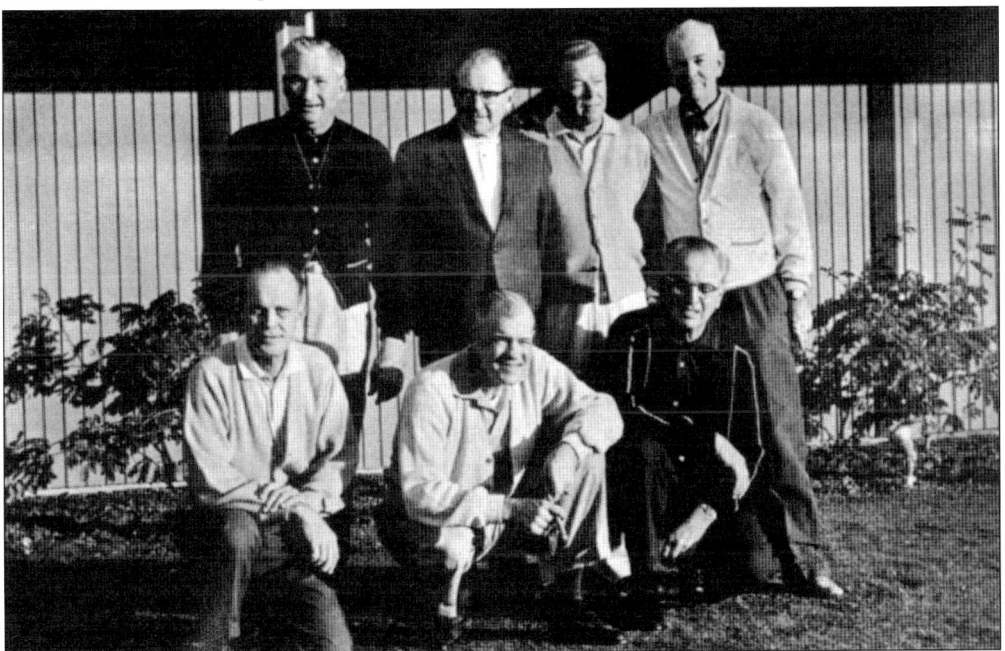

The LSM Men's Club directors, from left to right, are (first row) Gene Fellows, Frank Brence, and Van Varenhoust; (second row) Hal Grisamer, Ben Pifer, Wendell LaBelle, and Jim Newcom. One of the club's major tournaments was the President's Cup, which took place in November and December.

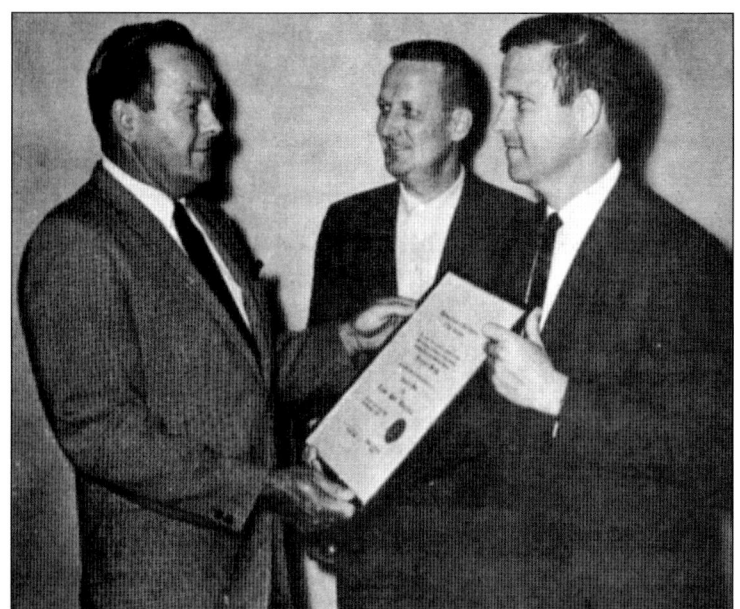

The top award for outstanding planning and home design was given to the engineers and developer of the Lake San Marcos community. Gordon Frazar (left) received the award from William Rick (right), chairman of the council awards program. In the center is Donald Campbell, president of Campbell, Miller & Associates in San Bernardino and engineer-planner of the project.

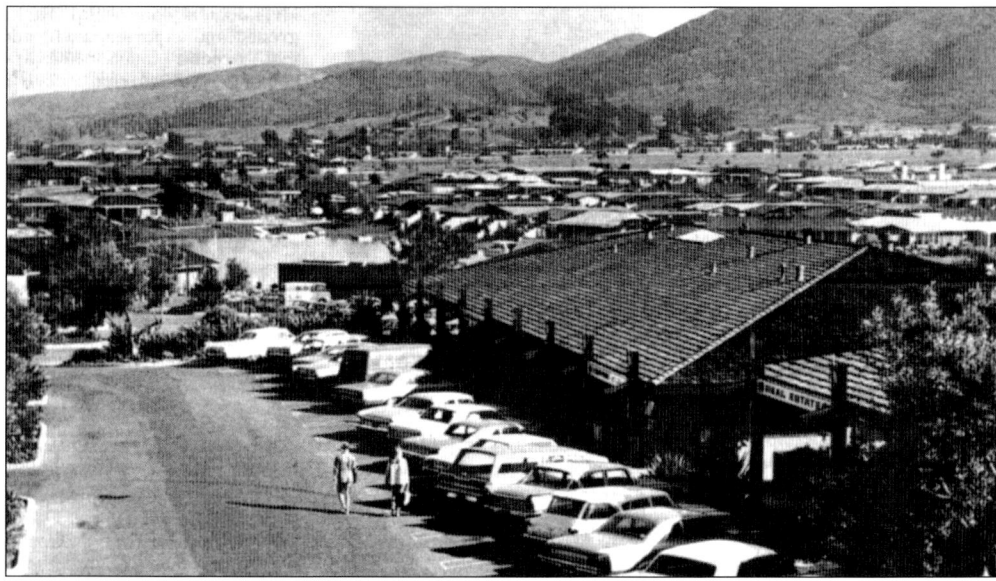

The shopping center was built with a view of the hills surrounding the lake. Some of the businesses in the center were the Barber Shop (Russell Kraft, manager), Liberty National Bank (Bill Word, manager), Pampered Lady Salon (Sharon Lane, owner), Ev-Lyn's Couture (Neil McElrath, owner), Orma's Gift Shop (Orma McComb, owner), Blue Sloop Coffee Shop (Jean and John Crosby, owners), Lake View Florist (Joan Slavinski, owner), Thomas Furst Interiors (Tom Furst, owner), Lake San Marcos Pharmacy (Bob Maxwell, owner), Shop Smart Market (Don Heffer and Wes Wilson, owners), LSM Cleaners and Coin Laundry (Frank Leidt, owner), Travel Mart (Bill Forshee, owner), Paint and Wallpaper (Bill Bell, contractor), investment counselor Sheldon Tyson, LSM Landscape Maintenance Nursery (Wes and Bob Steven, owners), dentist William Fowkes, optometrist Charles H Martin, Cassidy Medical Center, Quail's Inn Dinner House (Jack Schlendorf, owner); Quail's Inn Motel (Joan Nordyke, manager), Union Oil Service Station (Ed Ferguson, owner), and Lake San Marcos Art Gallery (Austin Deuel, owner).

Three
COMMUNITY DEVELOPMENT

In 1966, as Lake San Marcos was developing, the first residents decided they needed an honorary mayor. An election was held and proved to be great fun. Vice Adm. Donald Morrison was elected. Morrison, who moved to LSM in 1964 following his retirement from the Coast Guard after 33 years, thought that an honorary mayor should also have a council to help make decisions, so a coordinating council made up of elected residents was formed in 1968.

Even though these first elections were fun for the residents and were surrounded by much fanfare, there were some very real issues that affected them. These included traffic safety and speed limits, golf cart use, pet nuisances, golfing issues, safety and police protection, lake and lakefront rules and regulations, mall maintenance, the building of recreational facilities, the need for a post office, the development of cable television, the formation of a security patrol, and the organization of the Fourth of July picnic and boat parade.

By the mid-1970s, the focus of the coordinating council had become the security patrol. As LSM began to grow in size and prominence, there was a stronger need for an advisory organization to lend a unified voice on behalf of residents and address issues of increasing importance to the community. A nonprofit organization, originally called the Lake San Marcos Homeowners Association, was formed. Within several years, the name was changed to the Lake San Marcos Community Association. Soon thereafter, the coordinating council merged with the community association. To ensure continuity, the bylaws called for a nine-member board of directors to be elected from the community for staggered two-year terms. The community association board members then elected a president and other officers.

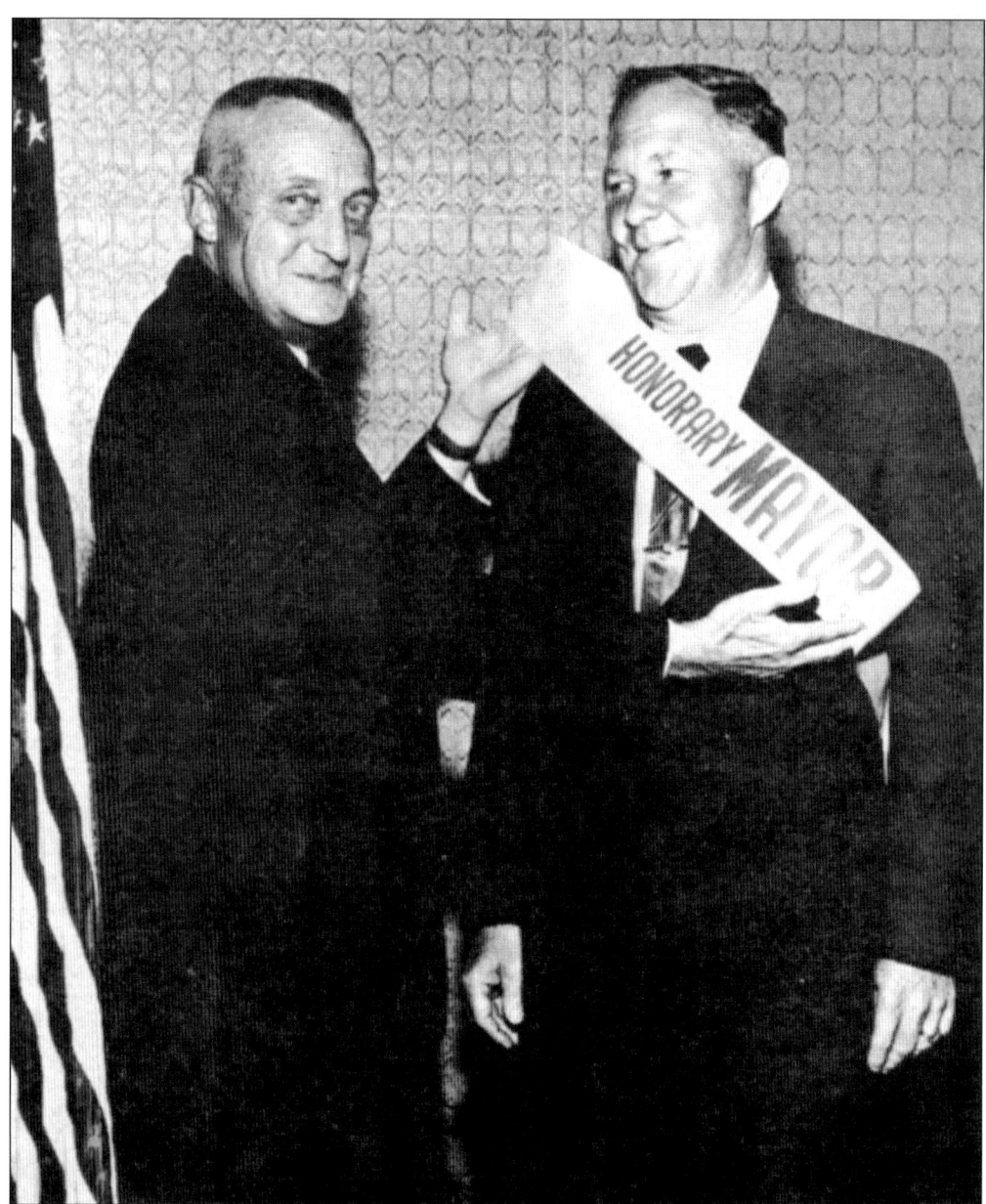
Charles "Charlie" Hahne (right) was elected the second honorary mayor of Lake San Marcos. He was pinned by retiring mayor Vice Adm. Don Morrison. This election came after a hard-fought, fun-filled campaign that started with a golf tournament and included horns honking, bells ringing, spectators cheering, and girls singing. It was followed by a land parade including a poodle wearing a beret and plaid jacket, and then a colorful boat parade. Hahne earned a reputation that caused people to say, "when a job needs doing, ask Charlie Hahne." Born and educated in Chicago, he founded Transformer Technicians Inc., which he ran until he retired. Married to Dorothea, he was a rock and mineral enthusiast with an extensive collection. He also held an interest in astronomy, played chess, was an expert marksman, and, in his spare time, served on the reserve police force and the San Marcos Fire Commission. He was chairman of the LSM Coordinating Council in 1968.

A CAMPAIGN TO REMEMBER

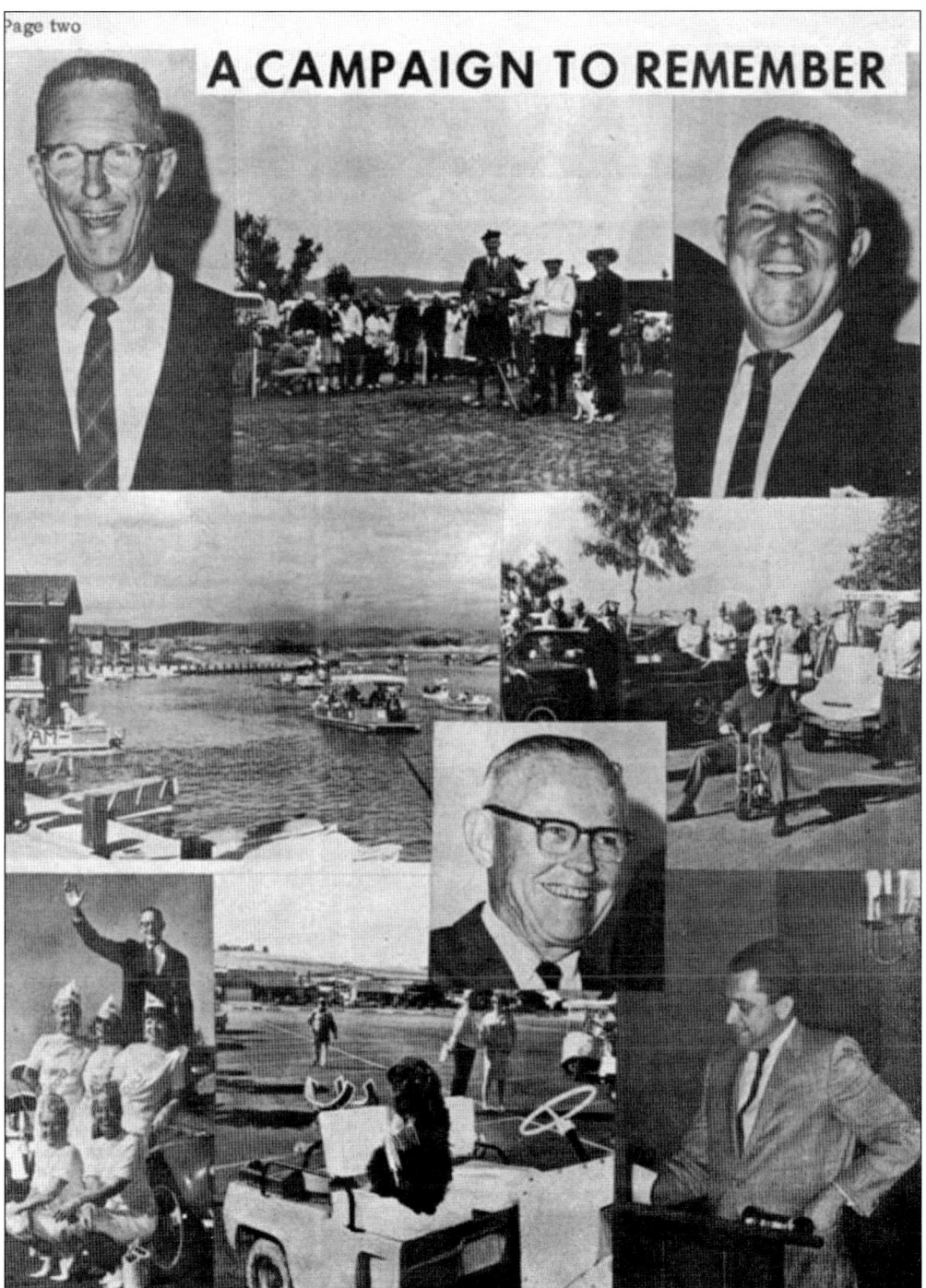

Election Day ran much more smoothly than the campaign, although everyone had a good time. The land parade brought forth everything from Charlie Hahne's official patrol car to Phil Hall riding a two-foot motor scooter. Mayor Don Morrison introduced the candidates, who in turn presented their individual platforms. At the end of the program, Mayor Morrison was given a standing ovation for the outstanding job he had done during the past year.

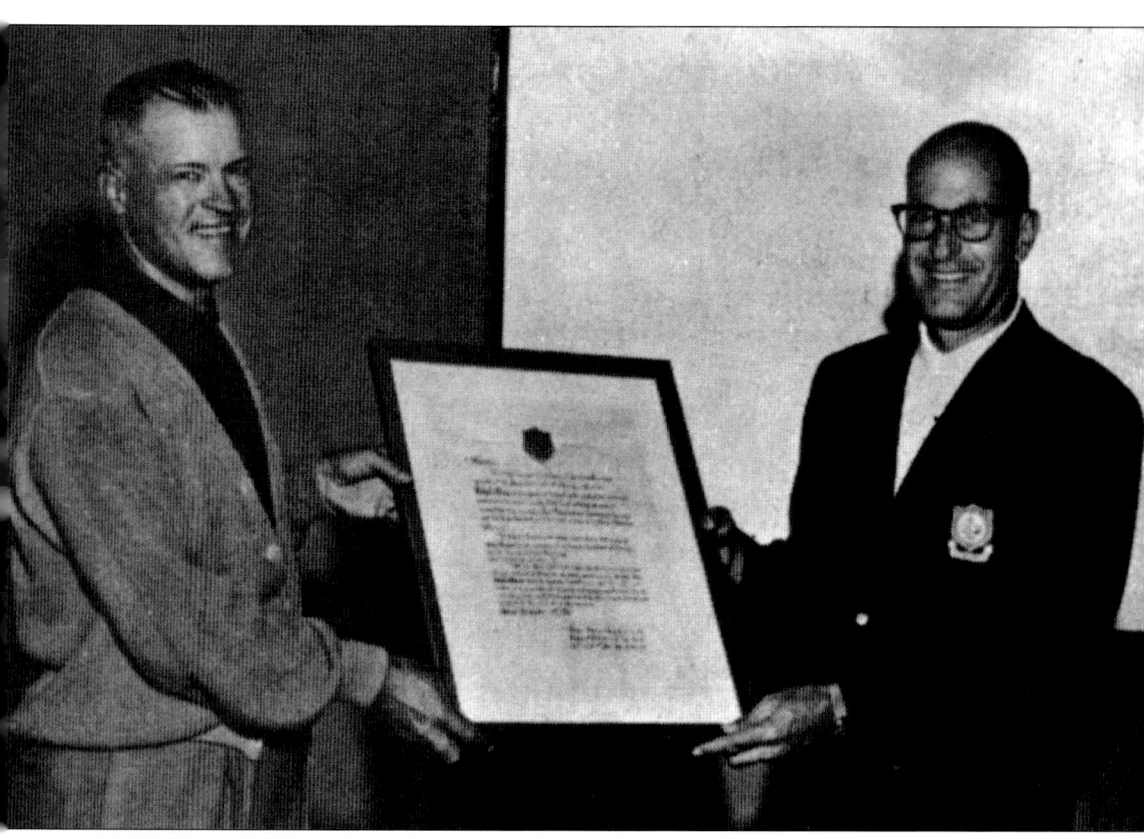

Ralph Meyer (left) received a framed scroll from the men's club as an expression of gratitude for his outstanding service. Pres. Frank Brence (right) made the presentation on behalf of the board of directors. Ralph had served as president in 1966 and as tournament chairman in 1965, and had been a board member since the club's inception in 1964.

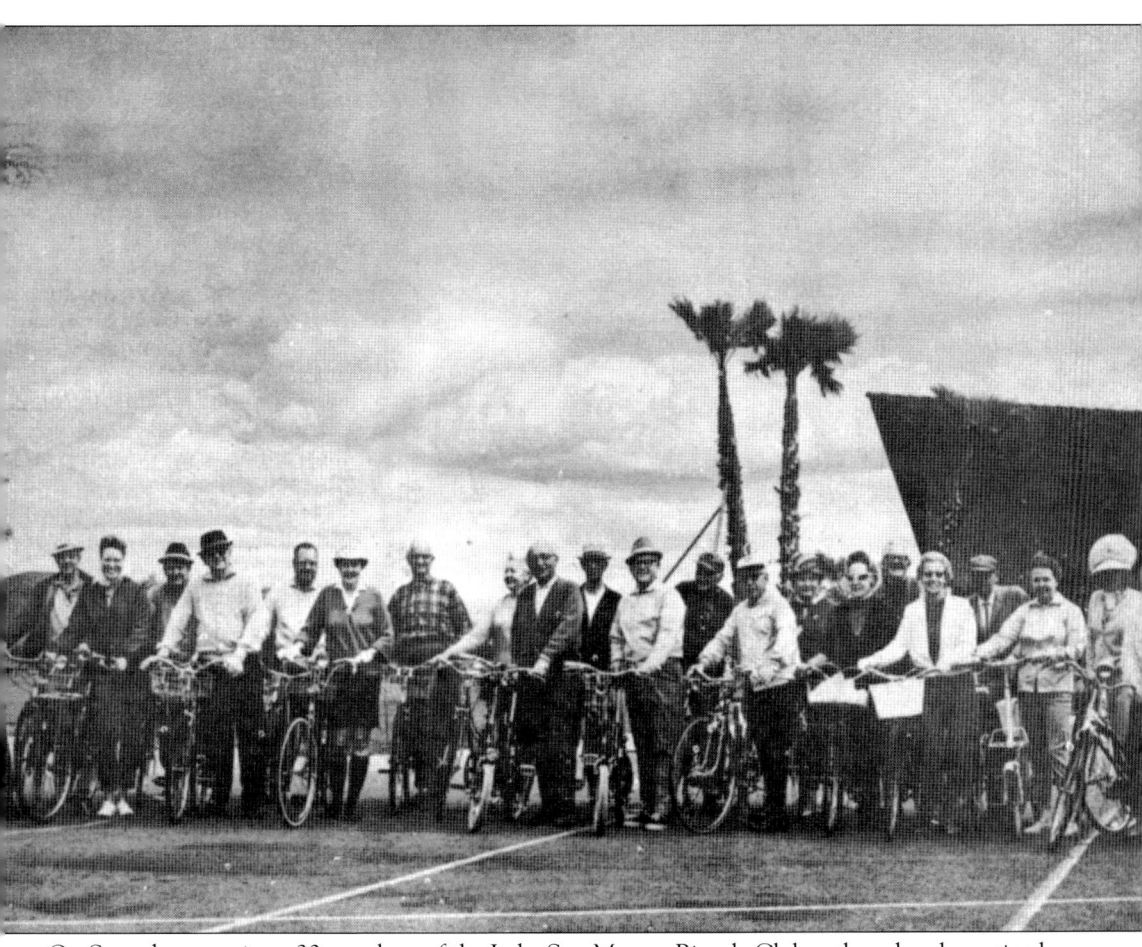

On Saturday mornings, 30 members of the Lake San Marcos Bicycle Club gathered and practiced "formation riding." The group, led by June Kassabaum and Bert Griffiths, then headed out for a six-mile ride through the countryside, ending with lunch at a fellow member's home or the recreation center. The group dubbed themselves the "Heaven's Angels" and become famous locally for their evening caroling during the Christmas season.

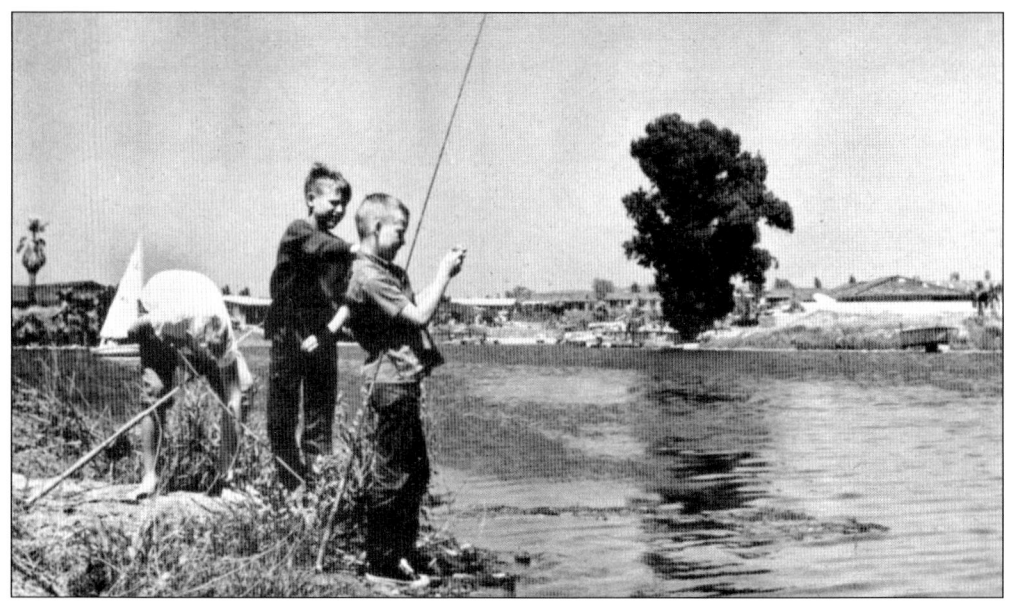

The second annual Huck Finn Day was held for 253 young fishermen. Ranging in age from five to fifteen, they caught a combined total of 1,902 fish, mostly bluegill. The lake also had catfish and bass. The winner, 11-year-old Eddie Harp, won a rod and reel for catching a one-pound, two-ounce catfish.

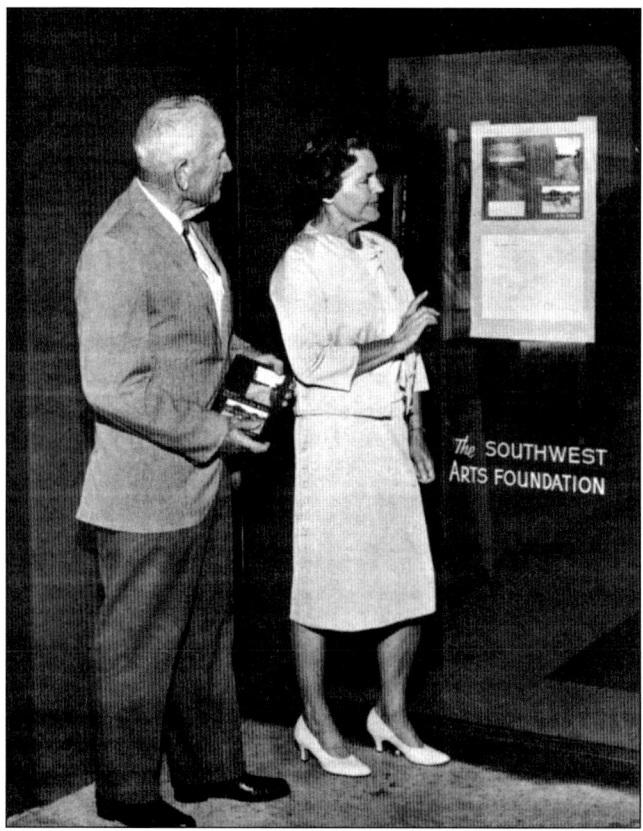

Trails and Tales of Baja author Pel Carter and his wife, Peg, are shown with the announcement of the publication of Pel's first book. It was displayed at the Lake San Marcos Art Gallery, which was also headquarters for the publisher of the book, Southwest Arts Foundation

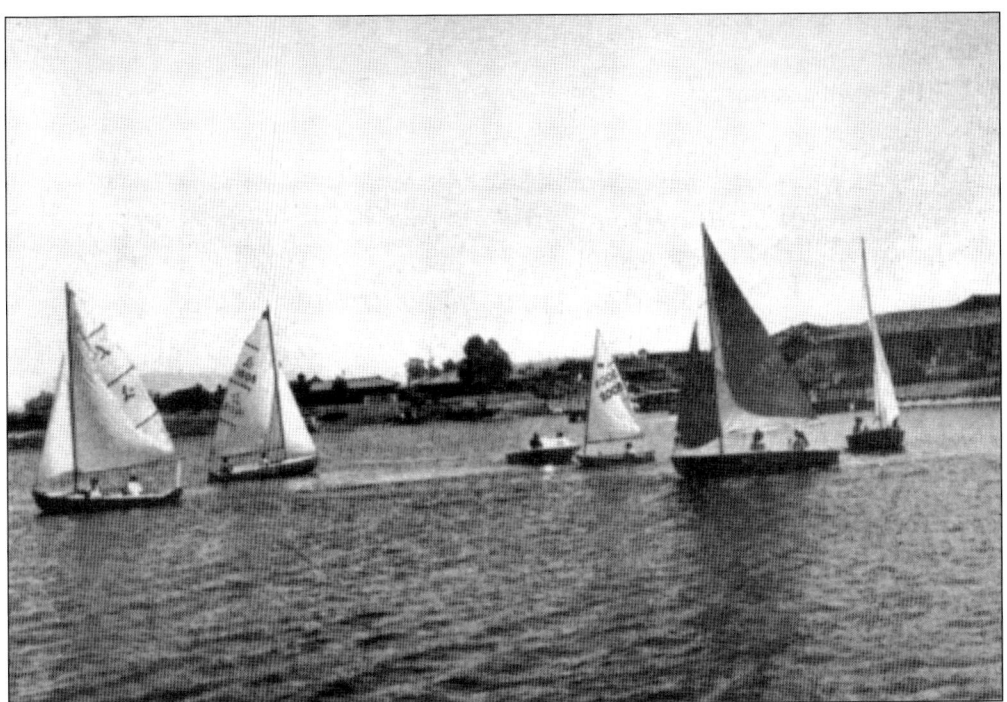

Sailing classes on Lake San Marcos were held every Monday and Thursday morning. They were free of charge to young sailors between 12 and 18 years of age. Lake San Marcos encouraged water sports of all kinds, and these classes were led by Max Smith and culminated with students racing in the annual Lido competition. Smith also volunteered his time to adult classes.

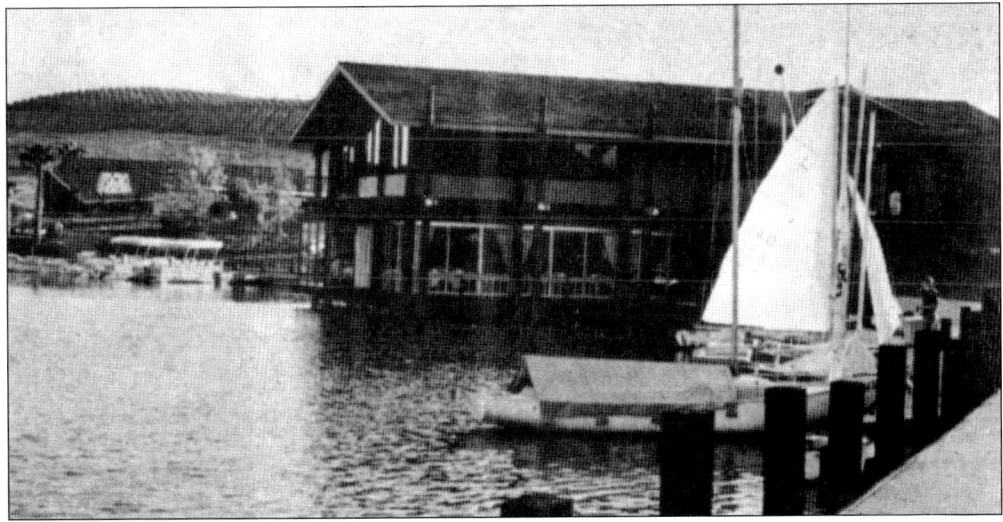

Dorothy Steven of LSM wrote about the secret of Lake San Marcos: "No one can tell you the whole secret. It is a combination of many things. But mostly it is the friendly people whose ages are as varied as their occupation and backgrounds. Here loneliness has found no breeding ground, and the social ladder needs no rungs."

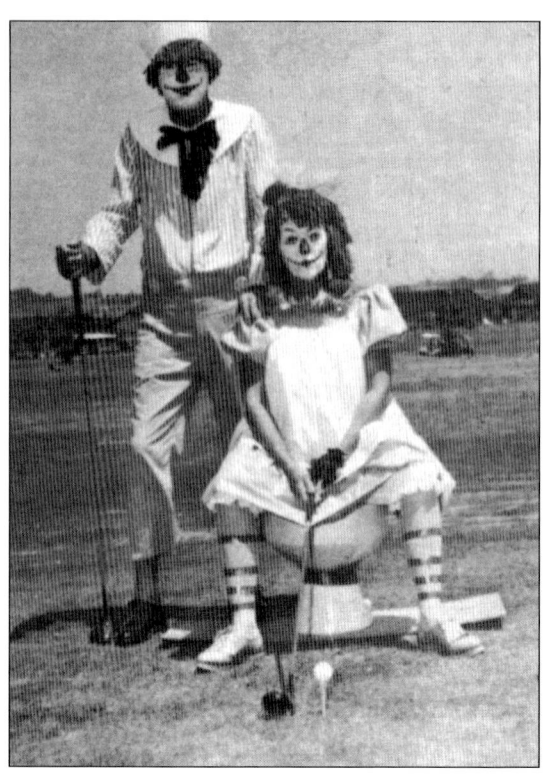

This photograph documents a day of goofy golf, costumes, and trickery. The dressed-up golfers teed off from mattresses, toilet seats, and rubber-hose tees, and used putters for drivers and drivers for putters. Eddie and Bill Ream walked away with the grand sweepstakes award for their fantastic Zulu costumes, and Bill and Marcie Chase were living dolls in their Raggedy Ann and Andy costumes.

Austin Deuel, Marine combat artist and owner of LSM Art Gallery, hosted the third annual LSM Invitational Art Exhibit. In the previous two years, exhibits had drawn over 10,000 viewers from all over Southern California. In the event's third year, 100 professional artists known for their realistic styles (no abstract or avant-garde paintings allowed) were invited to display their current works. Also, some 70 paintings from the Marine Corps National Gallery in Washington, DC, were on display at the gallery.

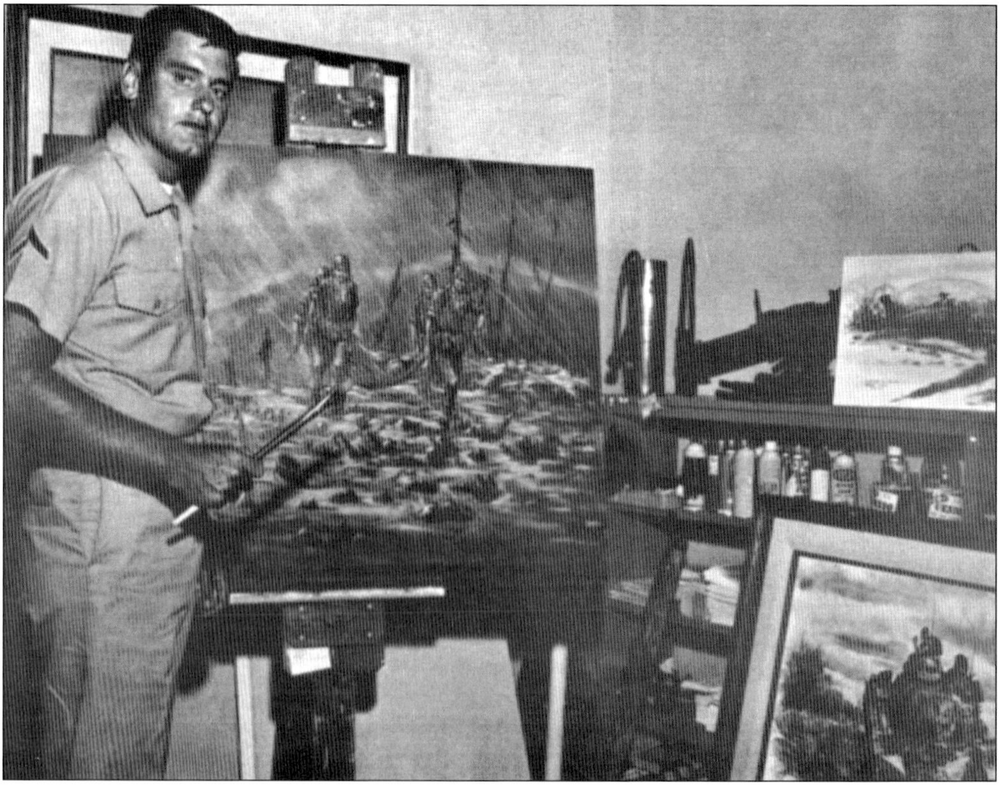

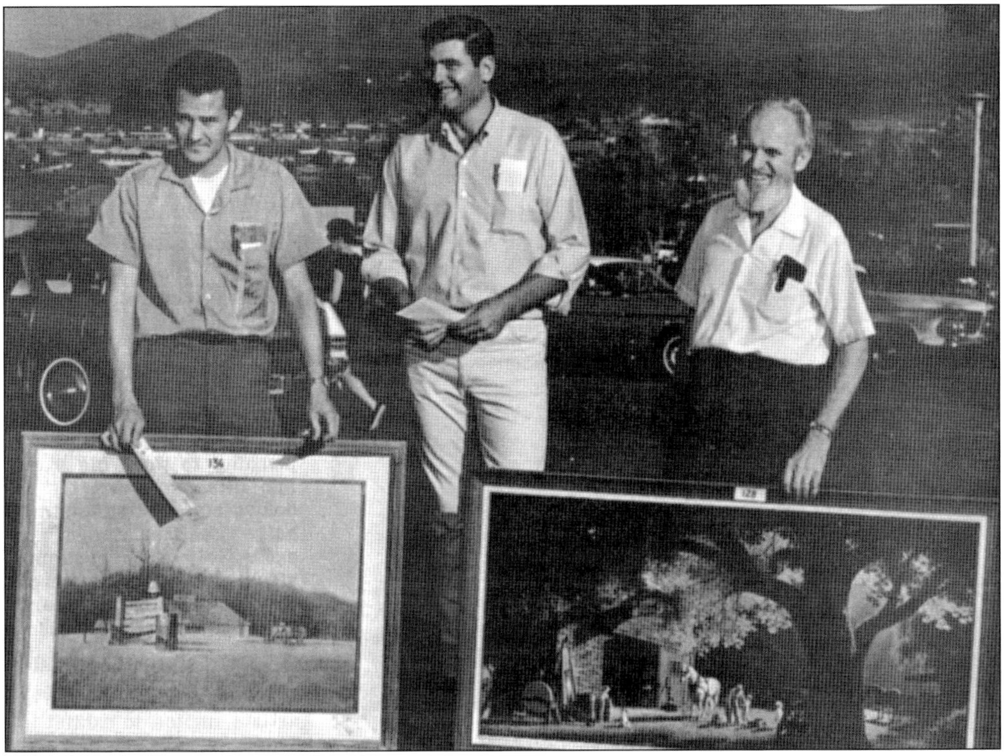

The LSM Invitational winners were Steven O. Scott's watercolor *Rural Autumn* (left), which received $400, and Paul Detlefsen's oil painting *Village Smithy* (right), which received $1,000. The prize checks were given by Austin Deuel (center), owner of the Lake San Marcos Art Gallery. The annual invitational art show attracted nearly 15,000 visitors over its two days, and the public voted for their favorite works.

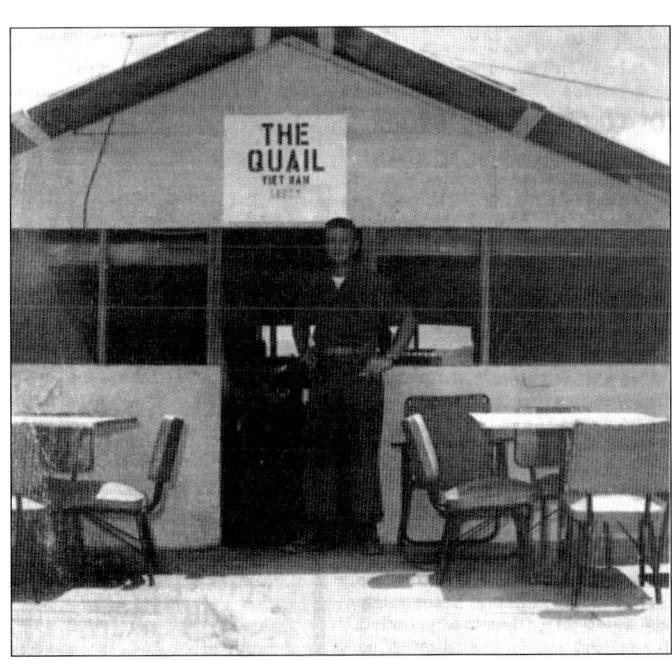

Quail's Inn bartender and Marine Harry Gamble opened the Viet Nam annex of Quail's Inn in Da Nang. Gamble said he much preferred serving his friends at Lake San Marcos and hoped to see them all soon. He had eight months to go to complete his 20 years in the Marine Corps.

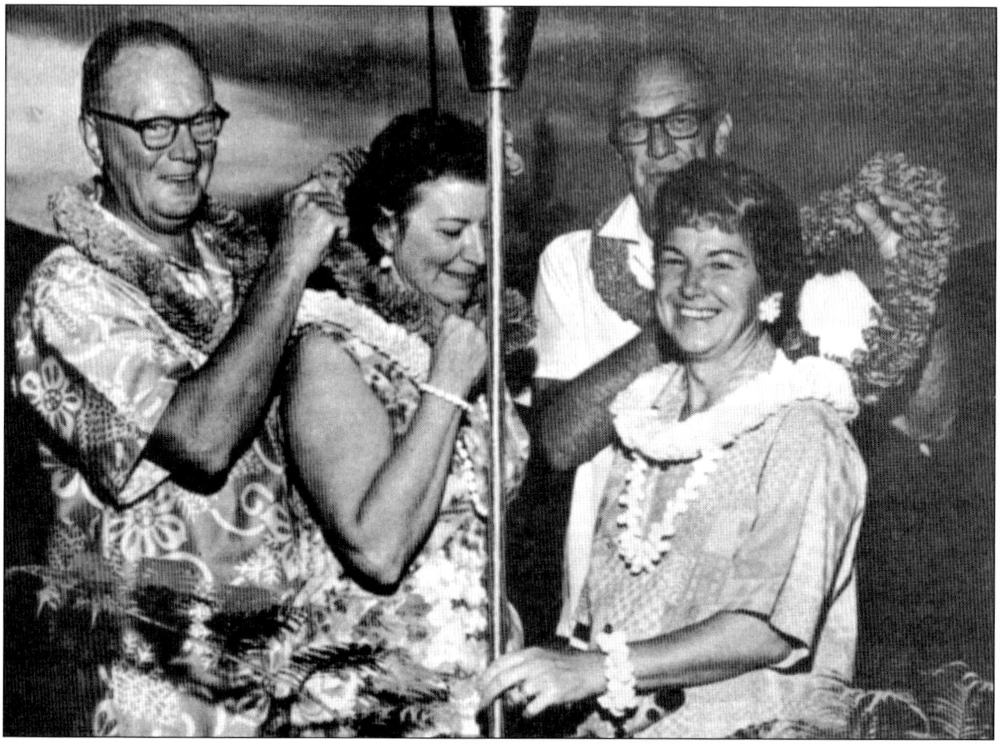

More than 200 residents turned out in colorful costumes for an evening of fun and entertainment at the third annual Lake Luau, which featured balmy weather and a full moon. Pictured from left to right are Gen. Ted Landon and his wife, Wilda, and George and Kay Dutton. Prizes were awarded for the best ladies' and men's costumes. Joan Slavinsky of Lake View Florist provided orchid and carnation leis for the occasion.

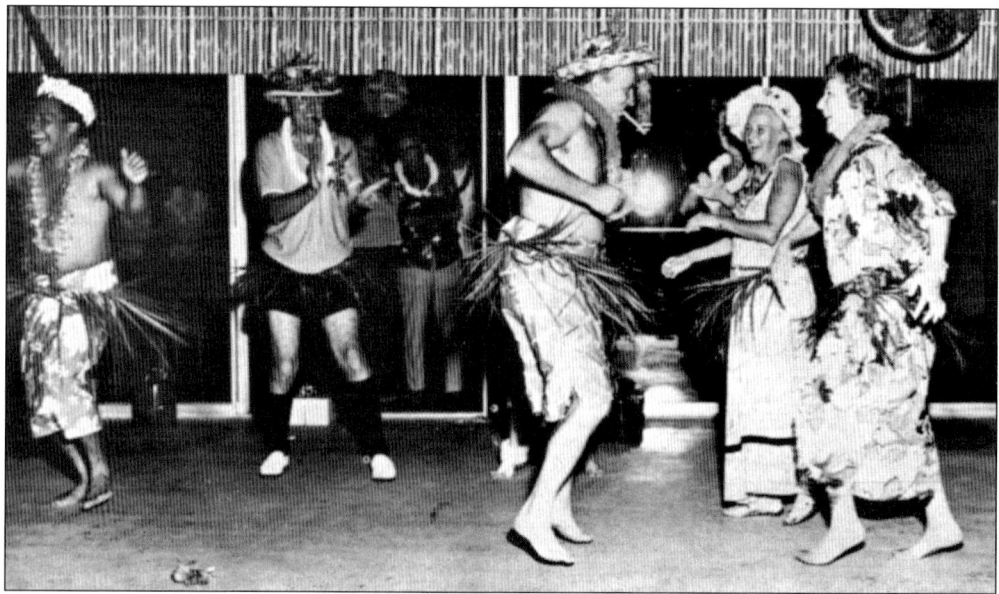

Residents got some encouragement from Bali Hai's number one entertainer, Arno (left), at the luau. Also shown dancing are, from left to right, John Wyatt, Gerri Frazar, and Helen Renn.

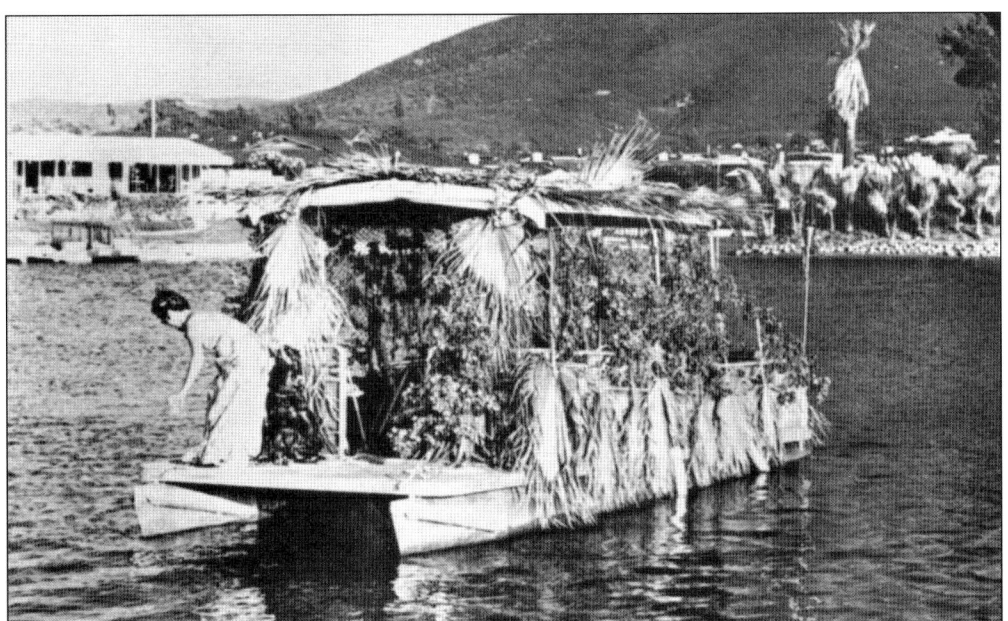

Residents caught the luau fever and came outfitted in native style. Decorated pontoon boats pulled up to the docks at the Quail's Inn Dinner House. The annual luau was a most popular event, and residents went all out with decorations and costumes.

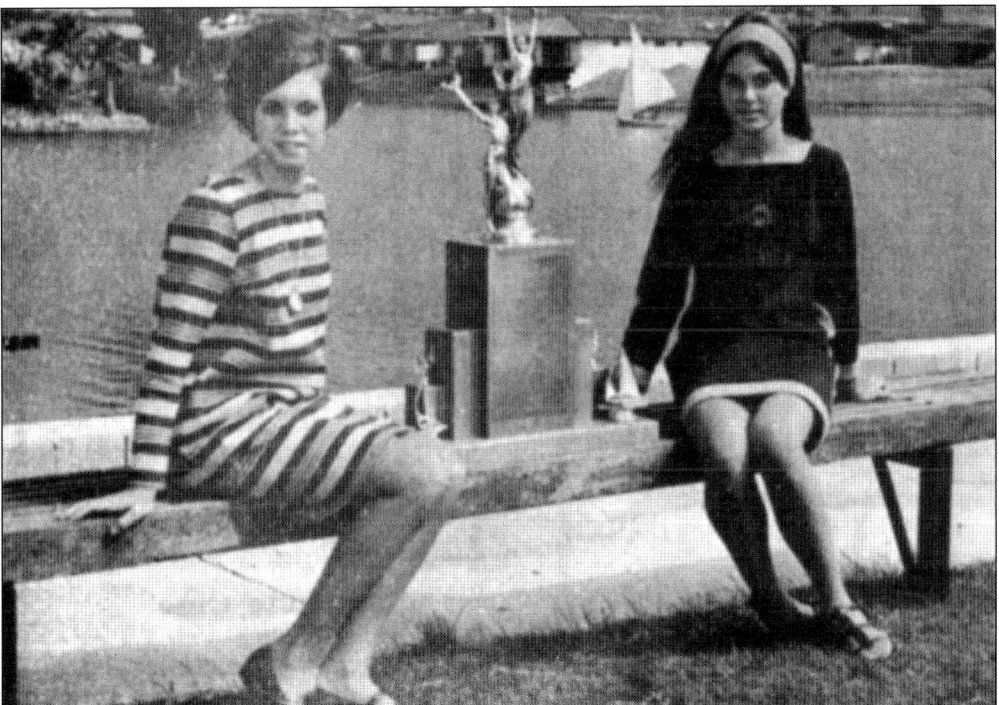

The winners of the second annual junior championship sailing races were two young ladies. Lorri Merritt (right) captained the winning Lido sailboat with Gwenn DeBit (left) crewing. They are seen with the perpetual trophy, which was to have their names inscribed and would be on display at the recreation center.

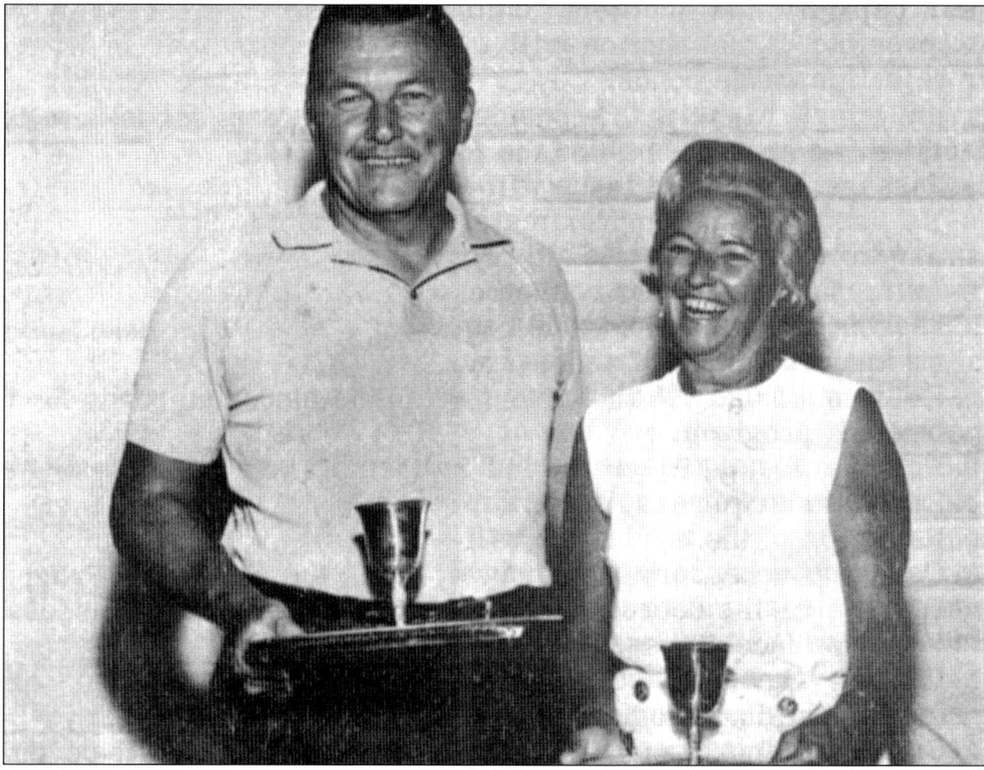

After Bob and Gerri Frazar tied for second place, they played a sudden-death round, which they lost, and took third place at the 1967 annual Lake San Marcos Invitational Golf Tournament.

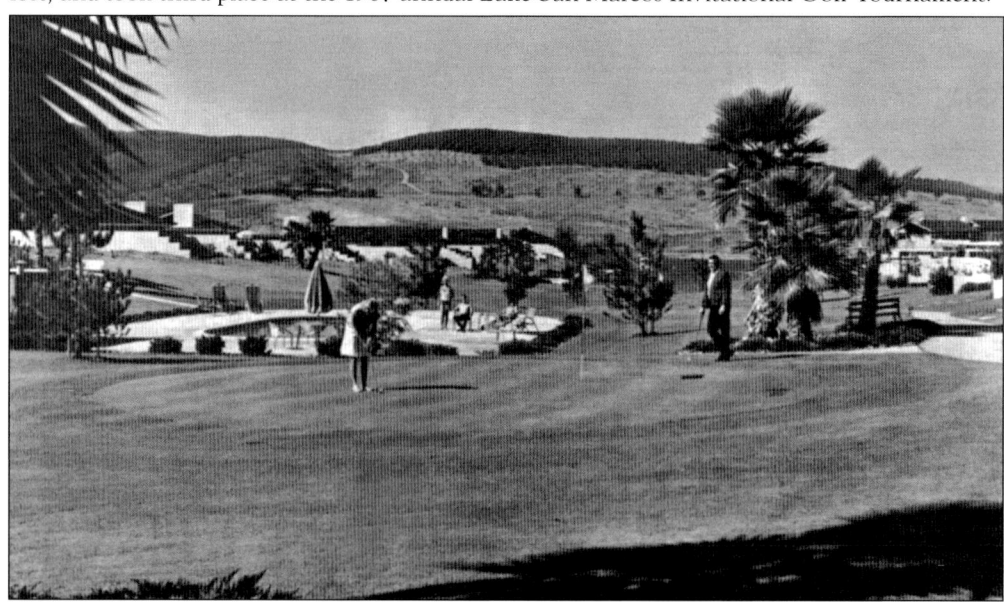

Mall 4 incorporated a pitch-and-putt golf course, nicknamed "Little St. Andrews," after the one on Mall 3 proved so popular. Mall 4 has 22 lakefront homes and 33 homes around the pitch-and-putt course. Another six lots would overlook a little area known as Lake Park, the small park located where the large water valve was used to take water out of the San Diego Aqueduct.

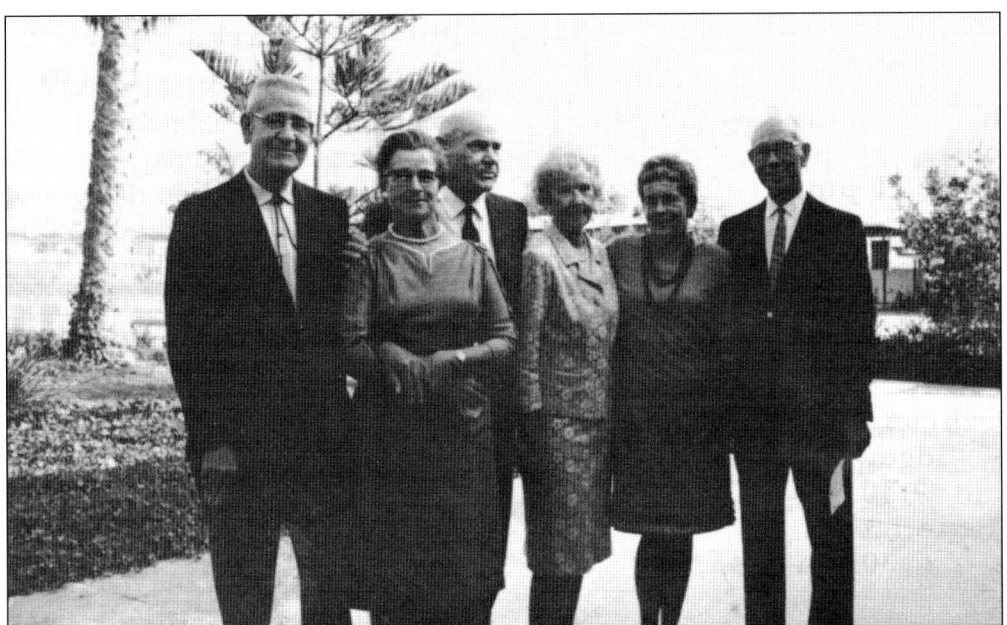

The 1967 LSM Bridge Tournament winners were, from left to right, Lloyd and Maggie Thompson, Dr Fred Mitchell, Gene Bekins, Thea Wilson, and Gary Corves. The tournament—the first of this type in LSM—was a long and hard-fought campaign. It proved so popular that another tournament was scheduled for the next year, and the tradition continues today.

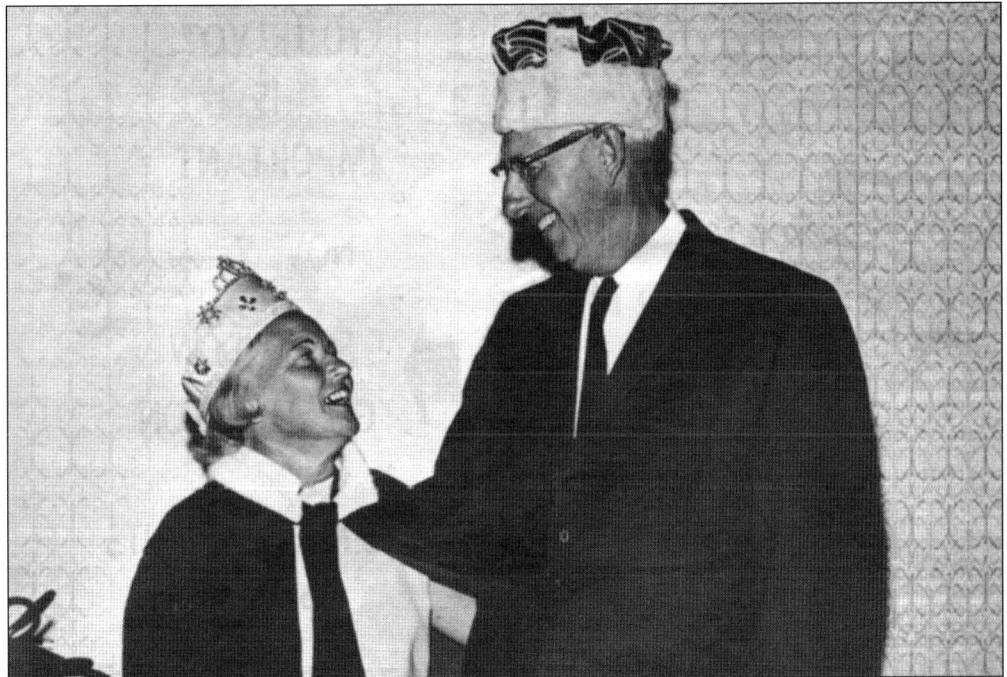

Gerri Frazar and Fred Brockett won the royal crowns in the annual Queen's Tournament for 1967. There were 94 players in this tournament, and these two won with a net of 62. The team was in the Santa Margarita Association, which won the association championship. The team captain was Maggie Thompson.

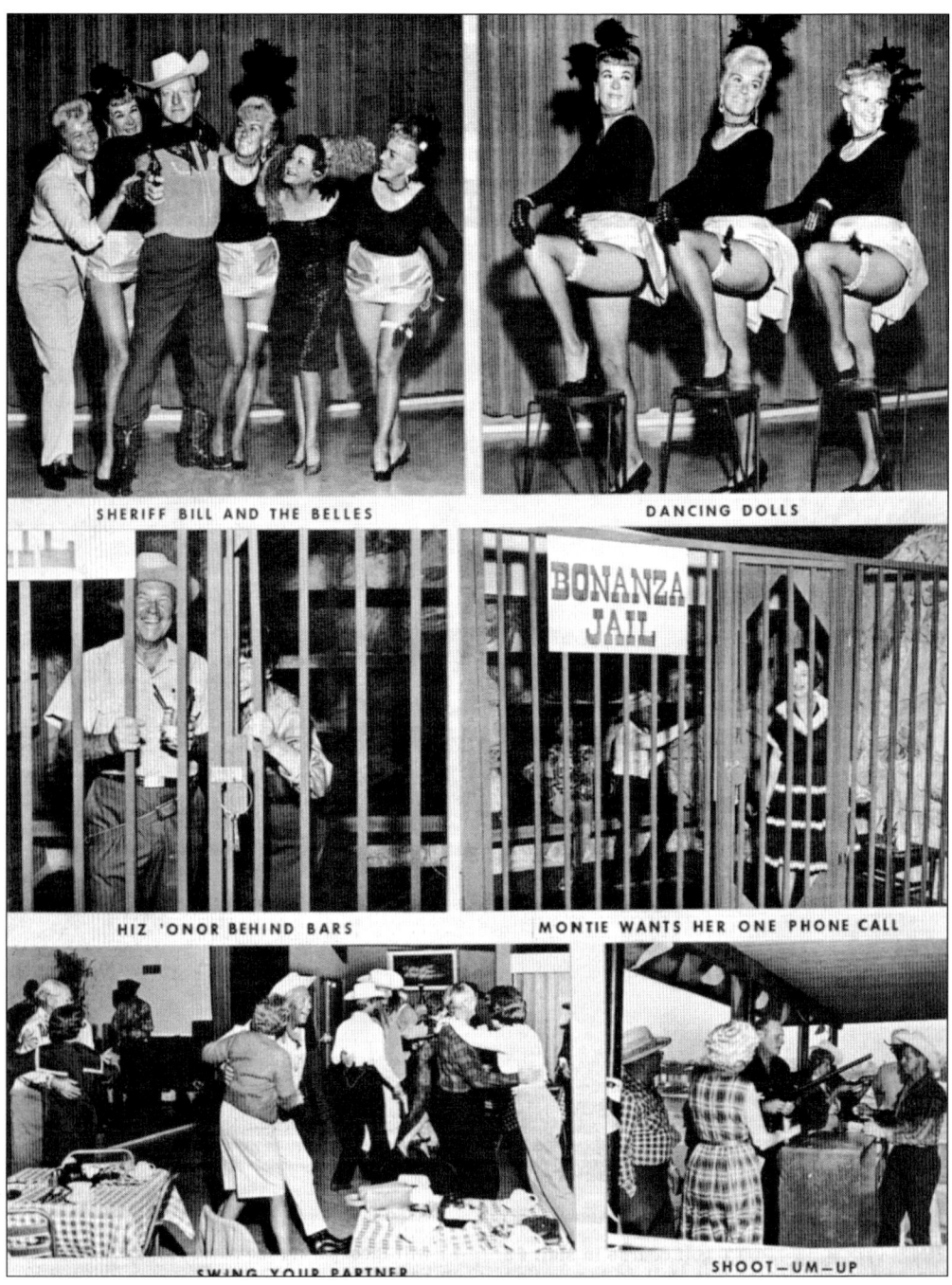

These images are from the 1967 Western Bonanza and Dinner Dance. Charles Hahne, John Beum, and Ben Farley built the jail and shooting gallery. Belles Grace Meyer, Eddie Ream, and Irene Garnjobst were choreographed by Anolyn Arden and Marcie Chase. Bill Ream tactfully policed the jailing and emceed the show. Prizes for the best costumes were determined by audience approval, and winners were Gene Bekins, June Lobdell, Peg Turner, Dewey Barber, Charles Hahne, and Cliff Bekins.

Fishing near the dam supplied the isolation and tranquility of a remote mountain wilderness. The privacy of the lake ensured peaceful areas of tranquility. Nearby was the hustle and bustle of a community with a shopping center and golf courses.

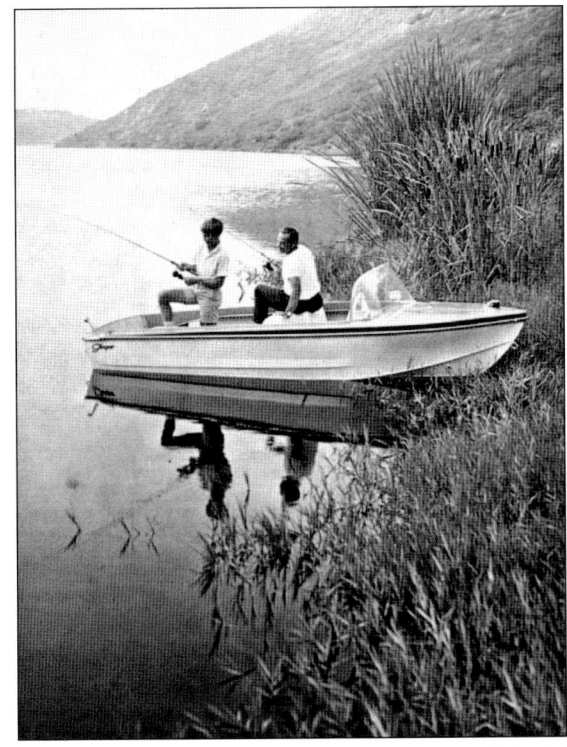

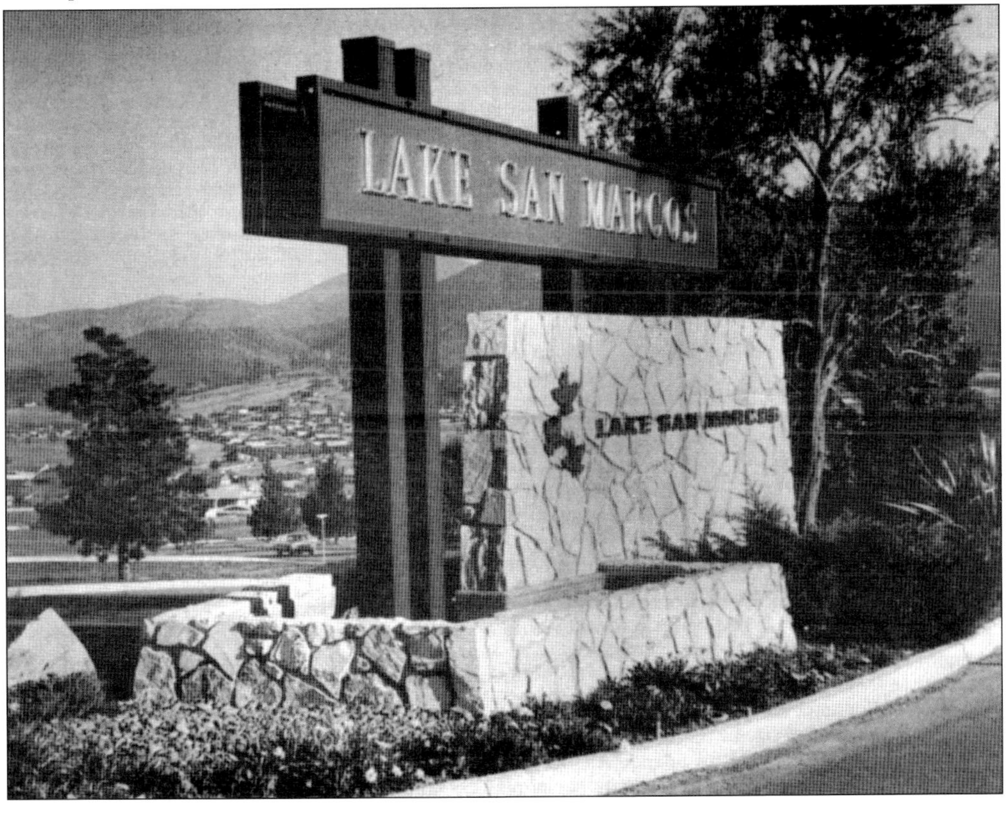

The new sign at the main entrance to Lake San Marcos on Rancho Santa Fe Road welcomed visitors. It remained at the entrance until 2013, when it was replaced. (Author's collection.)

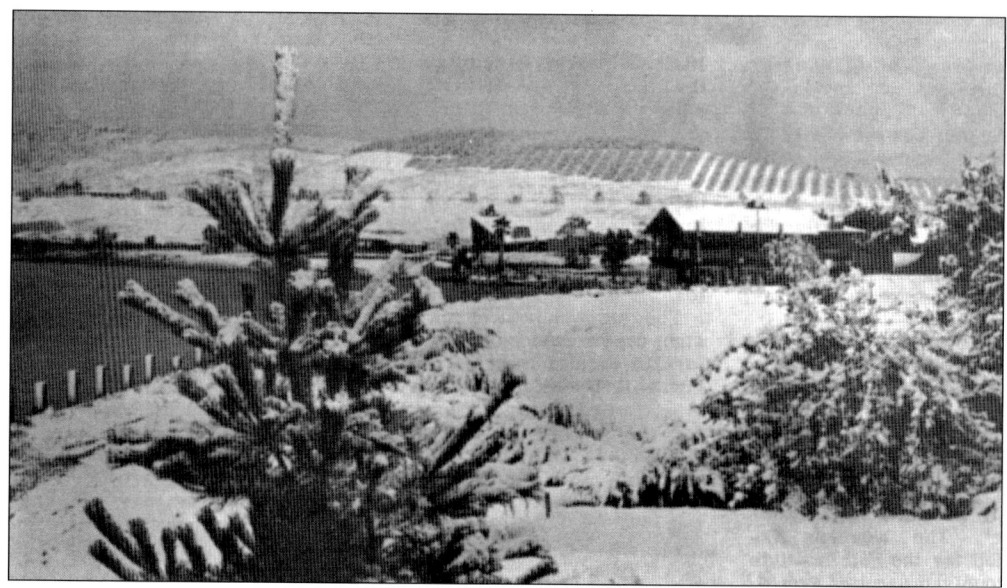

It snowed almost six inches in Lake San Marcos on December 13, 1967. Weather forecasters said this was a once-in-a-century occurrence, and it has not happened since. Dogs, children, and adults came out to play in the snow. There are truly few pictures like this one.

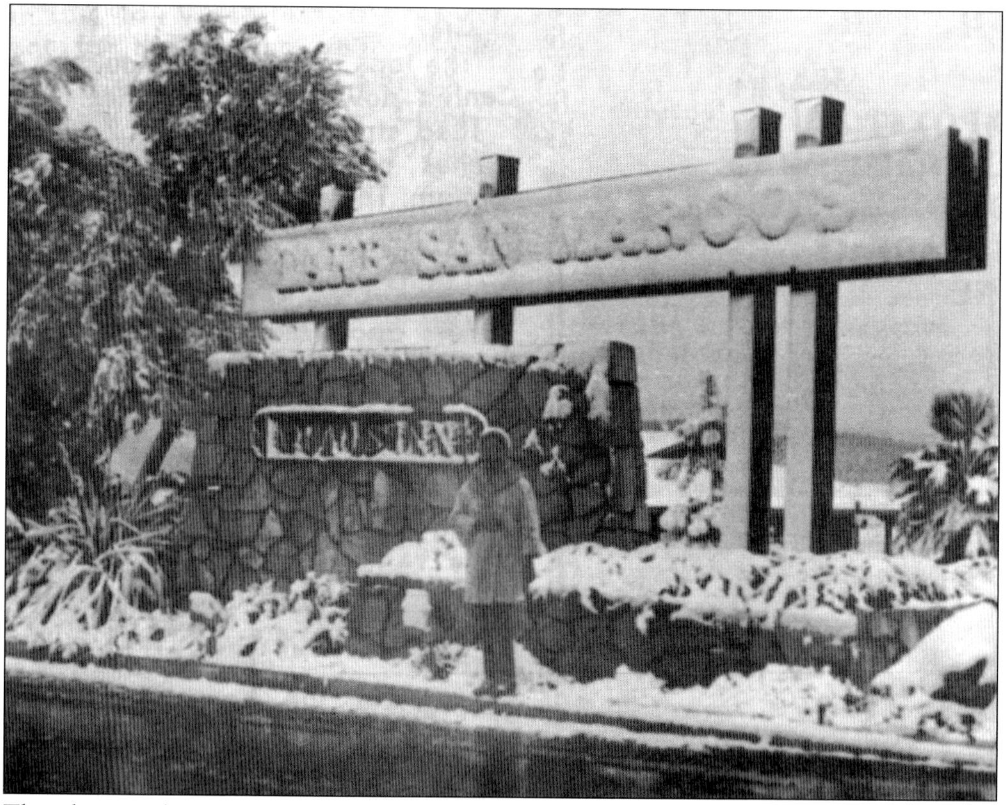

This photograph was taken by Glenn Dowdy of his wife, "Cookie," at the entrance to Lake San Marcos on December 13, 1967, the day it snowed almost six inches. (Author's collection.)

Four

The People

As the community grew, so did the need for leisure activities. The Quails Club was formed by residents and led by Frank Barton to develop community-wide clubs and social organizations. There were no dues or assessments. Various clubs were formed, including a welcoming committee (founded by Vivian Frazar and Ruth Barton), the yacht club (Harold Ide), and groups that focused on youth activities (Dorothy Steven, Ruth Sharp), arts and crafts (Betty Carlson and Mary Zoe Weeks), square dancing (Nadine and Check Pferdner), ballroom dancing (Dodie Heffer), women's bridge (Maggie Lynn), men's bridge (Walt Akers), mixed-couples bridge (Stubby Lynn), cards and games (John Wyatt), theater (Grace Meyer), potluck dinners (Eunice Isely), travel (Frank Isely), skeet and trap shooting (Wayne Rising), and shuffleboard (W. Hahne).

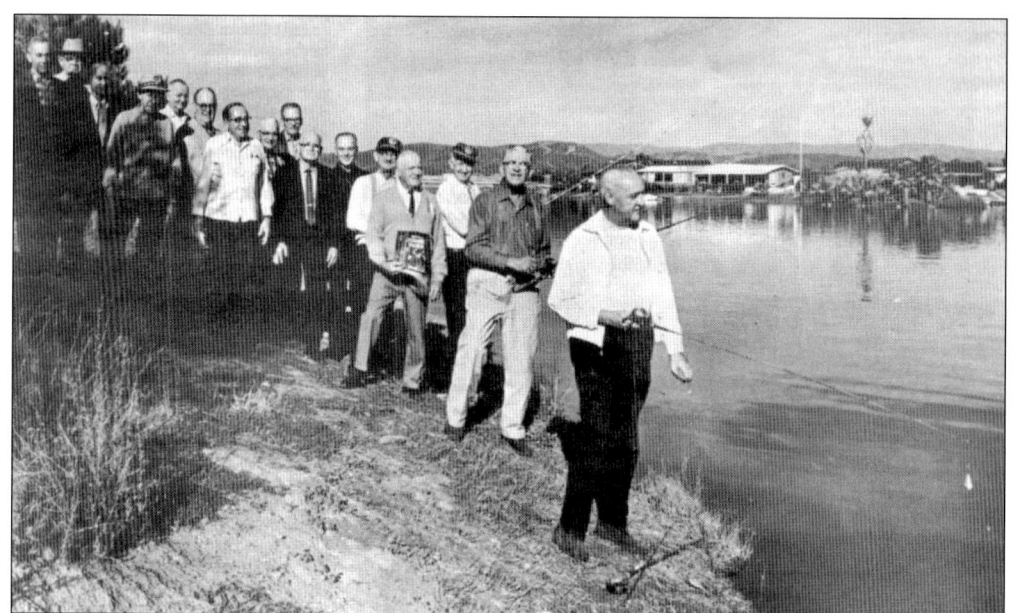

The Lake San Marcos Fishing and Casting Club formed at the suggestion of Herb Shefflin, a syndicated fishing columnist in Southern California newspapers for over 20 years. Harold Kelsey (far right) and Charles Sternberg (second from right) demonstrate overhead and side-arm casts in fly and plug casting.

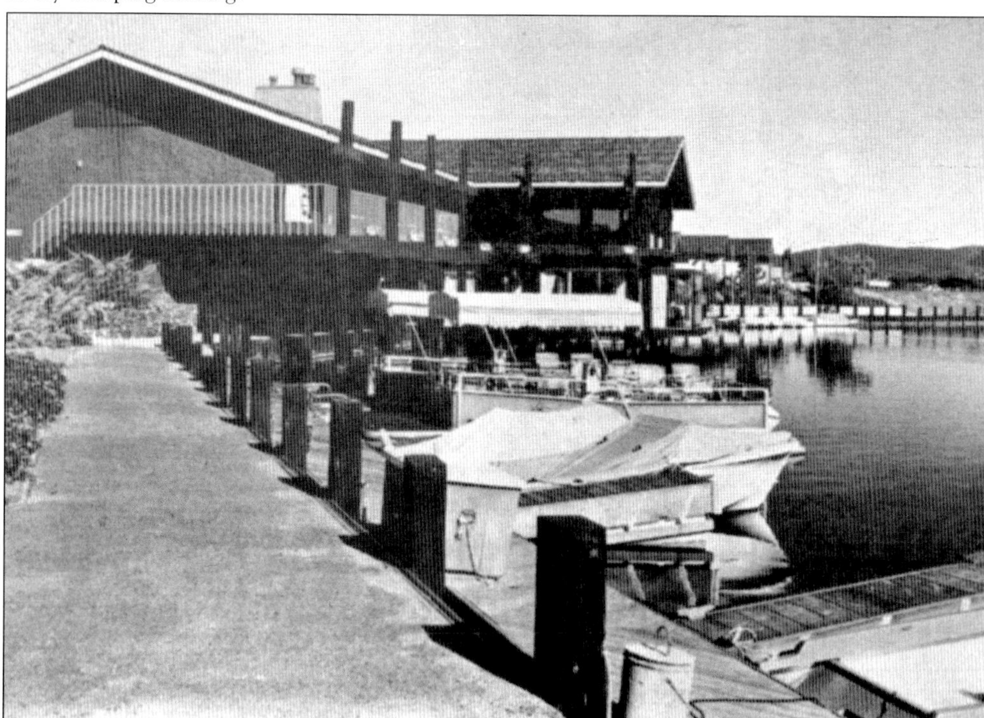

The Quail's Inn Dinner House was adjacent to the Quail's Inn Motel, which then had 76 rooms and would soon be expanded to 98. Patrons loved to sit in the Quail's Inn at dusk and watch the shadows on the hills.

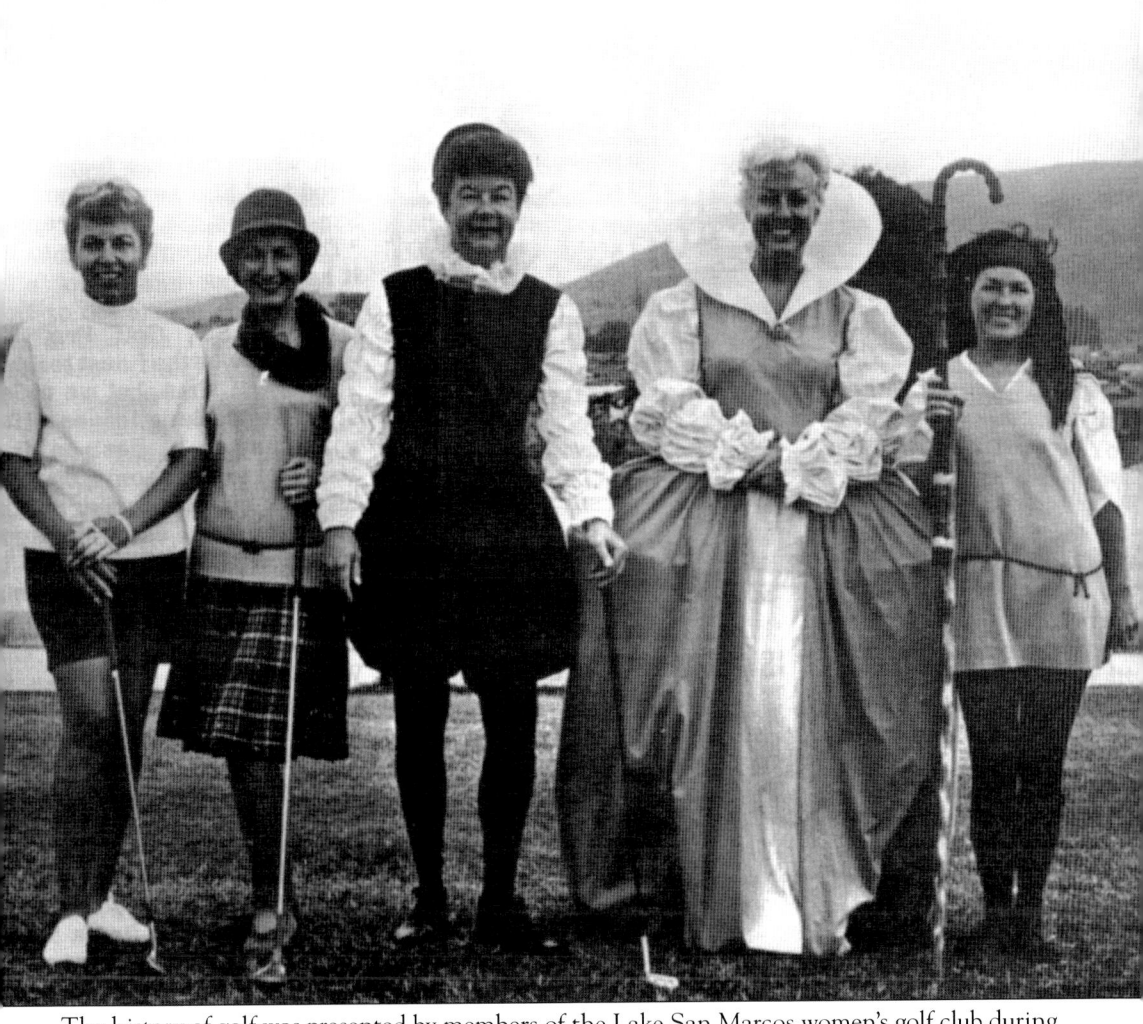
The history of golf was presented by members of the Lake San Marcos women's golf club during their fourth anniversary celebration in April 1968. From left to right are Dodie Heffer, Vee Skaff, Irene Garnjobst, Eddie Ream, (as Mary, Queen of Scots), and Marcie Chace.

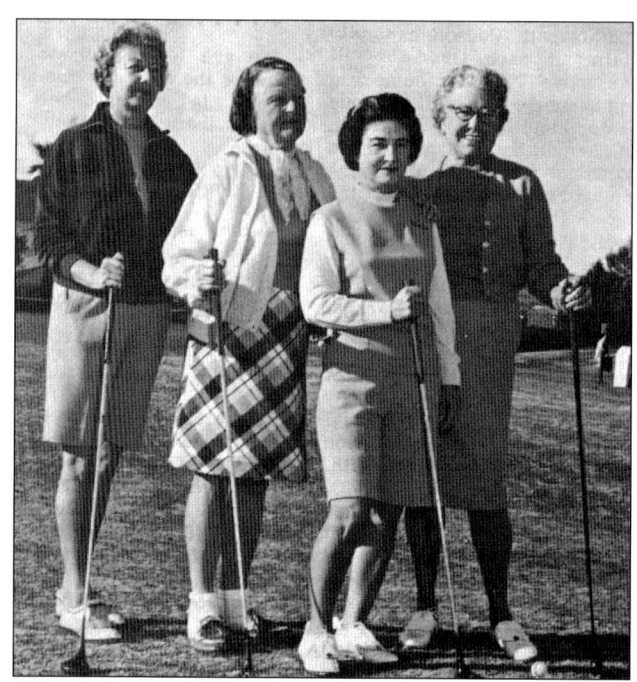

"Marie Ross Day" was held by the LSM women's golf club in honor of Marie Ross (second from left). Ross had won state championships and countless competitions all over the Northwest and Canada. She won the championship at Montebello in 1952, one at Candlewood in 1958, and played in the Augusta Open. A perpetual trophy had been donated in her honor. The first winner was June Lobdell. The men's club presented Marie with a beautiful bouquet of red roses. Pictured with Ross are, from left to right, Cecil Samuels, Olive Taylor, and Ruth Sternberg.

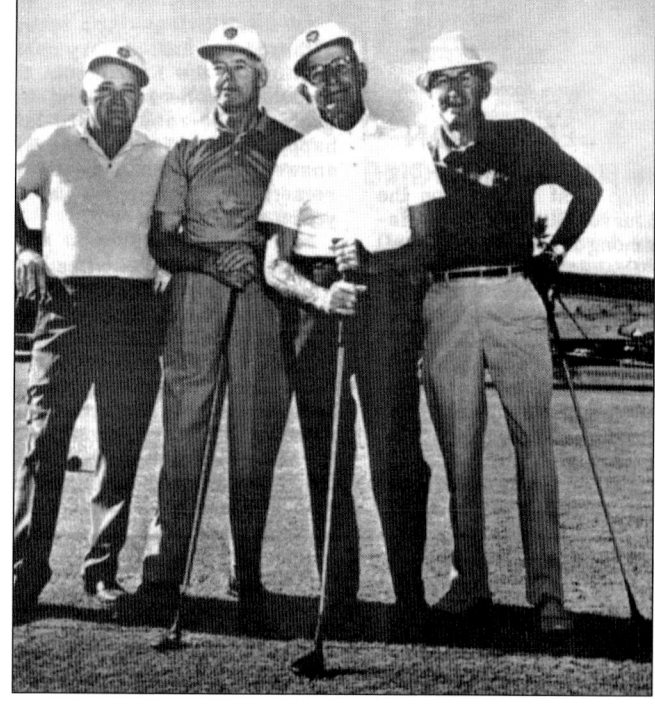

The men's club sponsored its own Fred Gates Tournament in honor of Gates's 81st birthday. The honoree's foursome included, from left to right, Joe Evans, Harry Edmunds, Gates, and Ernie Culp.

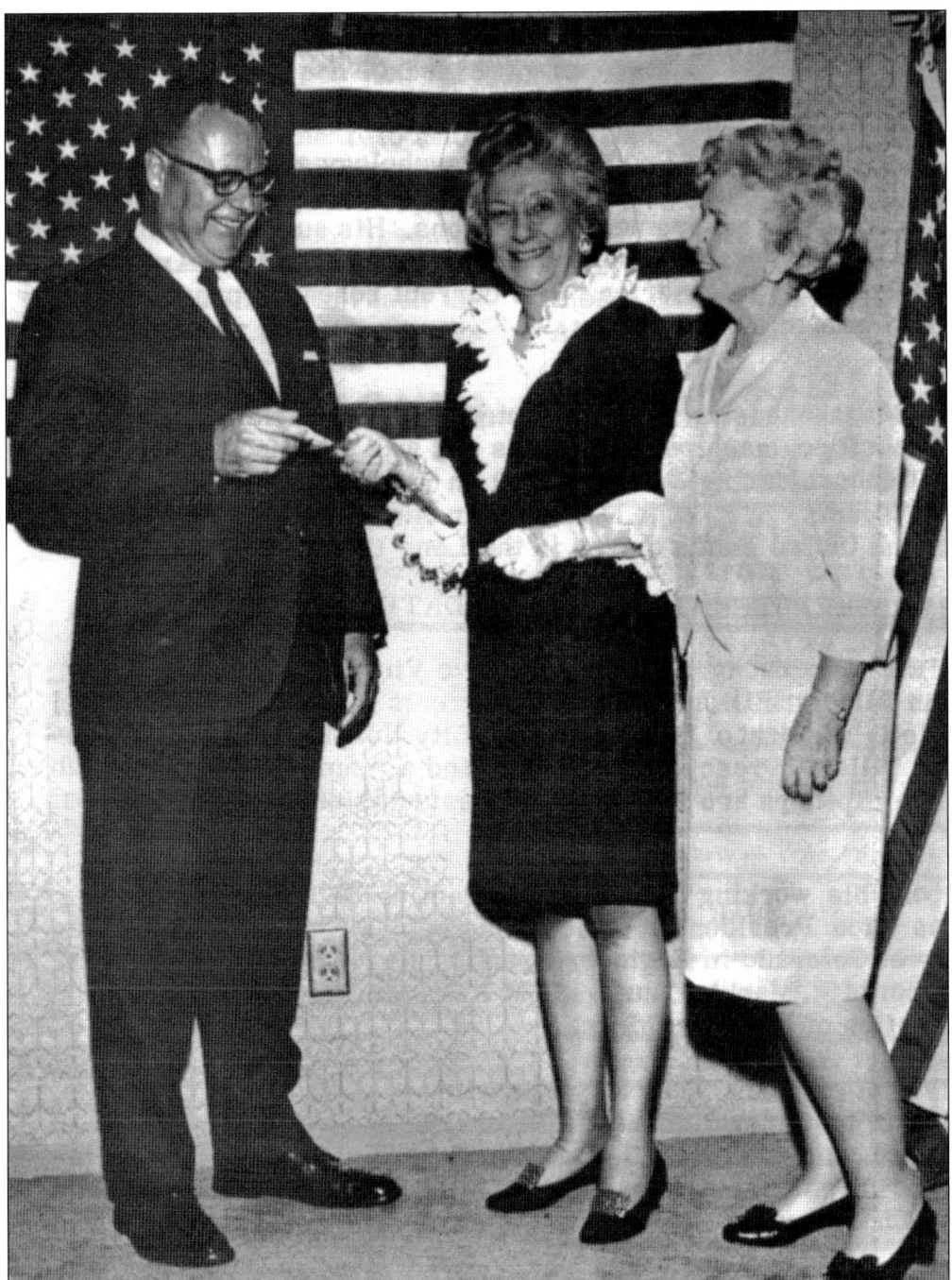

LSM residents responded to USO Day by raising $700 through the Lake San Marcos women's golf club, which sponsored the USO Golf Tournament. The tournament was directed by Mrs. Hal Grisamer and included 136 female golfers. Here, Regina Bekins looks on as Mrs. E.H. Kendig gives Otto Hirr, member of the board of directors for the San Diego USO, the $700 check.

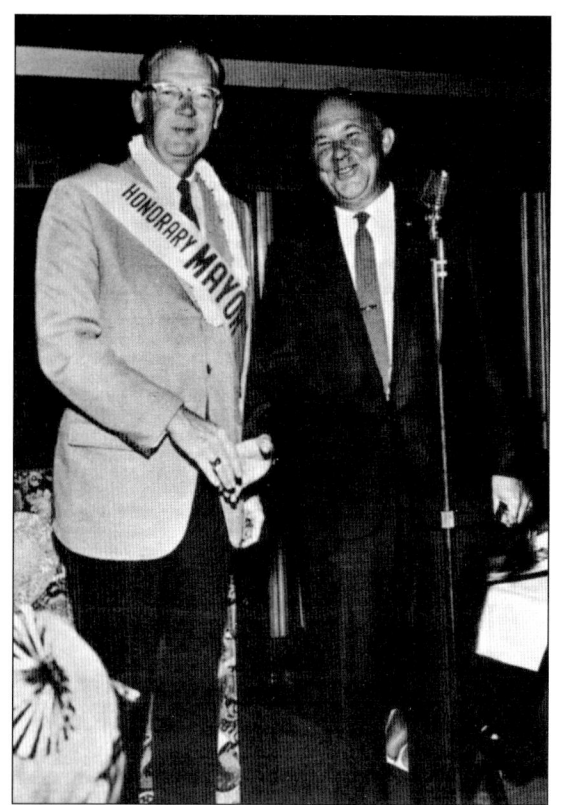

Former mayor Charles Hahne (right) congratulates 1968–1969 honorary mayor William Hipsher. Hipsher would not only serve as the honorary mayor of LSM but also as chairman of the LSM Coordinating Council. Richard Livingston would serve as vice chairman. The new procedure called for the coordinating council to elect a chairman from its elected membership rather than from mayoral campaigns.

Members of the 1968 coordinating council posed for this group picture. They are, from left to right, (first row) Wendell La Belle (men's golf club representative), Charles Hahne, Mrs. Frank Isely, Richard Livingston, and Allyn Blunt; (second row) Bob Wallman, John Wyatt, Don Heffer, Bill Hipsher, Fred Brockett, Ken Shaw, and Gordon Frazar. William Hipsher, who was executive vice president of the Mueller Company in Illinois, became the third Lake San Marcos honorary mayor.

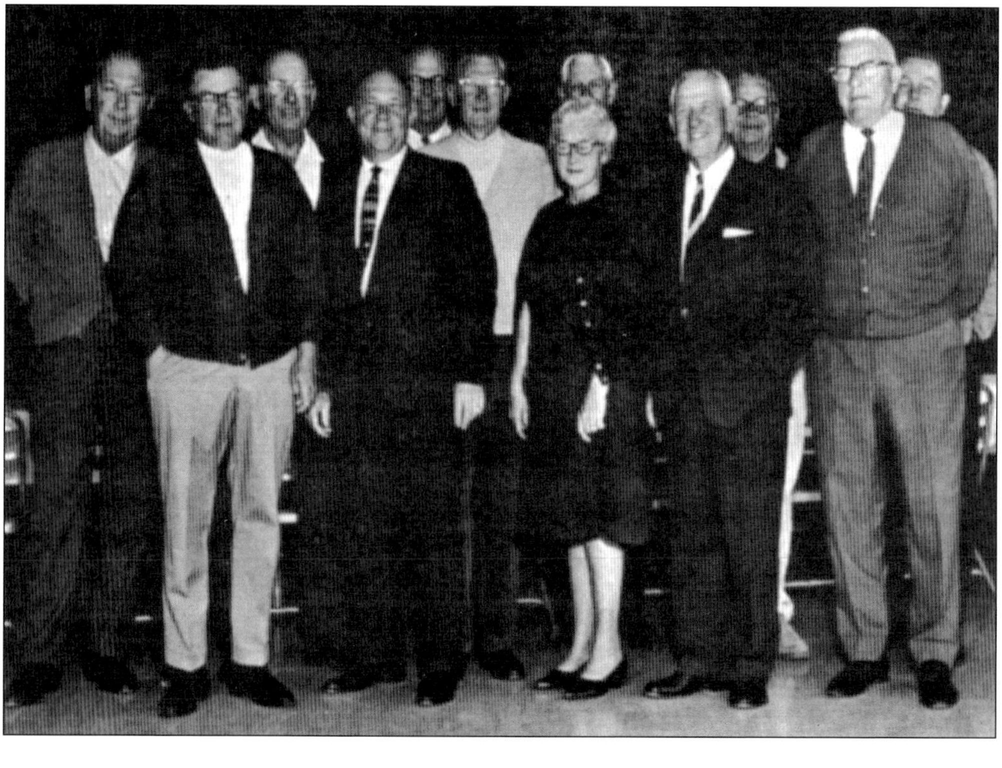

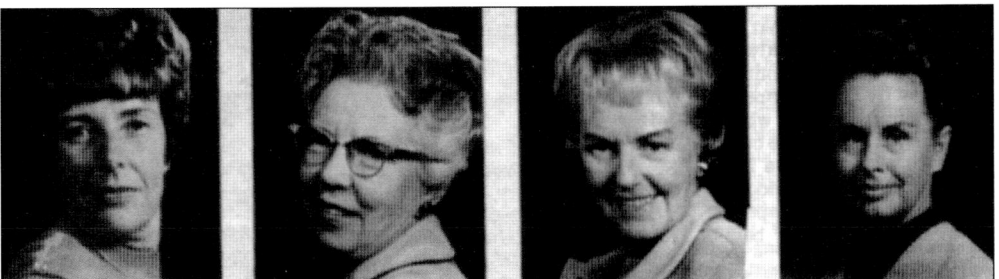

The women's golf club founders and past presidents are seen here. From left to right are Nadine Pferdner (1964), Kay Worman (1965), Grace Meyer (1966), and Ruth Sharp (1967).

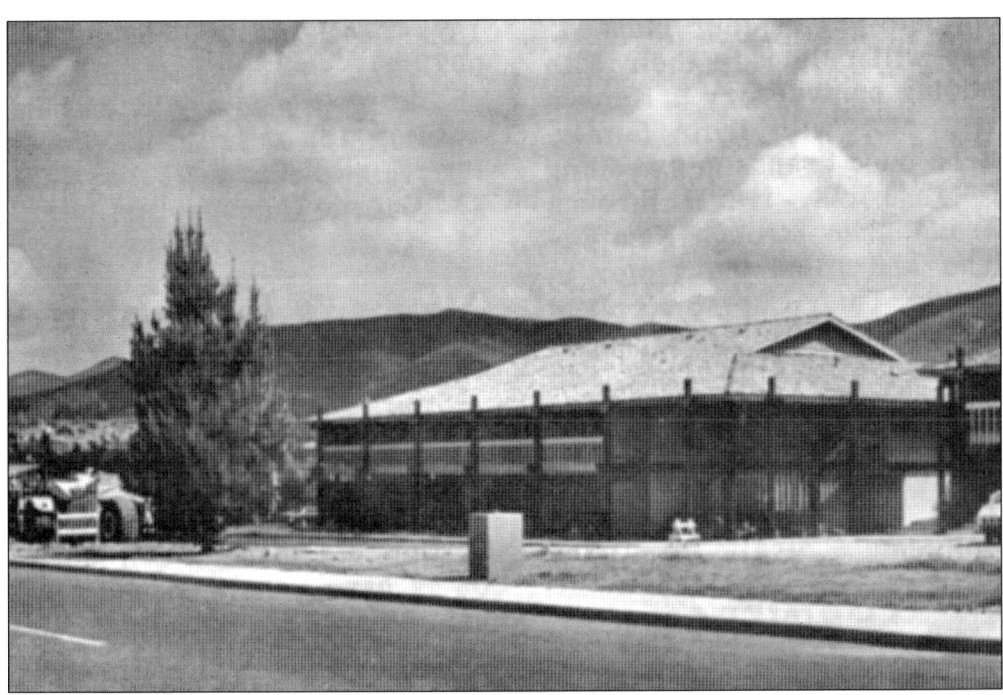

A 22-room addition to the Quail's Inn Motel brought the total room number to 98. The design and layout of the rooms had been attractively updated from the older accommodations. The furnishings were spectacular and included a color television in each room.

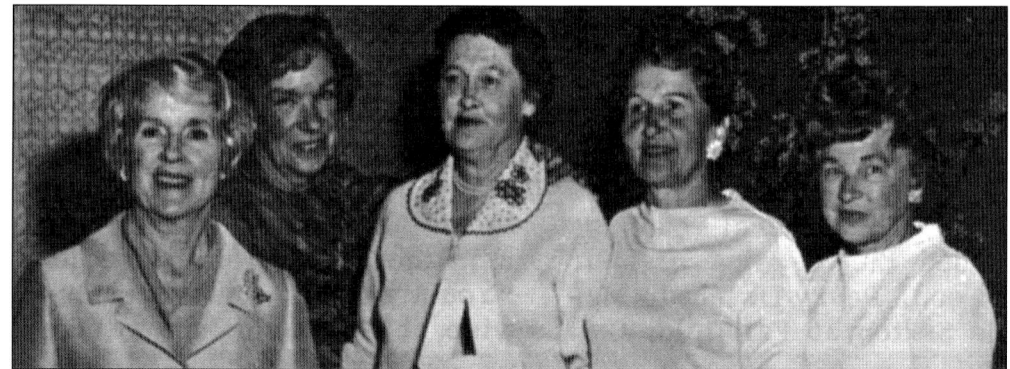

A party was given to honor the five original founders of the women's golf club. Shown from left to right are Mabel Hunt, Jean McGregor, Marion Griffiths, Marie Hall, and Ruth Hipsher. Afterward, the crowd enjoyed a buffet dinner in the Trophy Room at the country club.

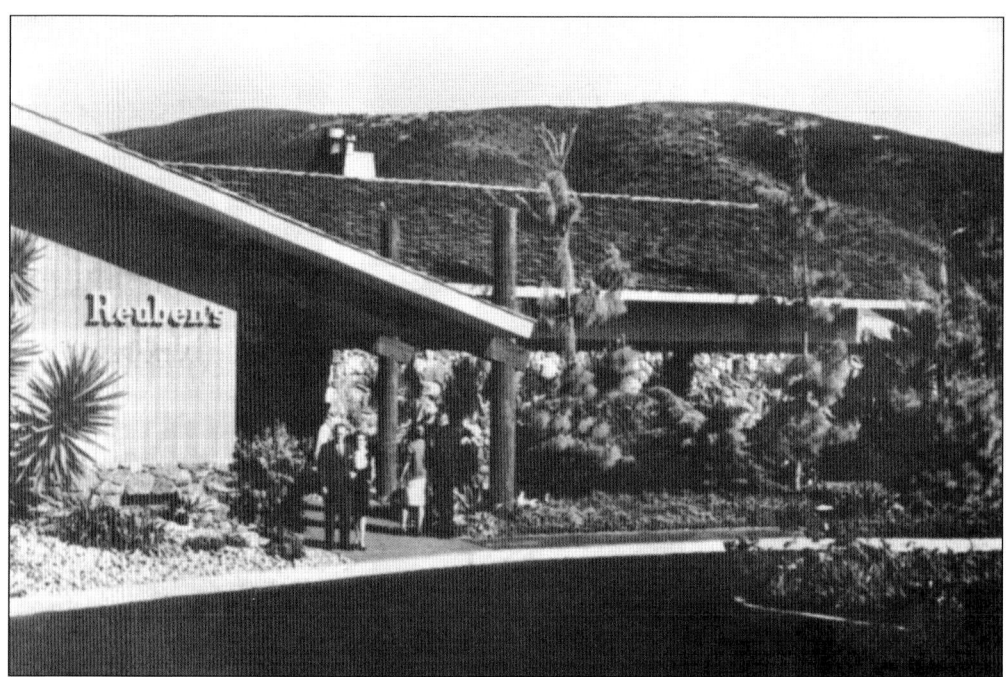

The Quail's Inn Restaurant became Reuben's after being remodeled with a Mediterranean theme. Every effort was made to have both the restaurant and the country club become a point of pride and enjoyment to all lake residents. Reuben's and the Quail's Inn Restaurant were favorites to more than just local residents, as people came from many miles to enjoy the lakeside views.

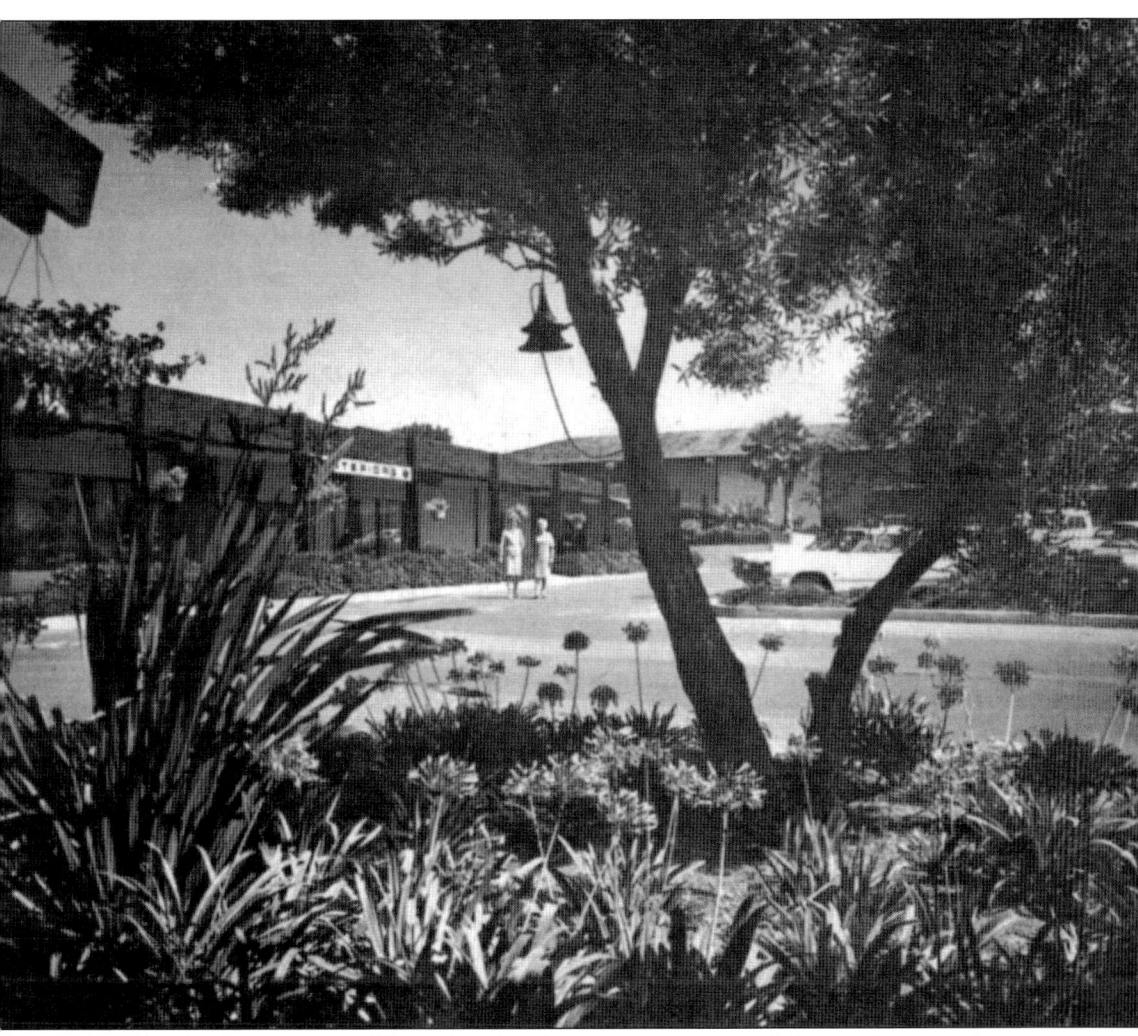
When the shopping center celebrated its fourth anniversary, most of the merchants and service people had been there from the beginning and were looking forward to many more years.

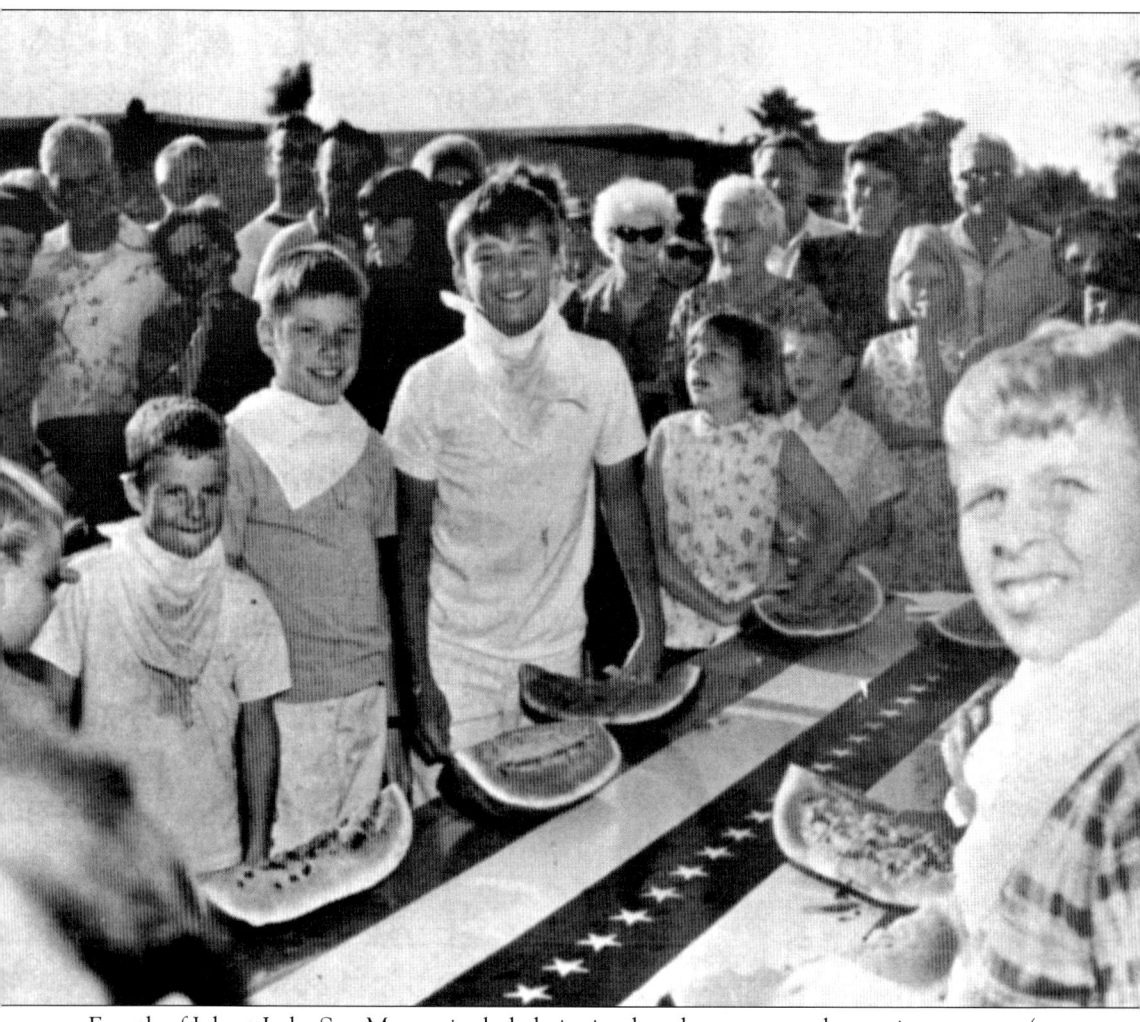

Fourth of July at Lake San Marcos included picnics, hot dogs, watermelon-eating contests (seen here), sack races, carnival booths, music, and bonfires. Many of the clubs sponsored booths and entertainment. The Women's Fellowship supplied hot dogs and home-baked goods. The women's Golf Club had a bargain book stall, and after sunset, an enormous bonfire was lit and everyone enjoyed watching the lighted boat parade sponsored by the yacht club. The festivities kicked off at 4:00 p.m., with the boat parade commencing at 8:30 p.m.

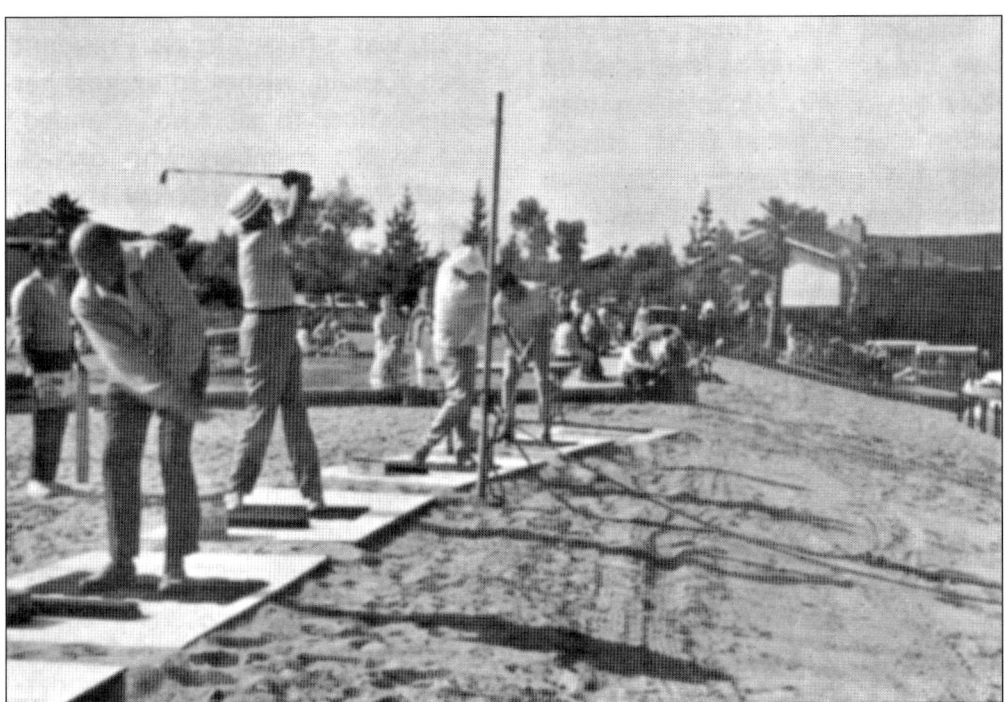

On July 4, golfers displayed their skill on the lakefront driving range, taking aim at a floating target. More than 1,000 used golf balls found their way to the bottom of the lake and are still there.

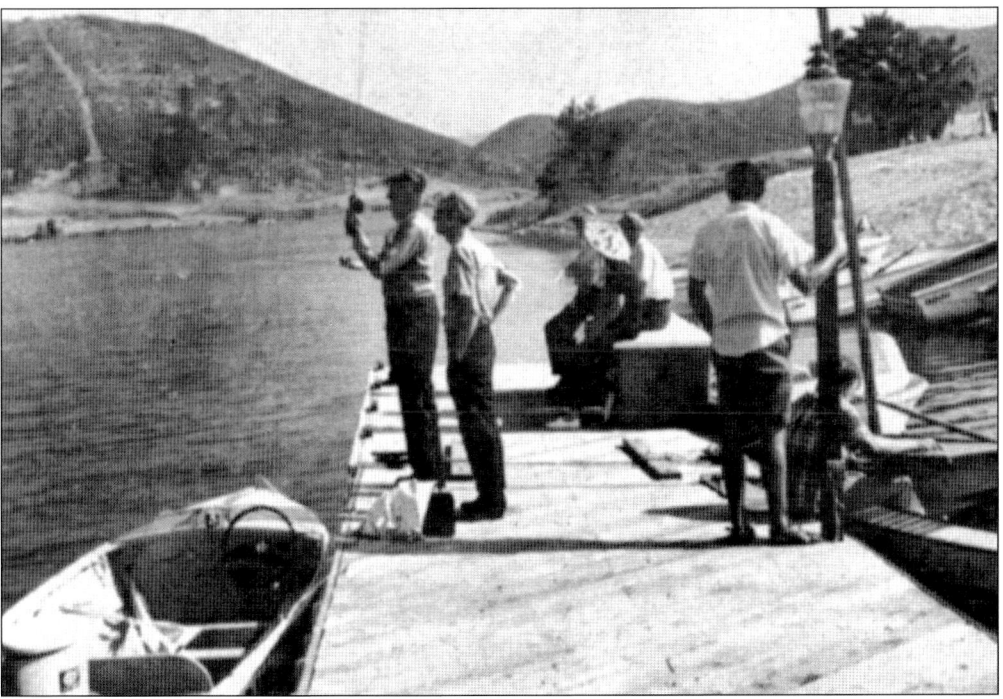

Seen here are fishing and casting club members Paul Cheney (holding the fishing rod) and Harold Ide (observing). The club's July meeting was held in the club room of the recreation center. The door prize, a fine fishing pole, was won by Al Hotz, the president.

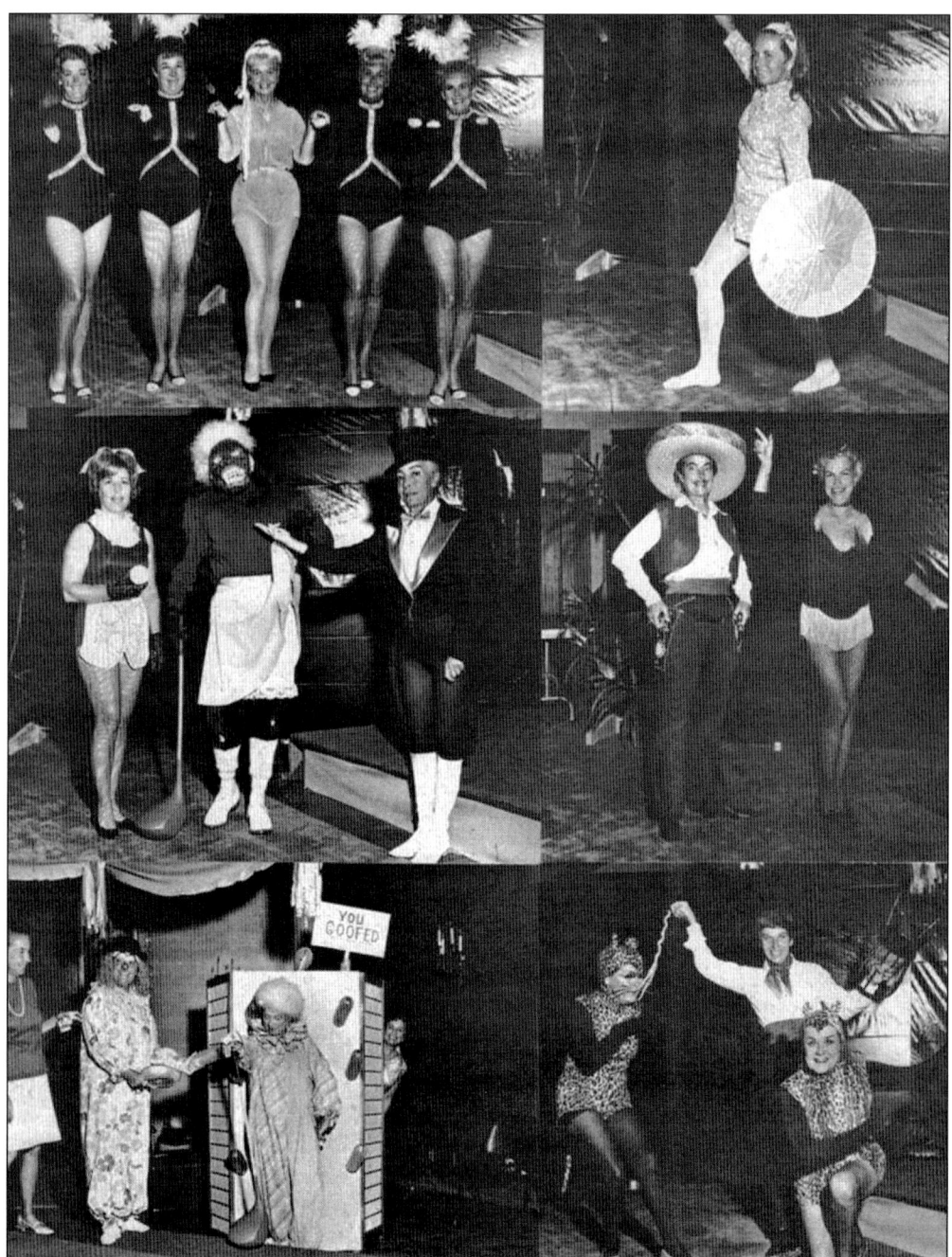

The circus was the theme of the third annual LSM Women's Club Invitational. Hostesses were dressed as clowns, and hot dogs and refreshments were served. Thursday evening, there was a Gala dinner, and tables were decorated with stunning stuffed caged animals. Following dinner, guests were entertained with the "The Circus," produced by Eddie Ream, with Anolyn Arden directing.

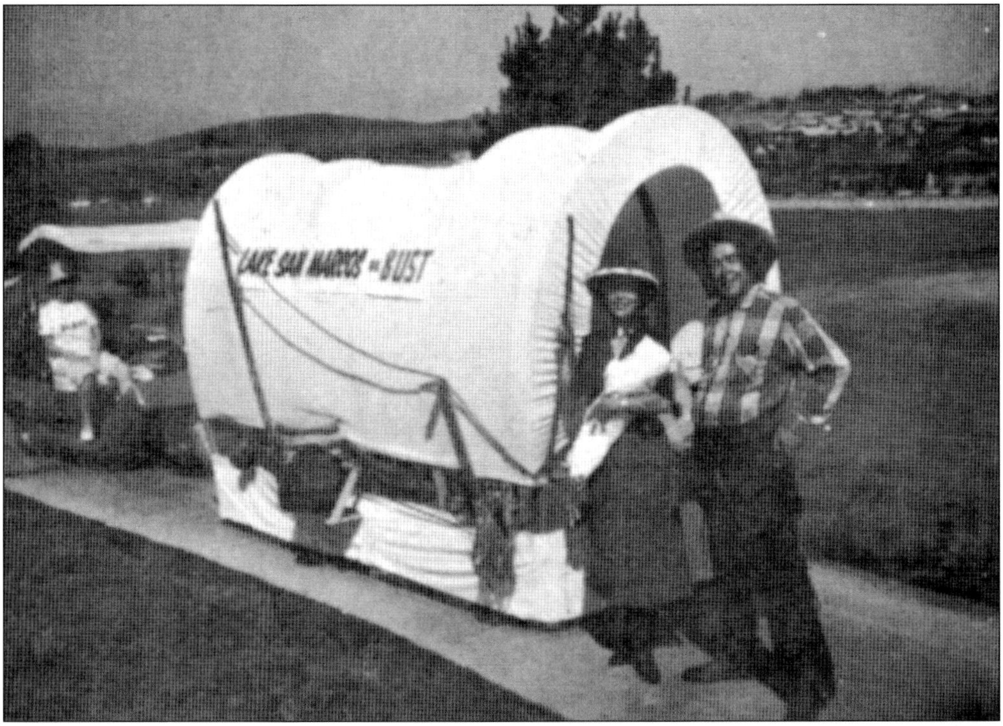

Once a year, on Goofy Golf Day, the men's club dedicated an event to emphasize the fun of the game. Costumes and decorated carts were original, imaginative, and hilarious. Above, the Wyatt Burps (John and Tensie Wyatt) were burly and unbathed, but they and their cart were filled with "spirits."

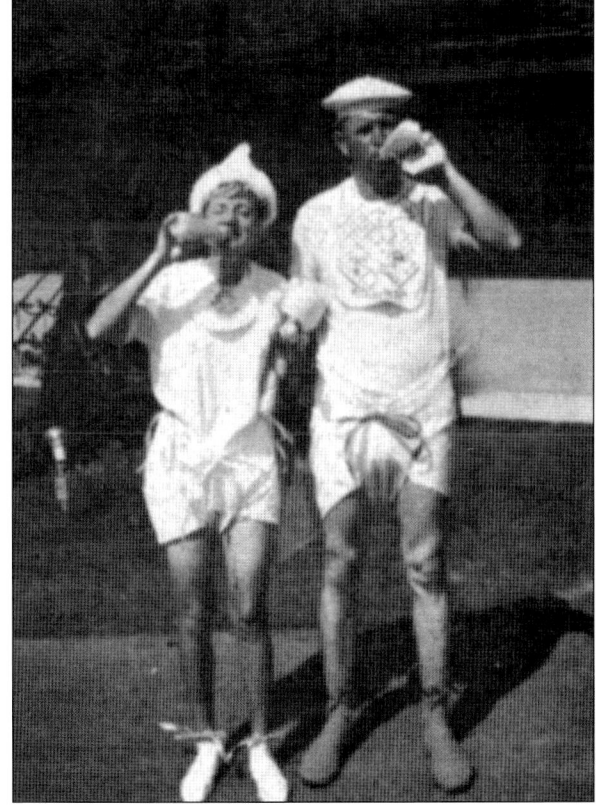

Jackie and Mary O'Connor stole the show on Goofy Golf Day by playing 18 holes in diapers, booties, and bibs. To make all players equal, unique hazards were scattered throughout the course. For example, on the 10th tee, a "one-hold biffie" was installed. All players were required to hit their tee shots seated on this relaxing donnicker.

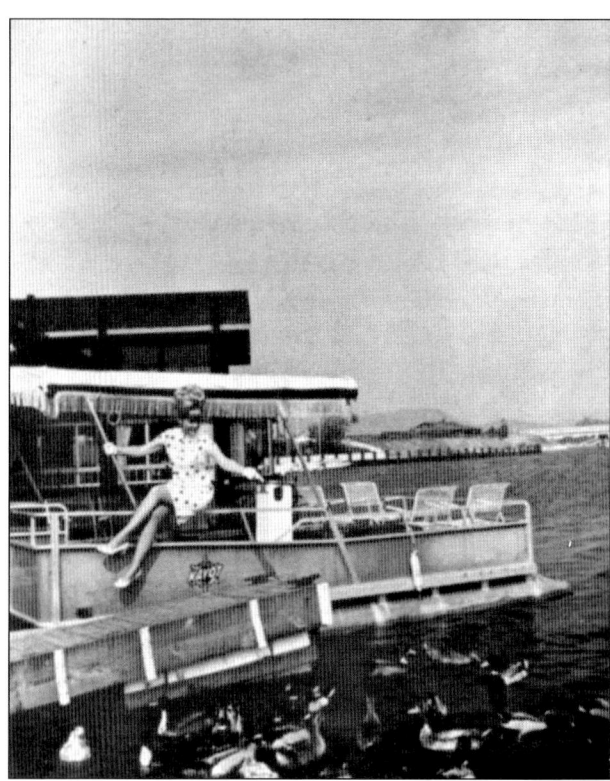

Duck-watching from Kayot boats was a popular activity on the lake and a constant source of amusement for visitors. Most of the ducks had become completely tame and seldom left the area.

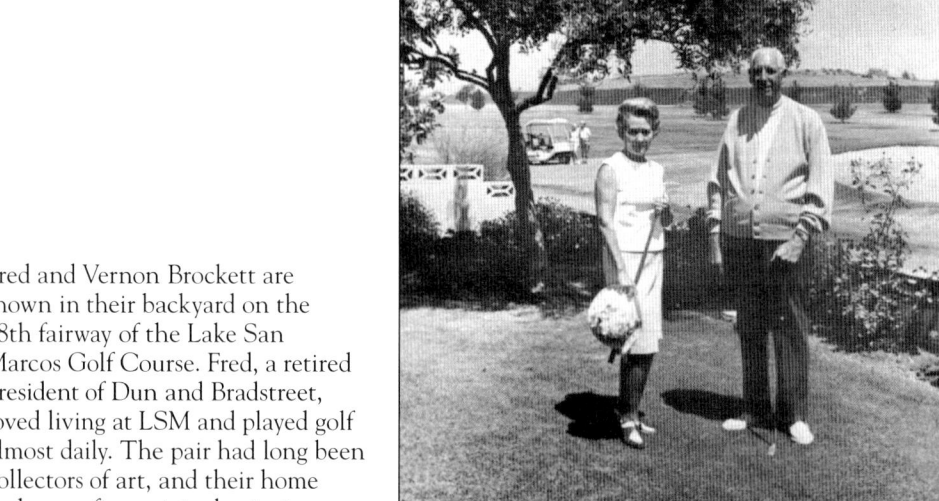

Fred and Vernon Brockett are shown in their backyard on the 18th fairway of the Lake San Marcos Golf Course. Fred, a retired president of Dun and Bradstreet, loved living at LSM and played golf almost daily. The pair had long been collectors of art, and their home had many fine original paintings.

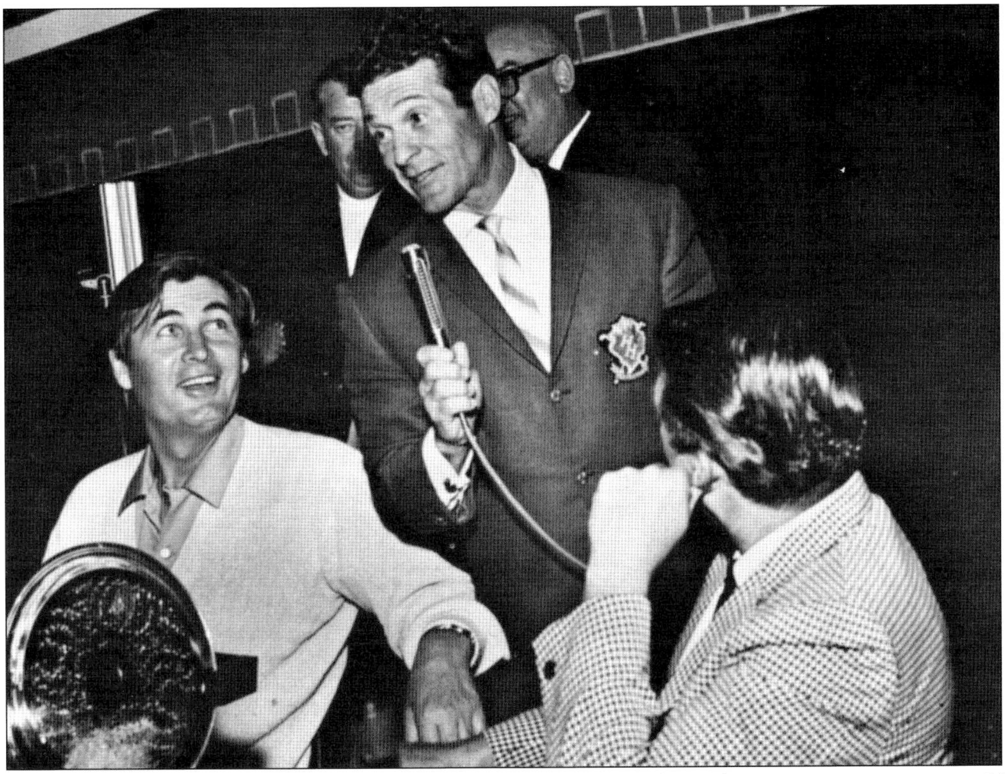

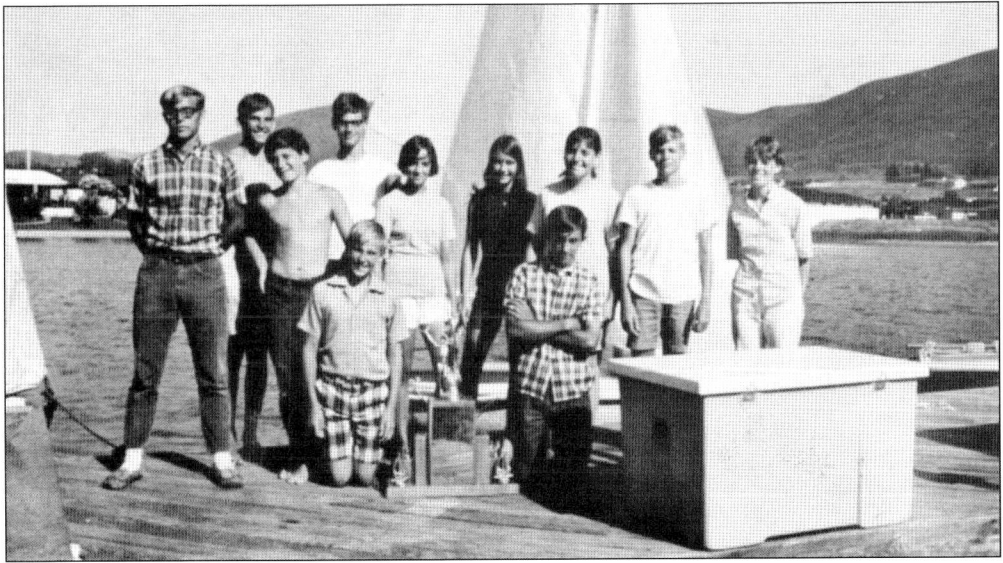

Celebrities Fess Parker (left) and Jack LaLanne come together after participating in a golf tournament. Lake San Marcos drew many Hollywood celebrities to the excellent golf course and lakeside amenities.

Jim Blaschke (left) volunteered to conduct sailing classes and to officiate at the annual Lido race. Members of the class were, standing from left to right, Chris Cutter, Ian Chamberlain, Jeff Swink, Gay Gadbois, Laurie Brindle, Sue Snavely, Tim Halloran, and Sharon Carew. Kneeling in front are the winners of the race, Kent Cutter and Bob Blaschke.

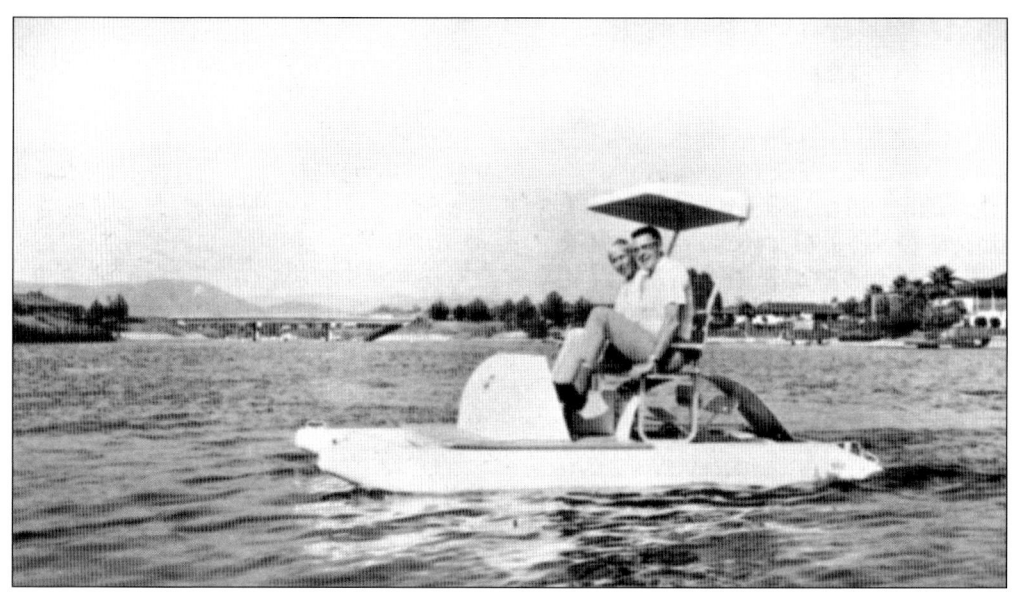

Bob and Dorothy Ann Christie demonstrated their new bicycle built for two. Water sports were, and still are, a large part of the recreation at LSM.

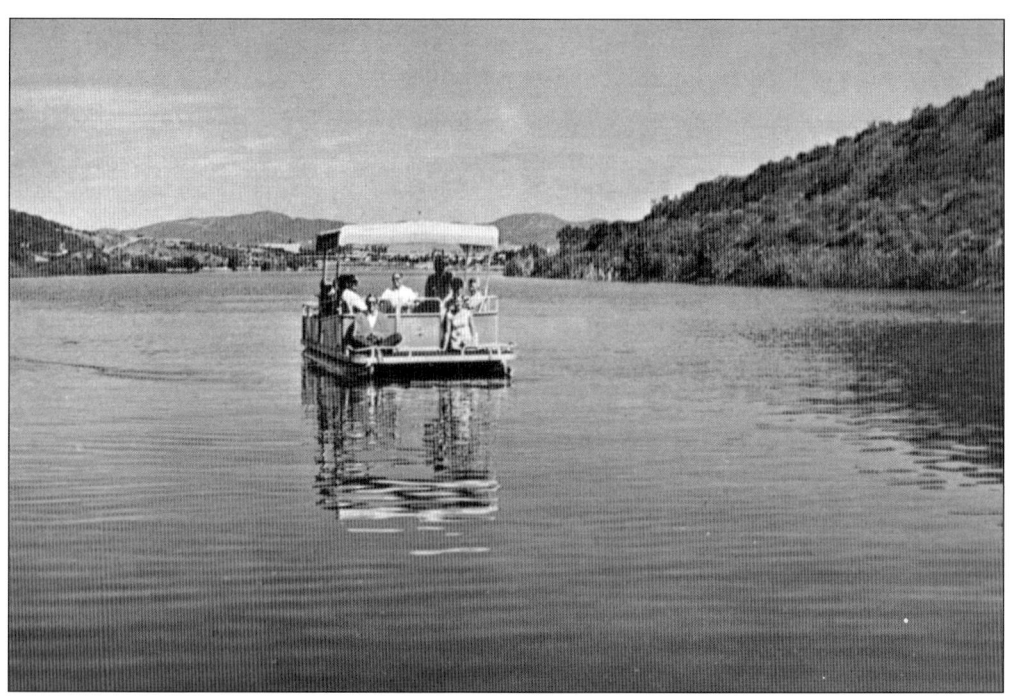

The "happy hour" residents took to Kayots, also known as patio boats, to enjoy late-afternoon rides around the lake and beautiful sunsets. This was a popular way to spend the evening.

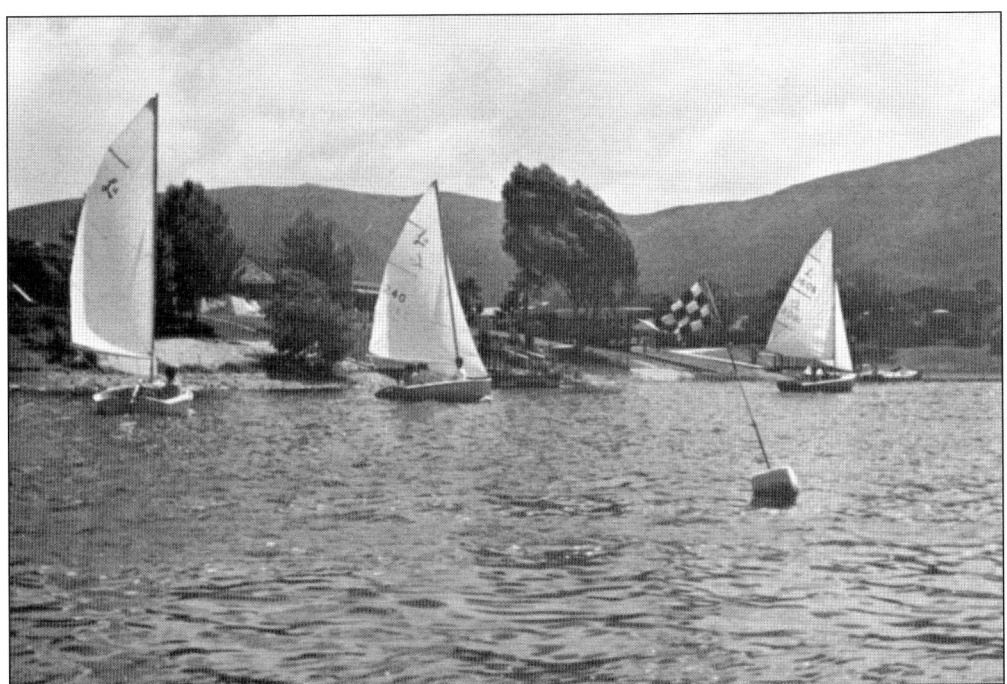

The Lido 14 races for youngsters included five teams, each sailing in three races. Max Smith volunteered his time to train the young sailors.

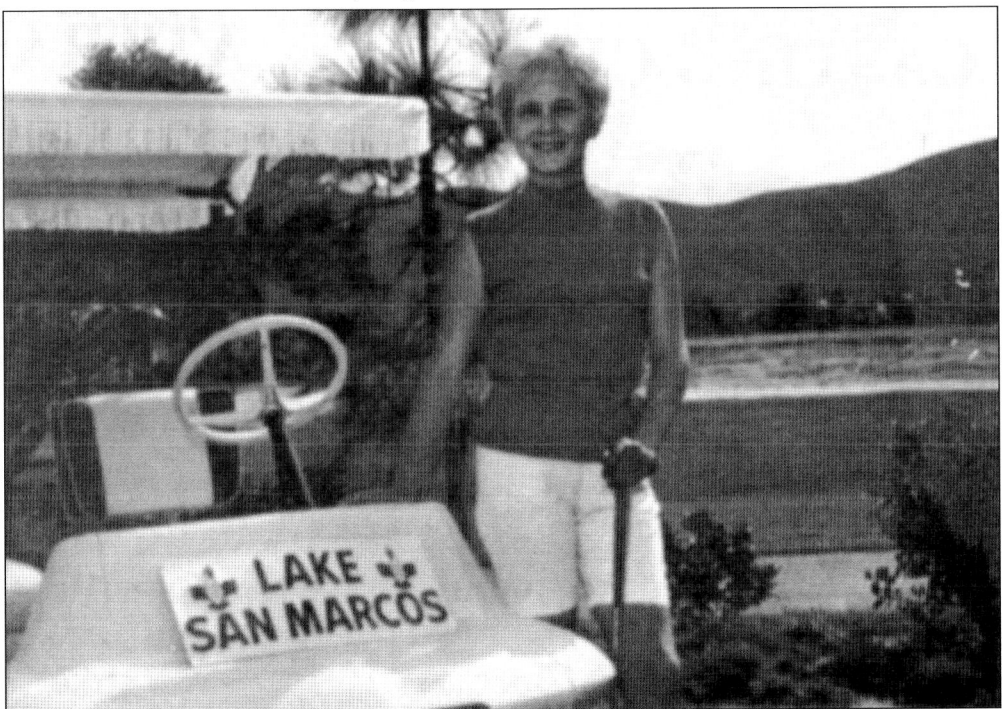

Golf professional Ruth Jessen played Lake San Marcos while staying the week at the Quail's Inn Motel. She loved the weather and had a chance to showcase her skills to local members before she returned to the circuit in March.

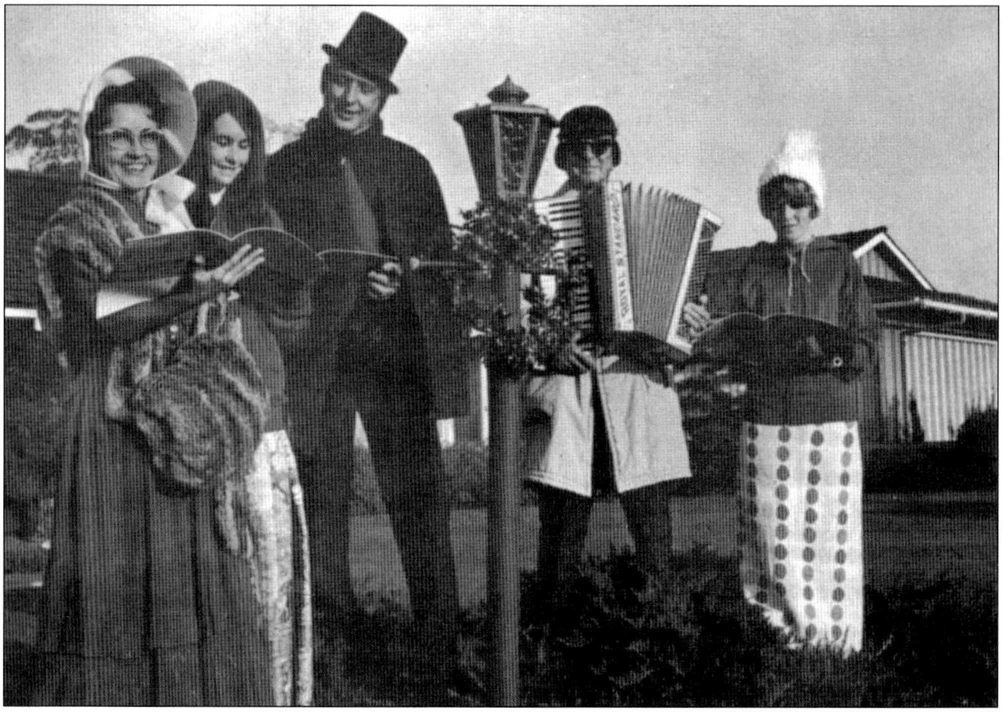

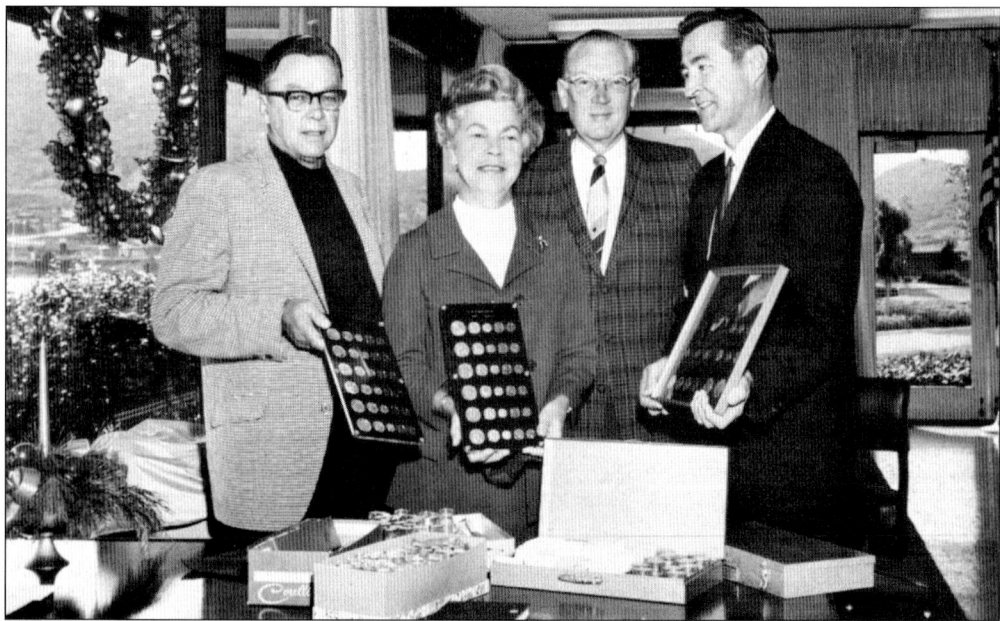

Rehearsing for their appearance at the Community Christmas Sing are, from left to right, Mary Eckert, Laurie Brindle, Harry Deuel, Leonard Cold, and Sharon Carew. The production was under the direction of Eddie and Bill Ream, and the evening was sponsored by the United Church of Lake San Marcos.

A $25,000 coin collection accumulated over 25 years by Mr. & Mrs. Wendell A. La Belle of Lake San Marcos was donated to the Friends of Tri-City Hospital. Receiving the gift on behalf of the foundation were LSM honorary mayor William Hipsher and Carlsbad resident Ralph Palmer.

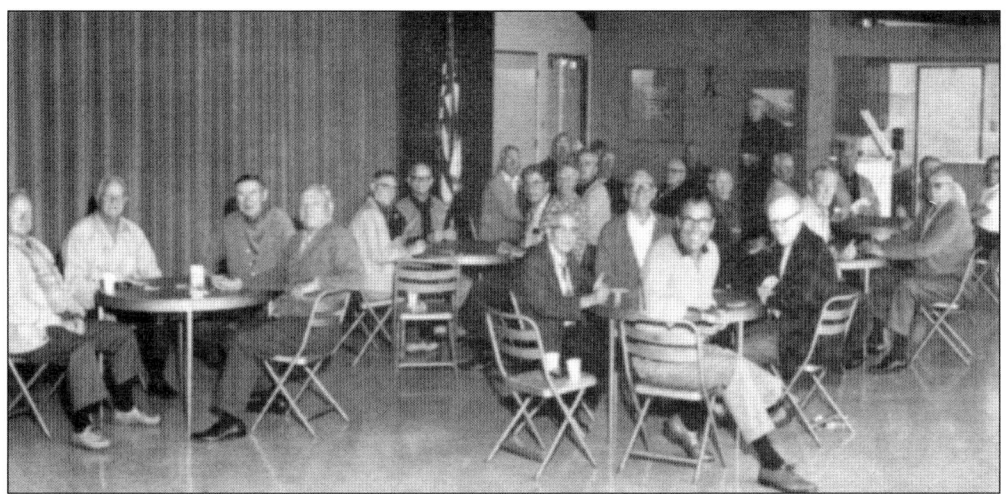

Starting at 9:30 a.m., Mondays and Thursdays are men's days at the bridge tables. Bridge is still played in Lake San Marcos.

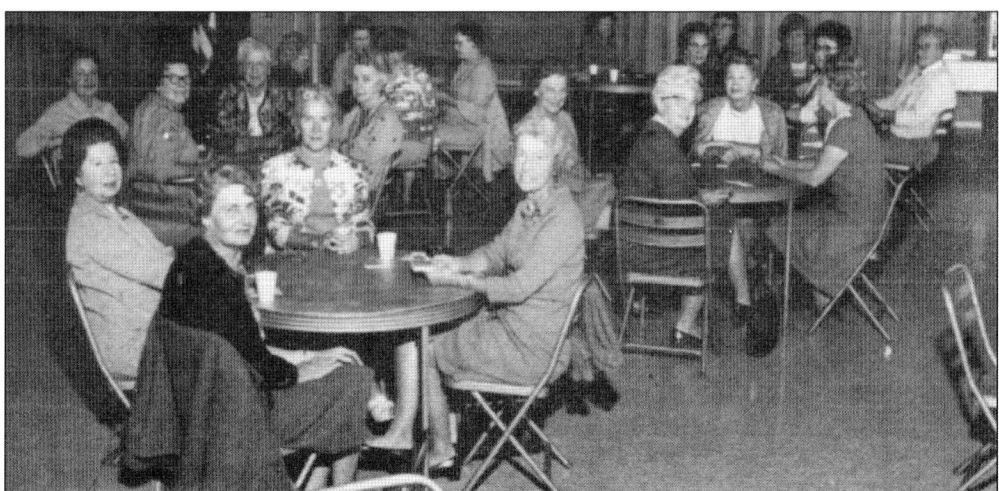

It was common to find women enjoying a round of bridge on Wednesdays at the recreation center. Next to golf, bridge would have to be considered the most popular game at the lake. These games afforded newcomers a means of getting acquainted with people in the area.

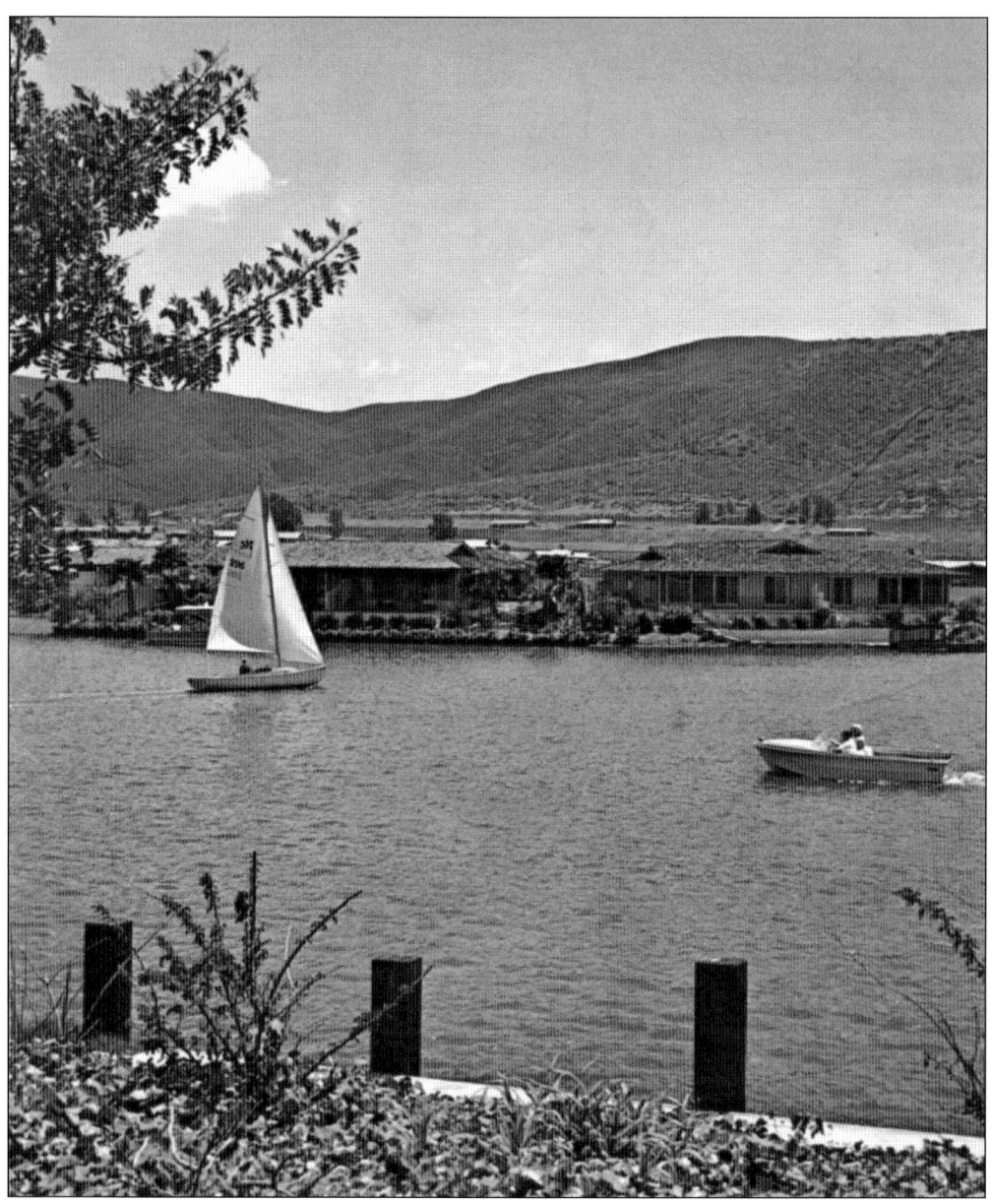
Sailboats and motorboats enjoyed a peaceful coexistence on the lake. With so many outdoor activities to engage in throughout the year, residents lived a healthy life filled with entertainment.

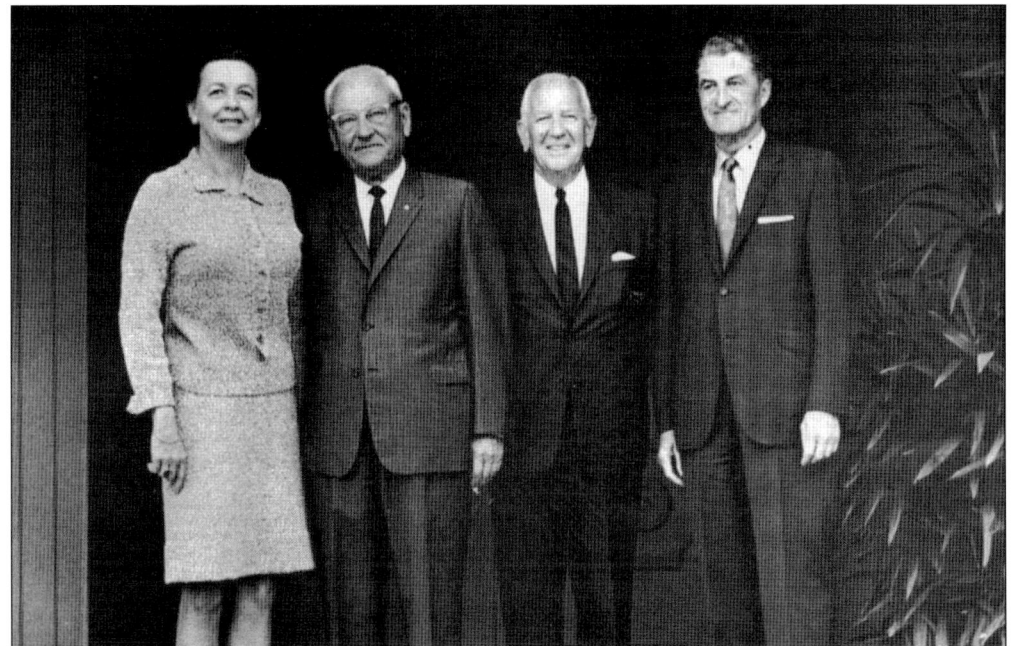

The coordinating council election winners for 1969 were, from left to right, Ora McKnight, George Wieman, Richard Livingston, and Wayne Albright. The title of chairman and honorary mayor was awarded to Richard Livingston after members voted at the first council meeting. Livingston, a Navy pilot in World War I, worked in manufacturing after the war and was president of Microsound Inc. before moving to LSM.

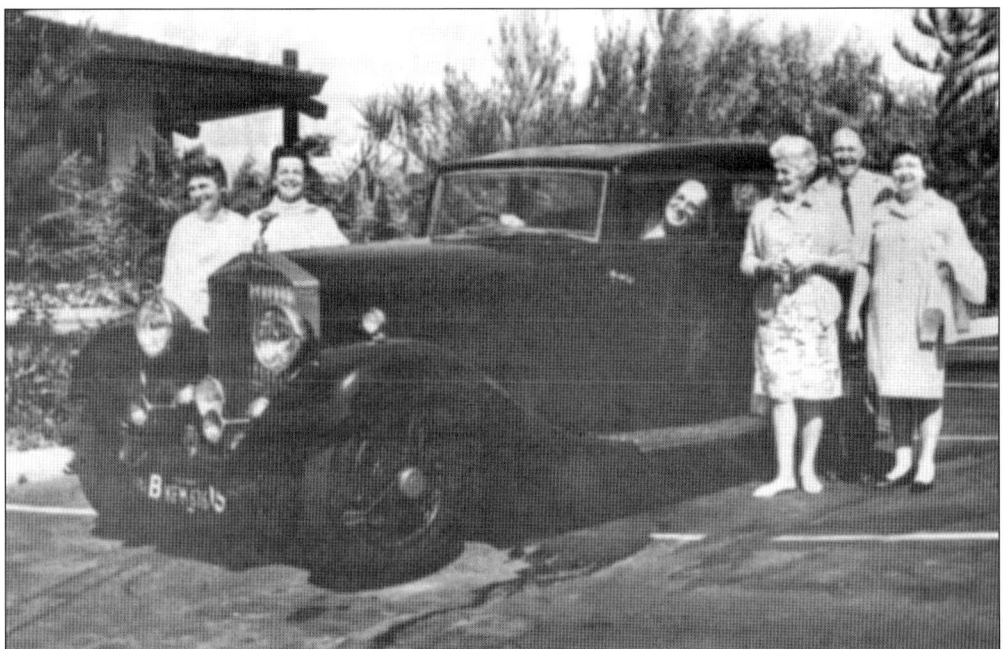

John Wyatt's 1934 Rolls Royce was displayed during a hobby and collectors show at the recreation center. Members of the committee spearheading the event were, from left to right, Jane Blair, Ora McKnight, John Wyatt (inside car), Mildred Sweeney, Charles Hahne, and Anne Blunt.

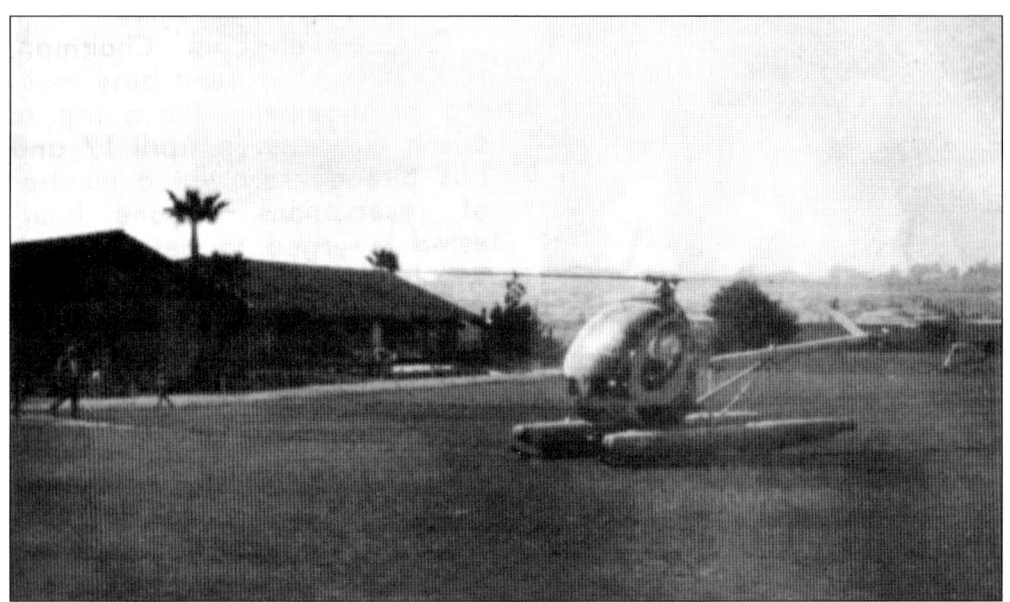

A helicopter demonstration was held by local law enforcement agencies at the country club. This photograph was taken by Marcie Chace. The helicopter was dubbed by some as the "flying golf cart."

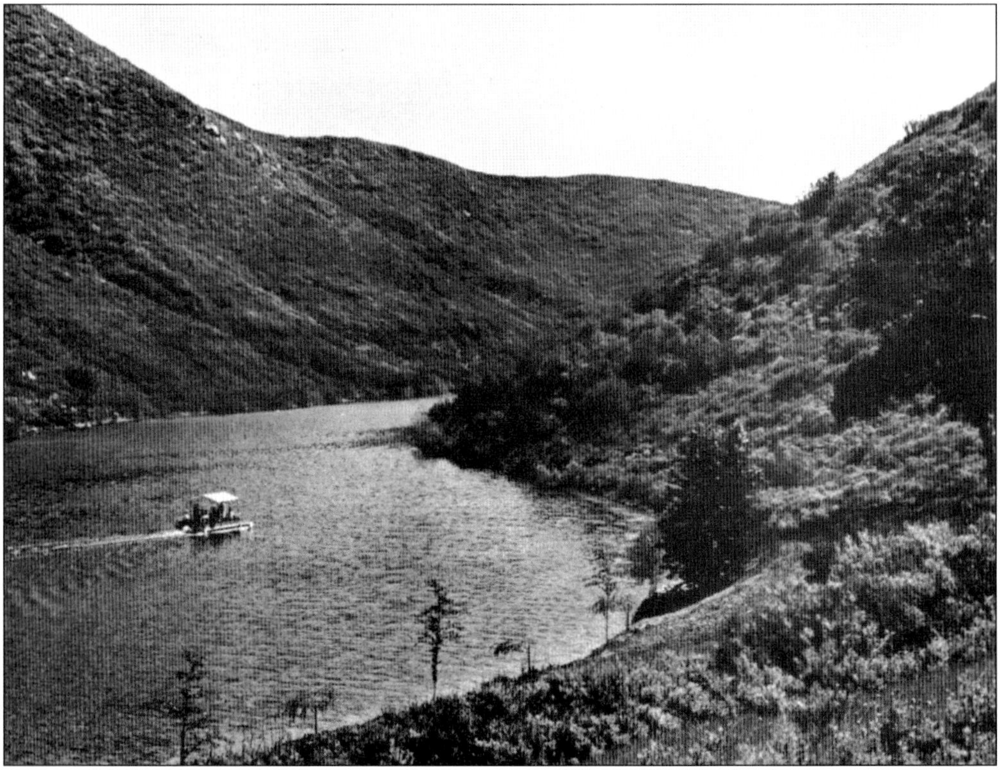

The southern end of the lake has been kept as natural as possible, with migrating birds, turtles sunning on the rocks, a few fishermen, and an occasional patio boat. No homes were built here, and the area is preferred for fishing and nature walking. It is accessible only by boat.

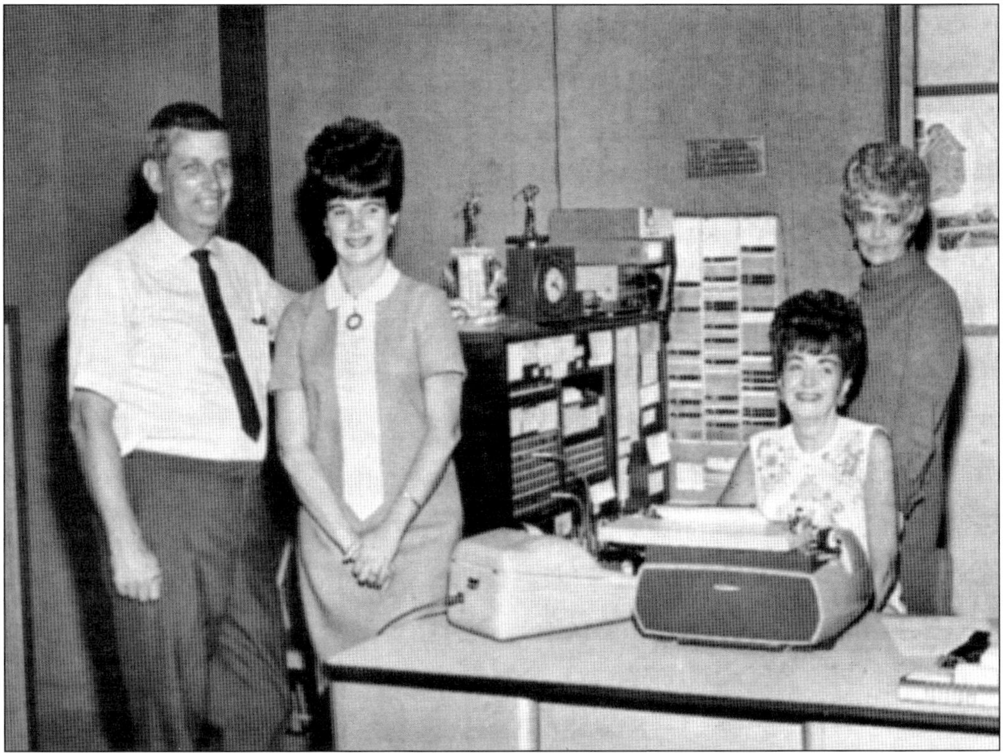

From left to right, Quail's Inn Motel general manager Harry Davis, Joan Nordyke, Marge Delongpree, and Sharon Sorensen are shown here. These were some of the key people who made the wheels go round in Lake San Marcos.

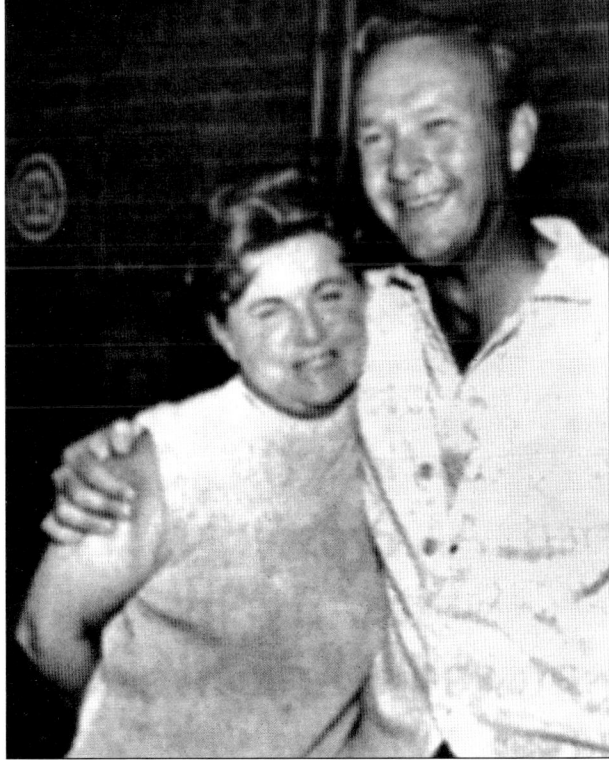

Betty Montank promised never to wash the spot on her cheek where her hero, golf professional Arnold Palmer, gave her a kiss when they met at the Tournament of Champions in May 1969.

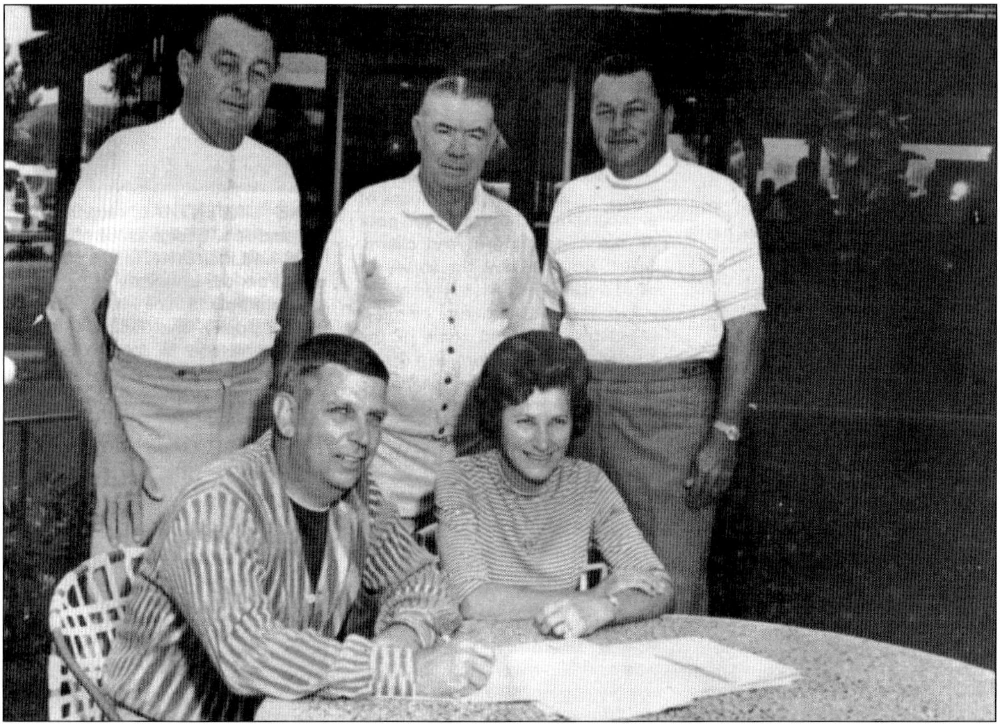

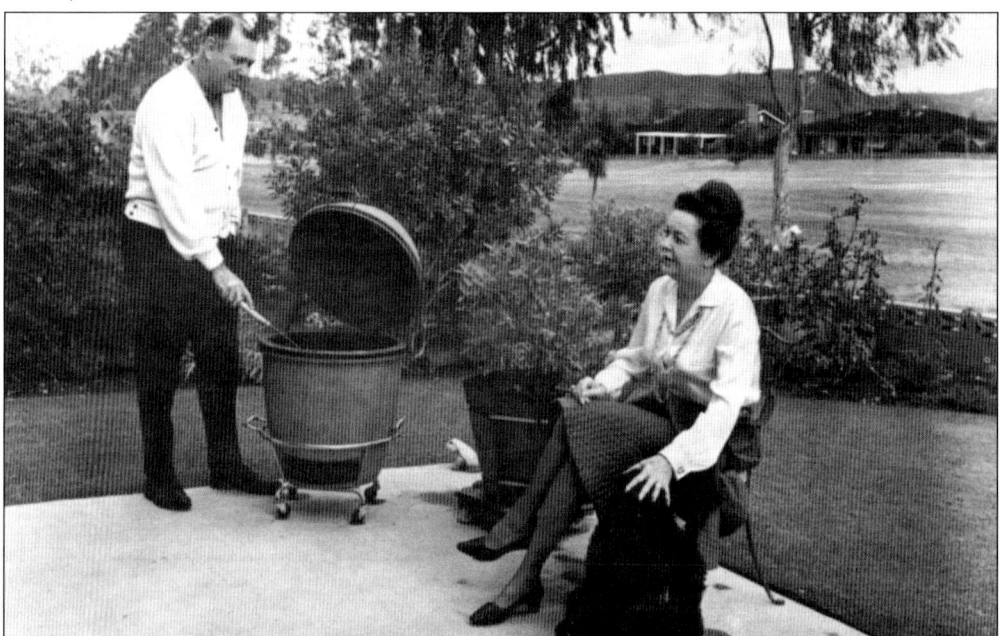

The members of the final planning session for the sixth annual Frazar Invitational Tournament were, from left to right, (first row) Harry Davis and Vee Skaff; (second row) Gordon Frazar, Mans Smith, and Bob Frazar.

Tom McKnight is seen here with his wife, Ora, in the backyard of their Lake San Marcos home. Tom flew for the Air Corps for 17 years, after which he developed his own electronics manufacturing business. Tom was also capable of producing an outstanding barbeque.

Shown here from left to right are Austin Deuel, Vivian Deuel, and their father, Harry Deuel. Deuel, also known as the "Great White Quail Dog" because of his involvement and many duties at the lake, was public relations director of Citizens Development Corporation from its infancy. He assisted in the development of the shopping center, served as advertising and business manager of *Quail Call* magazine, and held the position of director for the recreation center. He opened his new firm, Total Graphics, in San Marcos in August 1969. Vivian Deuel married John Herron not long after this photograph was taken. Austin Deuel, an artist, owned the Lake San Marcos Art Gallery, which had earned the reputation of being one of the finest in Southern California. He was also responsible for the annual Lake San Marcos Invitational Art Exhibit, which drew thousands of visitors.

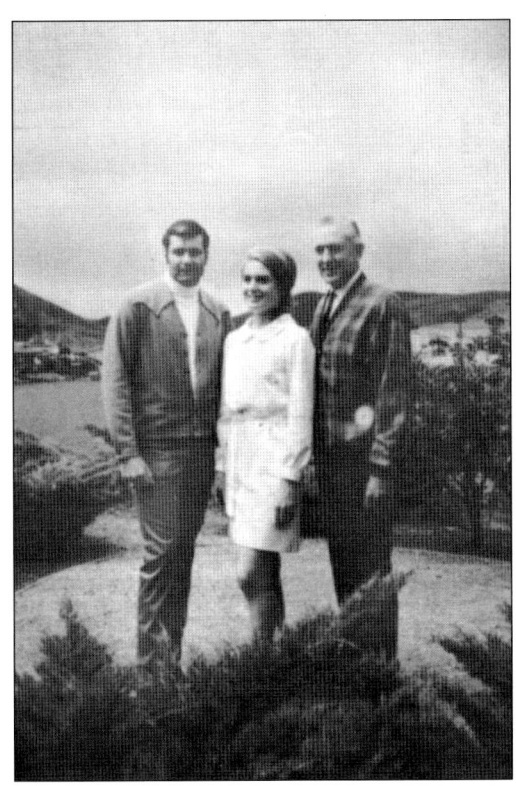

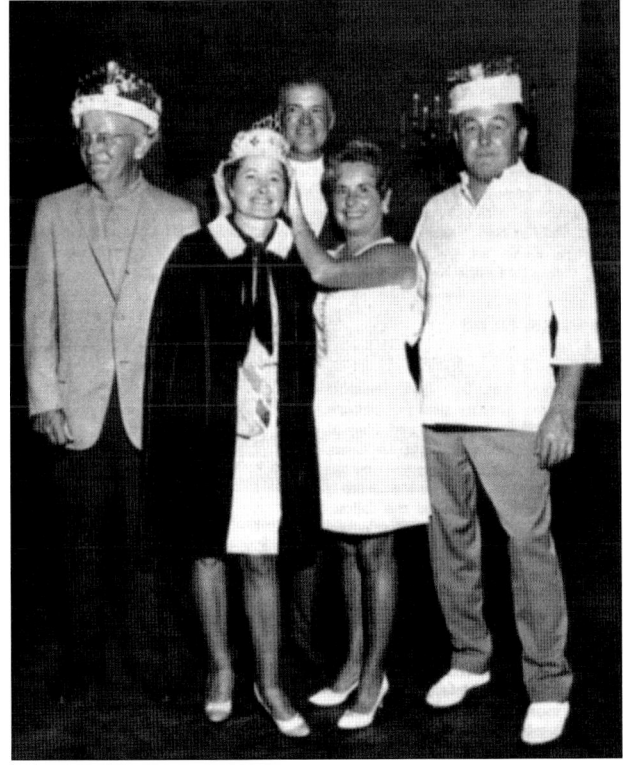

New queen of the links Millie Grisamer received her crown from retiring queen Ruth Sharp at the Queen's Tournament. The courtly consorts were, from left to right, Art Benton, Frank Brence, and Gordon Frazar.

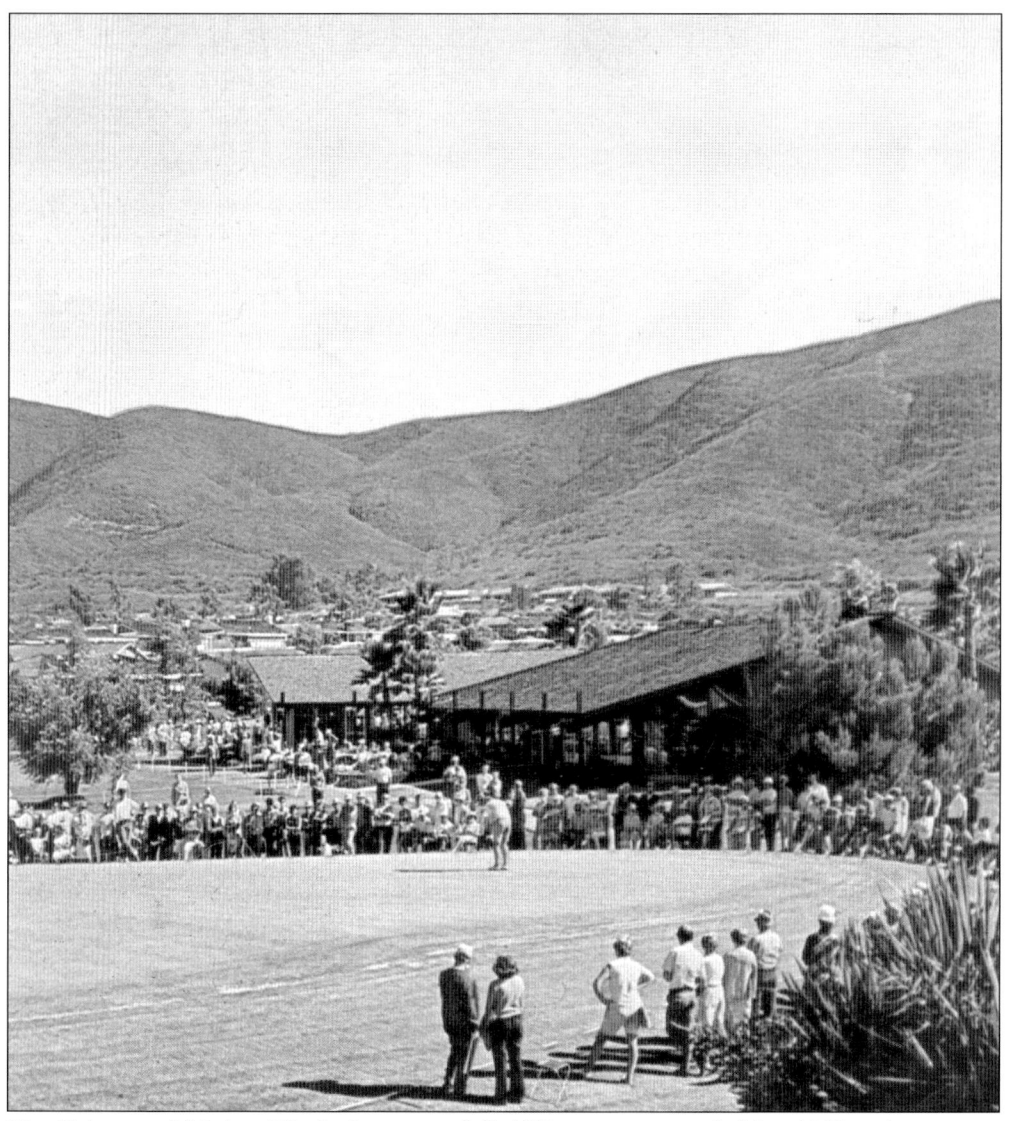

The 11th annual Mickey Wright Invitational Golf Tournament was held in 1969 at the country club. The tournament was named for female golfer Mary Kathryn "Mickey" Wright, who was inducted into the World Golf Hall of Fame in 1964. It drew an estimated 4,500 spectators on the final day of play.

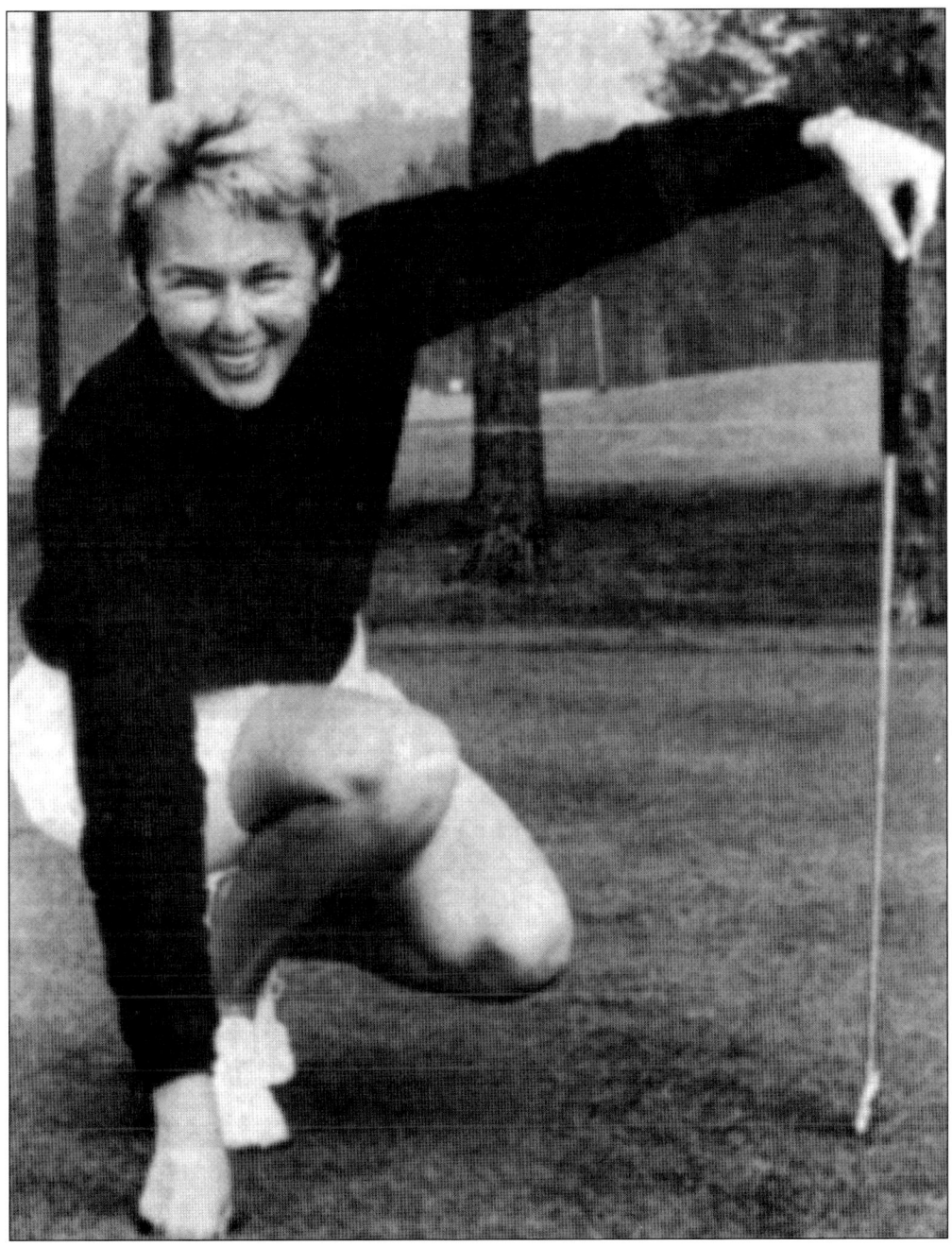
Mickey Wright herself headed the long list of famous names playing in the Mickey Wright Tournament. There was television as well as major press coverage throughout the five-day event.

RONALD REAGAN
GOVERNOR

State of California
GOVERNOR'S OFFICE
SACRAMENTO 95814

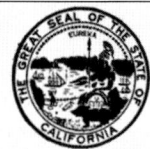

It is a great pleasure for me to send you greetings and welcome all of you to beautiful Lake San Marcos for the 9th Annual Mickey Wright Tournament to benefit retarded children.

It is a great source of satisfaction to me knowing that individuals and organizations are seeking and finding ways to help our children, and especially those children who need particular attention and an assurance that they are loved and accepted by those with whom they come in contact. It is that extra measure of encouragement and love that tips the balance toward progress for them.

I commend the North San Diego County Association for Retarded Children for the time, effort and heart devoted to these children.

Best wishes for a most enjoyable and memorable tournament.

Sincerely,

Ronald Reagan
RONALD REAGAN
GOVERNOR

The Lake San Marcos Country Club received this letter from Gov. Ronald Reagan when it sponsored the Mickey Wright Tournament.

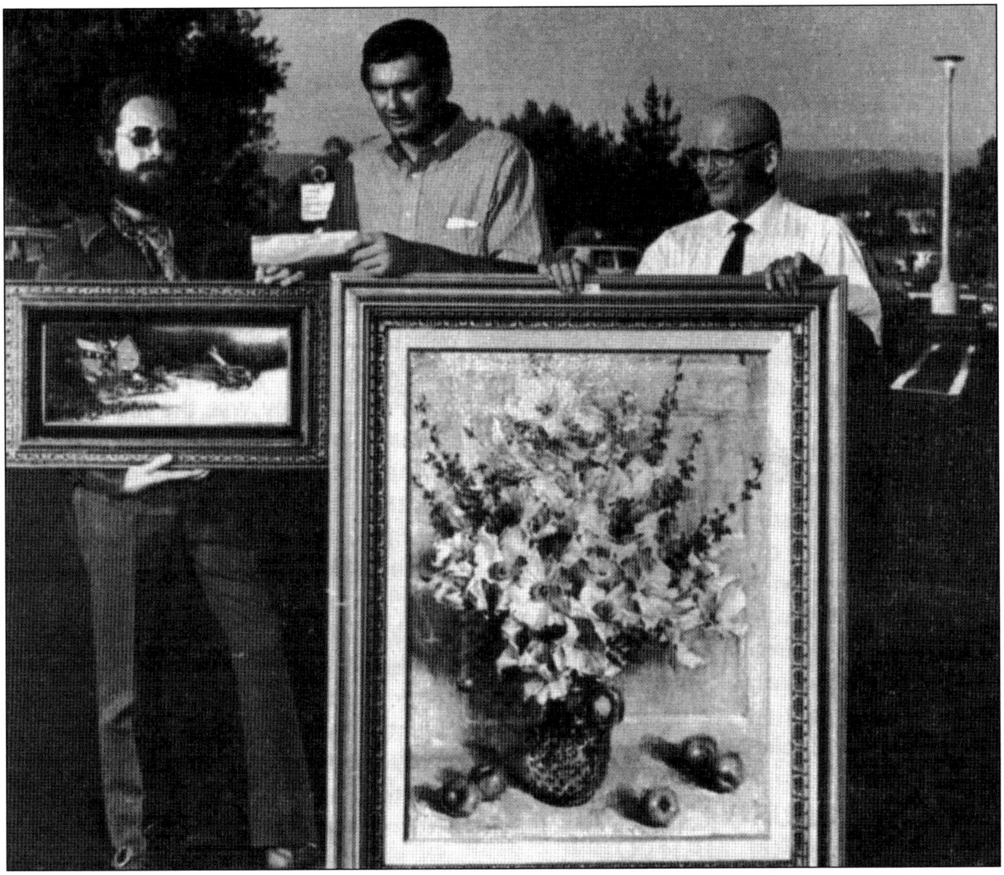

Winners of the 1969 arts festival at Lake San Marcos were Herbert Parrish of Ramona, who won the $1,000 prize for his floral oil painting *Matilijia Poppies* (right), and Ken Ebert, who took home $500 for his watercolor *Morning in Missouri* (left).

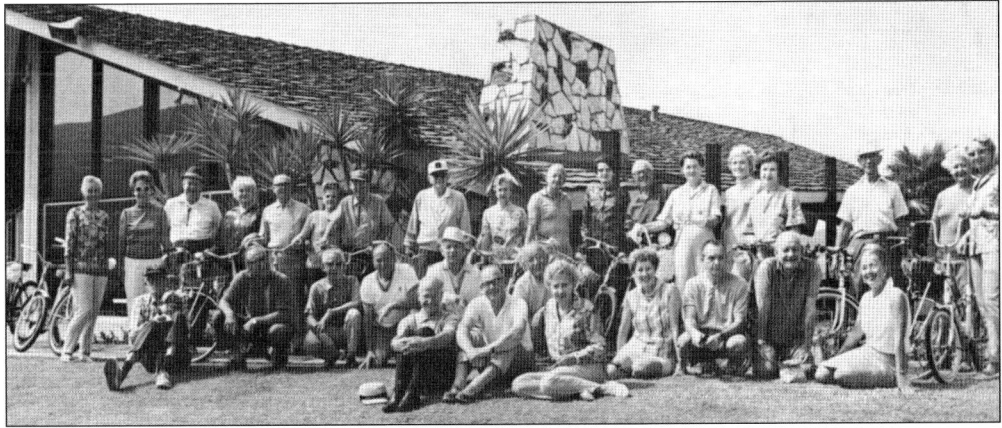

The Lake San Marcos Bicycle Club gathers here in front of the recreation center. In the center foreground is world-famous cyclist Dr. Clifford Graves (founder of the San Diego Council of American Youth Hostels). Dr. Graves had cycled across Europe eight different times. Also pictured in the front row are members Dick Putzier (left) and head "Angel" Millie Mittricker (right). (Author's collection.)

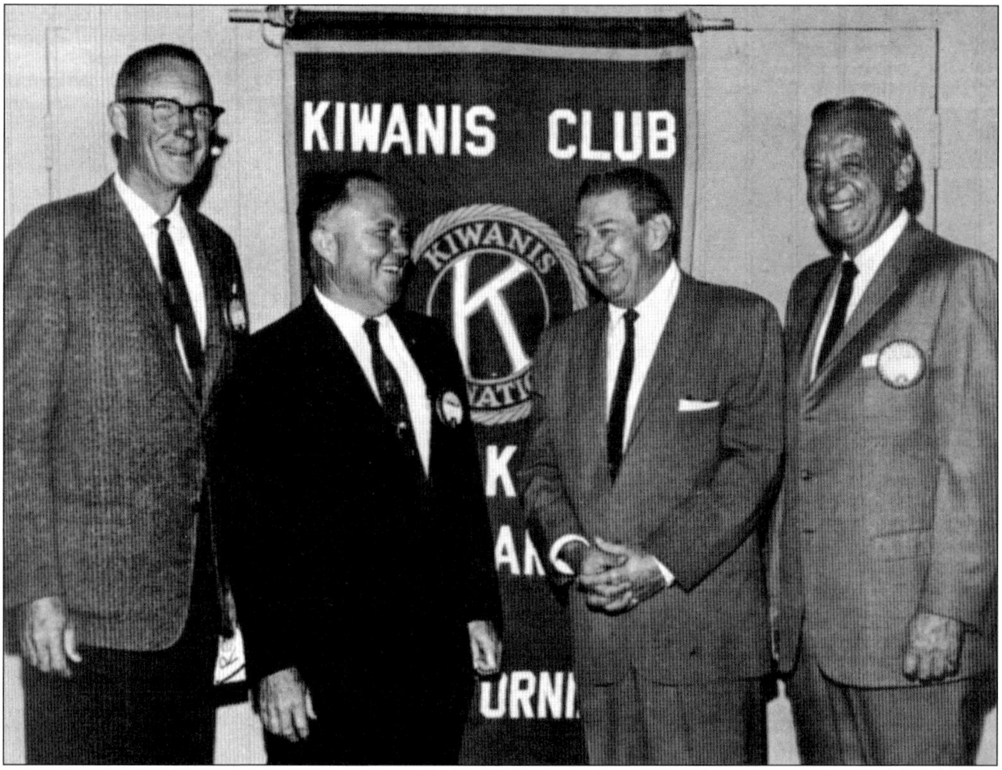

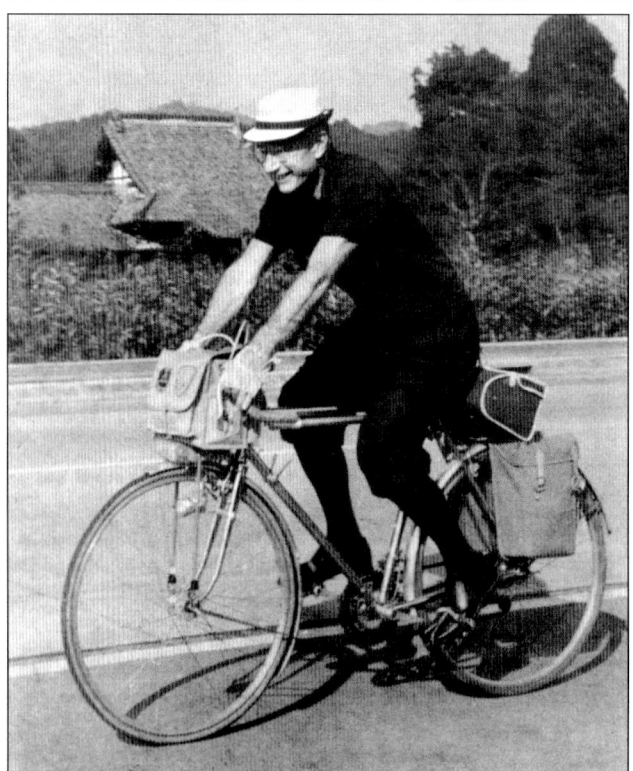

LSM Kiwanis hosted the San Marcos Rotary in 1969 to hear an address by Harry Von Zell, the announcer for the George Burns and Gracie Allen radio and television shows. Pictured from left to right are outgoing Kiwanis president Scott Dow, 1969 president elect Charles Hahne, Von Zell, and Wendell Campbell. (Author's collection.)

Dr. Clifford Graves, La Jolla surgeon, is shown on one of his international bicycle tours. He was guest speaker at the Bicycle Club meeting in January 1969.

Finalists in the men's championship playoffs Art Benton (left) and Russ Frakes wish each other luck.

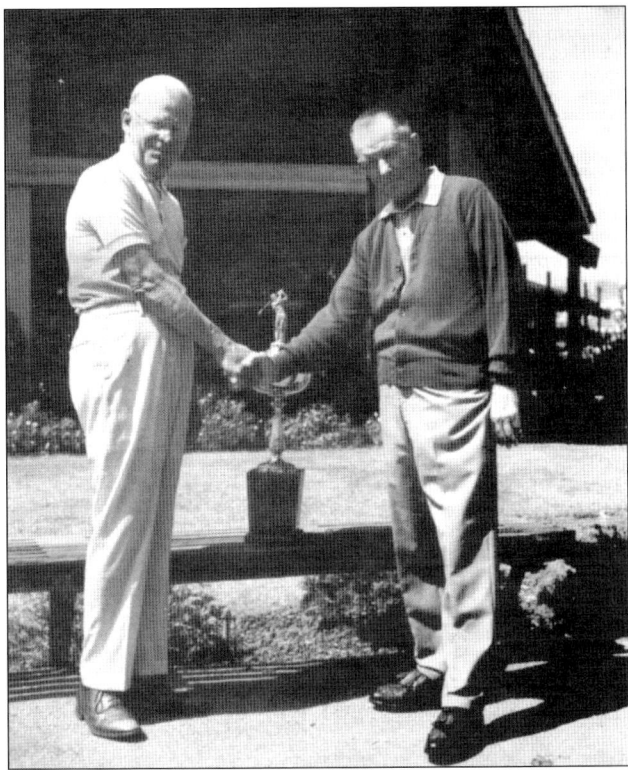

Resident Lonnie Lindanger and his wife, Ruth, are shown in their 1918 Ford Runabout. Lonnie wooed and won the fair Ruth in this jazzy car, and they were married in Riverside in 1919.

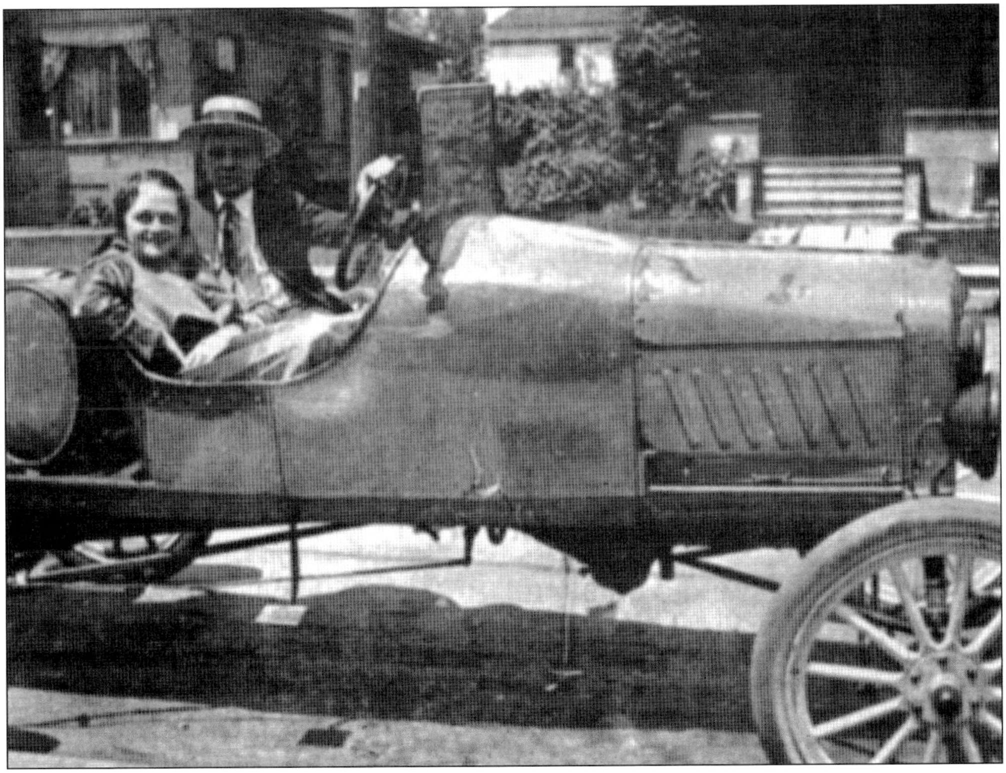

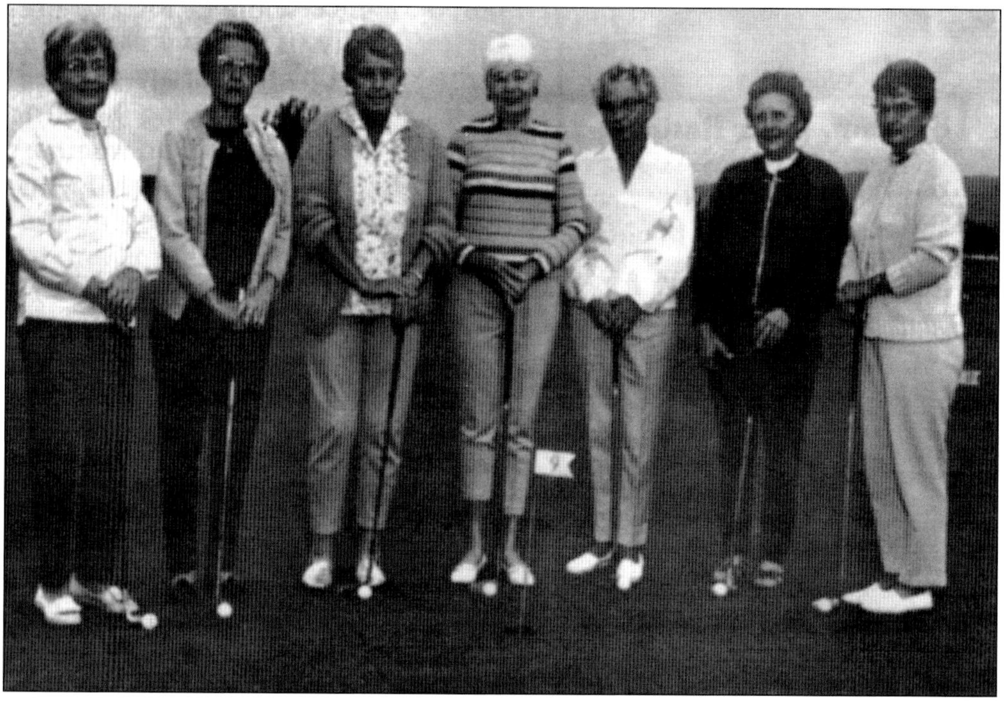

Winners of the nine-hole section's eclectic golf tournament were, from left to right, Olive Wilson, Gretchen Wardell, Ethyl Fleming, Grace Munn, Ree Blanchard, Alice Hall, and Myrtle Emerson.

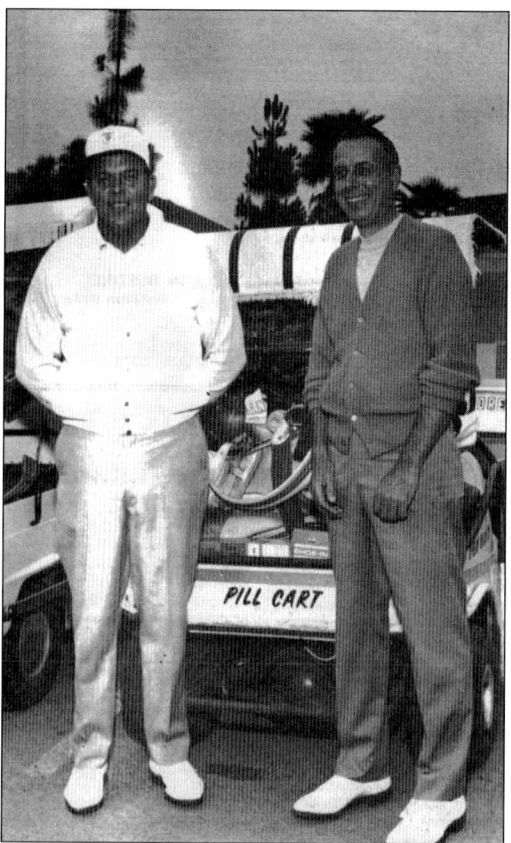

Curt Davis (left) and Lake San Marcos's own genial pharmacist, Bob Maxwell (right), won the Frazar Invitational for the second year in a row, and not without stiff competition. They said, "Lightning does strike twice." Their happiness is evident in this photograph.

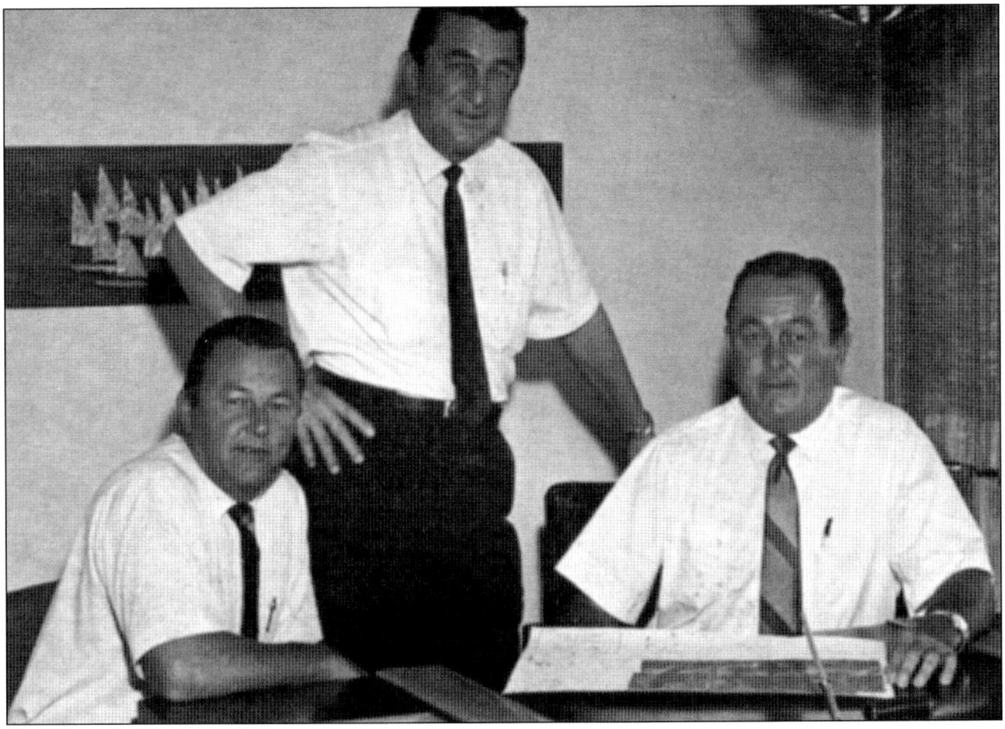

The Frazar brothers—Bob, Don, and Gordon—were the creators and master planners of Lake San Marcos, the first development in San Diego County to have all utilities, including television, placed underground, and the first lakeside development in California.

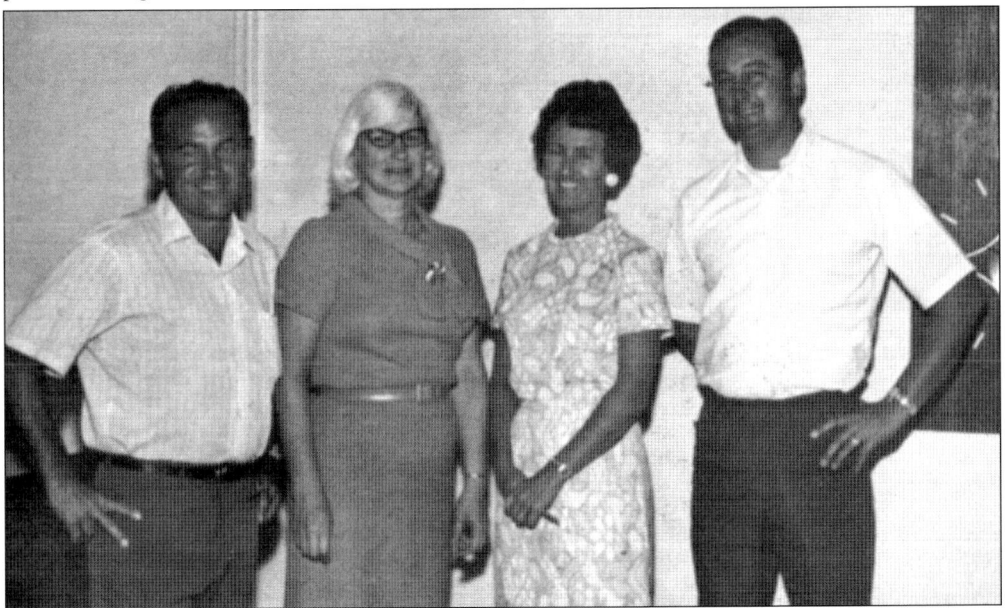

From left to right, administrative office staff members Richard "Tony" Buckman (construction consultant), Vi Pfeiler (executive secretary), Glennis Rath (office manager), and Ron Frazar (coordinator) are shown here. These were some of the key people who made Lake San Marcos the success story it was.

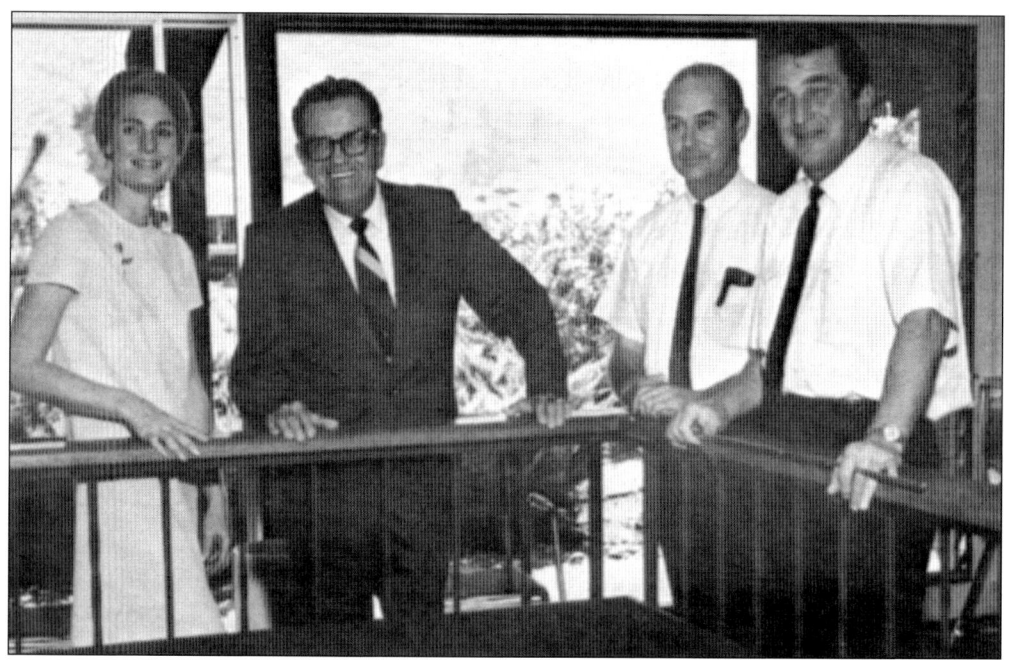

This is another photograph of the key information center staff. Fom left to right are Vivian Herron, Larry Wiley, Bill Corbin, and Don Frazar. The information center was located at the entrance to Lake San Marcos from Rancho Santa Fe Road, where Seaglass Condominiums are now located.

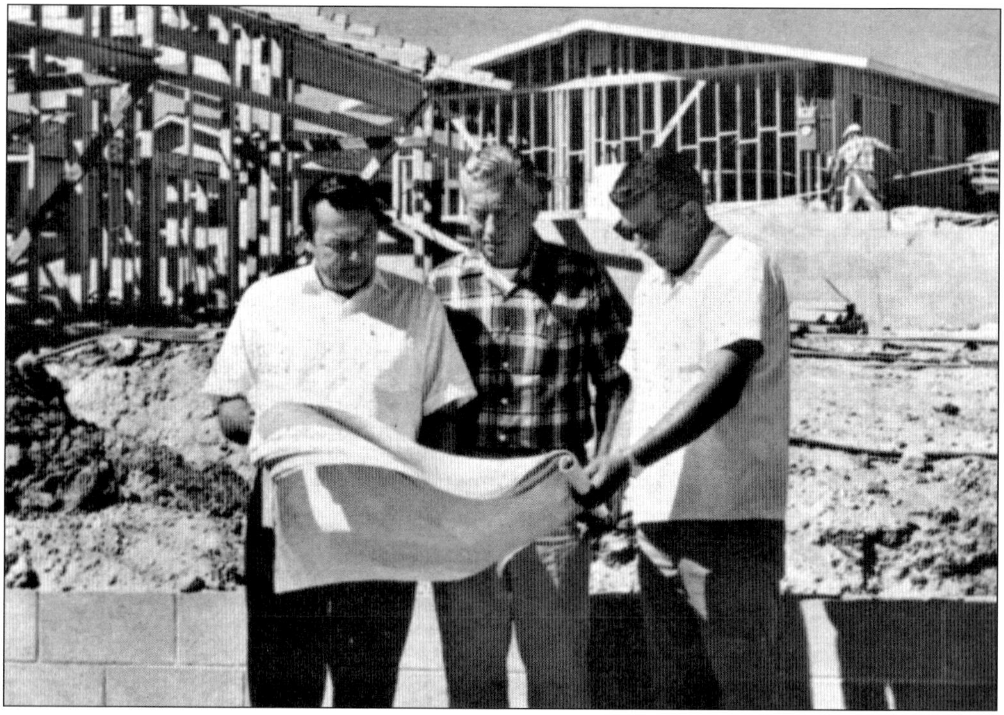

Construction manager Bob Frazar consults with building superintendents Dale Van Ripper and Roy Rockdale. Approximately 150 lakeshore homesites would line the banks when development was completed on both sides of the lake. Today, there are more than 2,500 homes in Lake San Marcos.

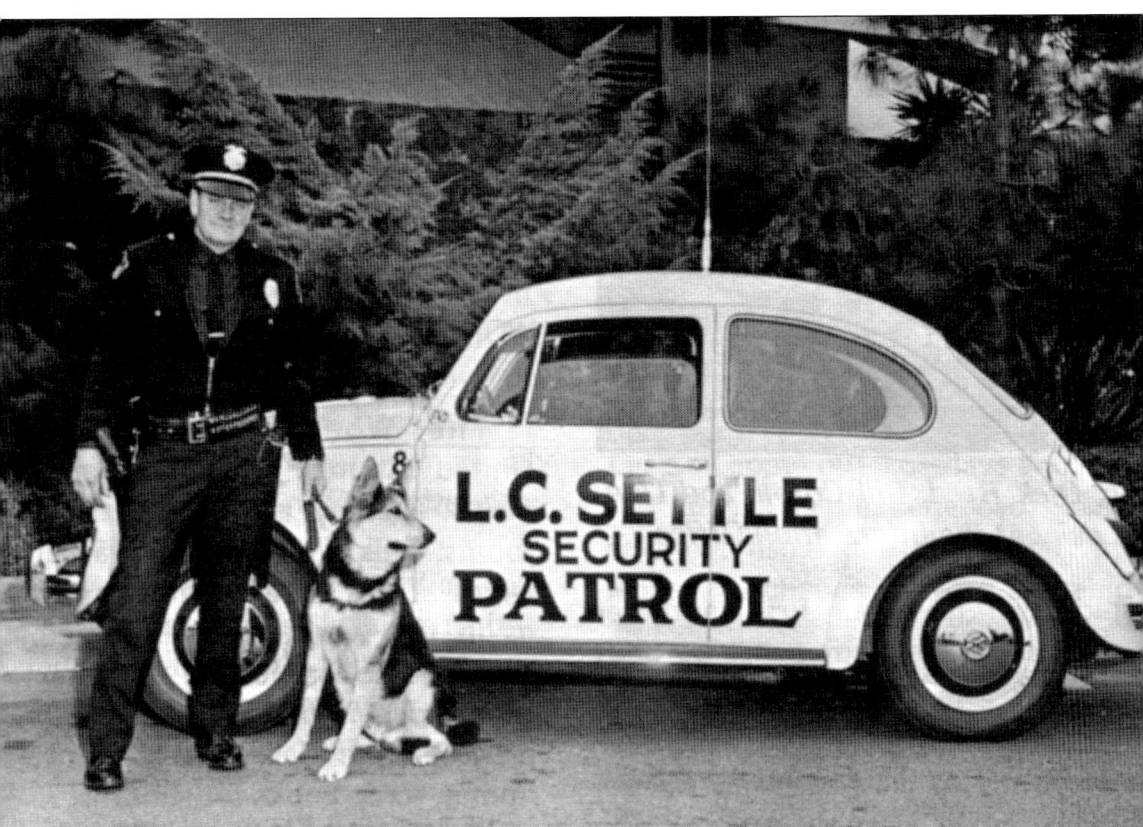

Lake San Marcos was once protected by the L.C. Settle Security Patrol. L.C. Settle is pictured here with Prince, one of his five trained German shepherds. The security patrol worked closely with the county sheriff's department and was in constant radio communication with the Quail's Inn Motel switchboard throughout the 12-hour nightly patrol. The patrol service began October 1, 1969, at a cost of $1,299 per month. CDC volunteered to pay $200 a month, and the shopping center merchants and professionals agreed to pay $100 per month, leaving only $900 per month to be paid by 360 resident subscriptions. As of September 11 of that year, 180 people had sent in their checks. Liberty National Bank volunteered to handle the record keeping at no cost, and L.C. Settle Security Patrol Service agreed to furnish decals to all subscribing members without fee.

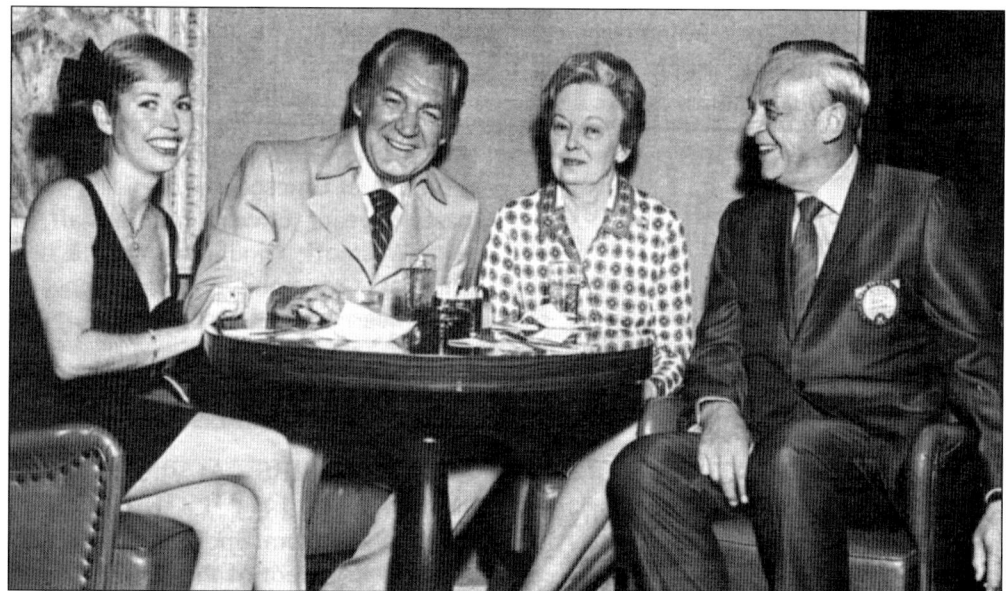

Hollywood actor Forrest Tucker and his wife (left) are seen having dinner with Wendell and Betty Campbell at the Trophy Room. The group was entertained by Forrest's hilarious stories of his time on stage, television, and the big screen. He told of President Nixon's recent visit to Lakeside Country Club in Toluca Lake and of the locker room sessions that included the president, Bob Hope, Jimmy Stewart, Fred McMurray, George Gobel, and himself. The Tuckers and their two youngsters were guests of the Campbells during their stay at the lake.

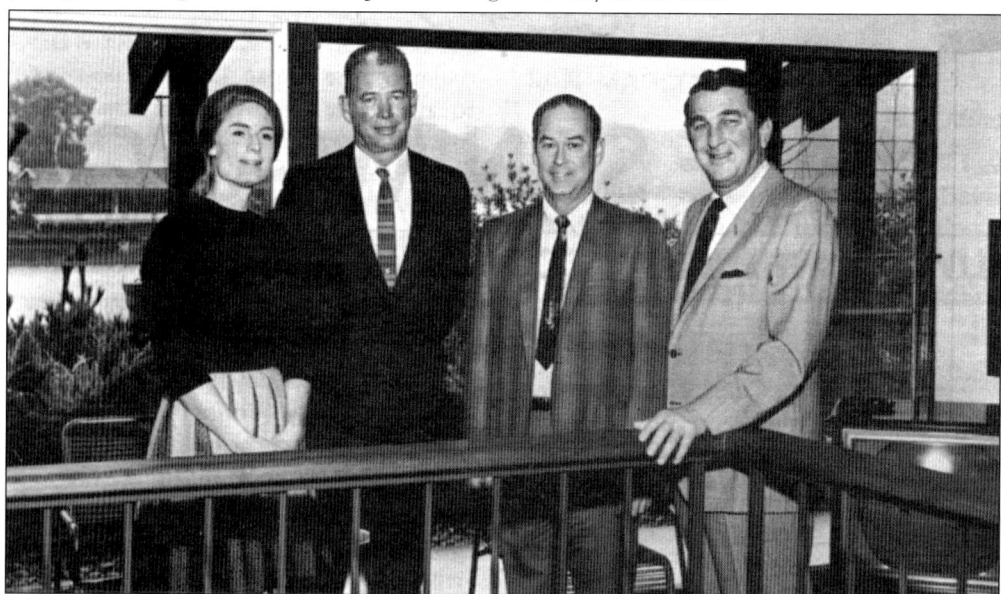

From left to right, Vivian Herron, Dick Reed, Bill Corbin, and Don Frazar were responsible for serving the needs of residents on a daily basis at the information center. Herron answered thousands of questions and helped almost all new residents with everything from color selections to escrow signing. Don Frazar reported at the time that the newest homes in the Highlands were selling in the $29,500 range, and many would have excellent views. He felt fortunate that they were able to continue the 7.75 percent interest rate.

Pam Barnett, a young professional golfer on tour with the Ladies Professional Golf Association (LPGA), was visiting LSM for a short visit and looked forward to playing some golf. Here, she is speaking with LSM golf professional John Juris. Barnett said all of the ladies on the LPGA tour were very impressed with the Lake Course during the Mickey Wright Tournament and noted the friendly attitudes of the members.

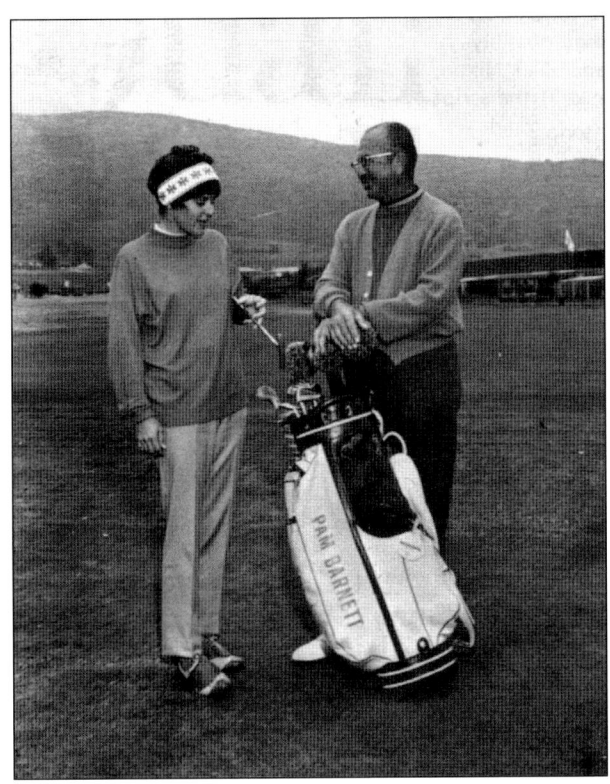

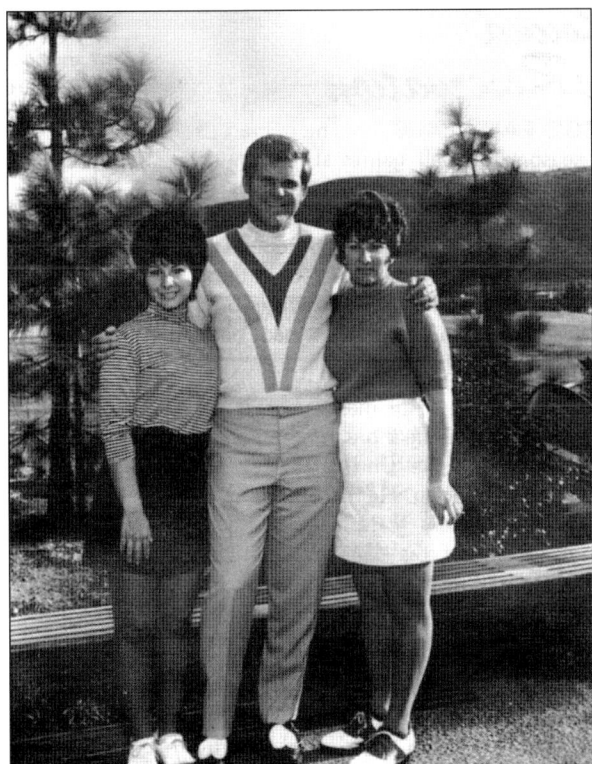

Famous golfing sisters Janet (left) and Donna (right) Caponi were houseguests of the Montank family; they are shown here with Neil Jr. Janet was on her way to play in the $40,000 Burdin's Invitational in Miami, and Donna was headed for New York, where she would be receiving the Golden Tee Award at the Metropolitan Golf Writers Association dinner and the Most Improved Woman Golfer Award from *Golf Digest*.

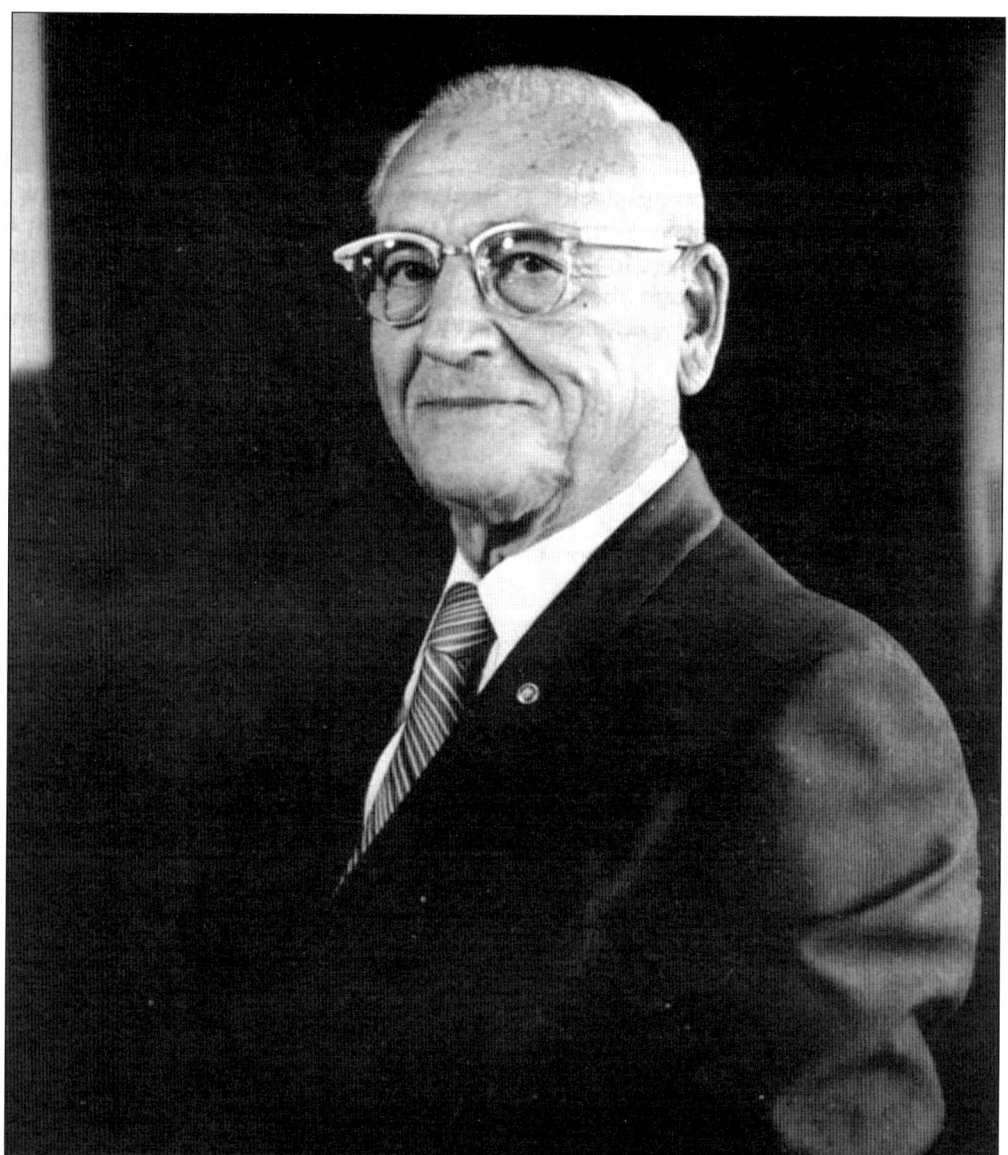

George C. Wieman was named honorary mayor and coordinating council chairman for 1970. He had served as vice chairman and chairman of the Patrol Service Committee the previous year. George retired from the Crown Zellerbach Paper Company in Los Angeles before moving to Lake San Marcos. Unfortunately, he was unable to complete his term, passing away unexpectedly in November 1970.

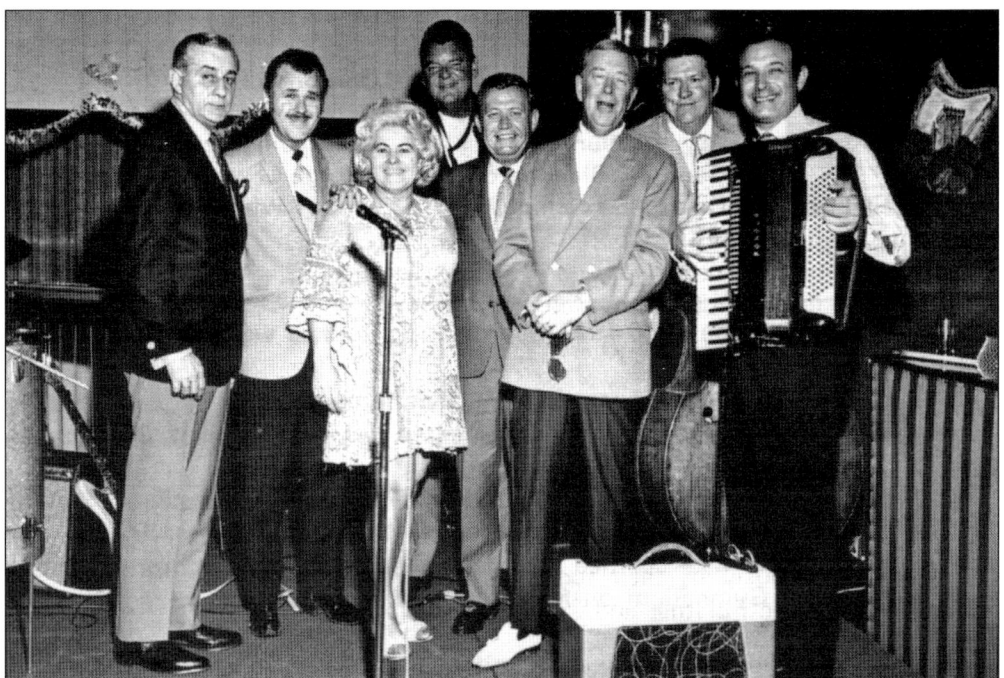

Red Rowe of Ramblin' Red Rowe's Rhythm Makers was a longtime radio and television star and an LSM resident. Red assembled a group of music professionals to entertain for the men's golf club. From left to right are Les Mack of CBS-TV, Roy Lanham, Mary Ann Lanham, Bill Hamilton, Noel Boggs, Red Rowe, Red Wootten, and Ernie Villice.

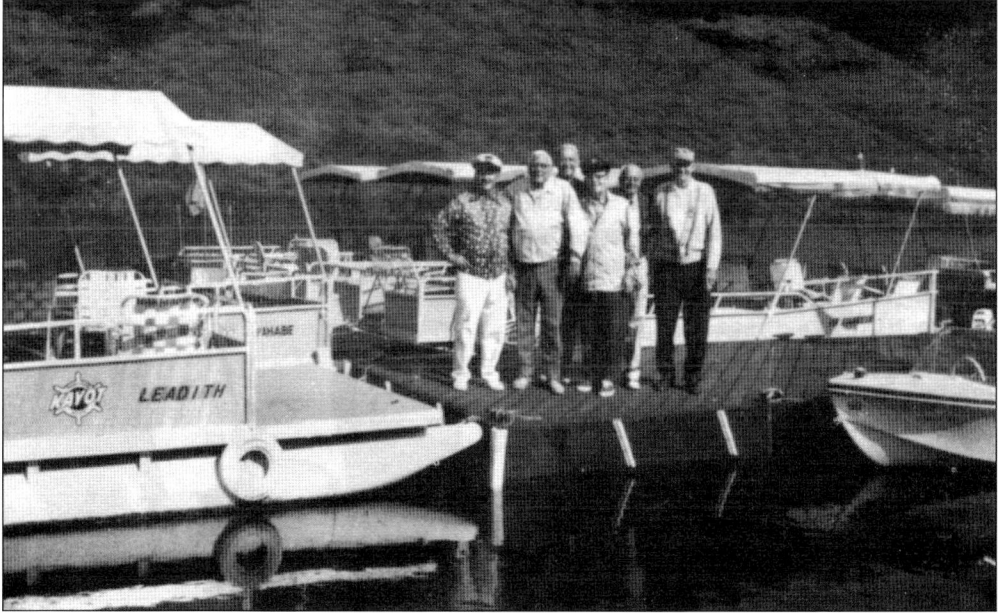

Yacht club officers pose on the new dock at the picnic grounds. From left to right are 1970 commodore Allyn Blunt, Wendell Campbell, Lea Glaze, Ron Strong, and Paul Cheney. The picnic grounds at the south end of the lake were a popular gathering place for yacht club functions and were accessible only by boat.

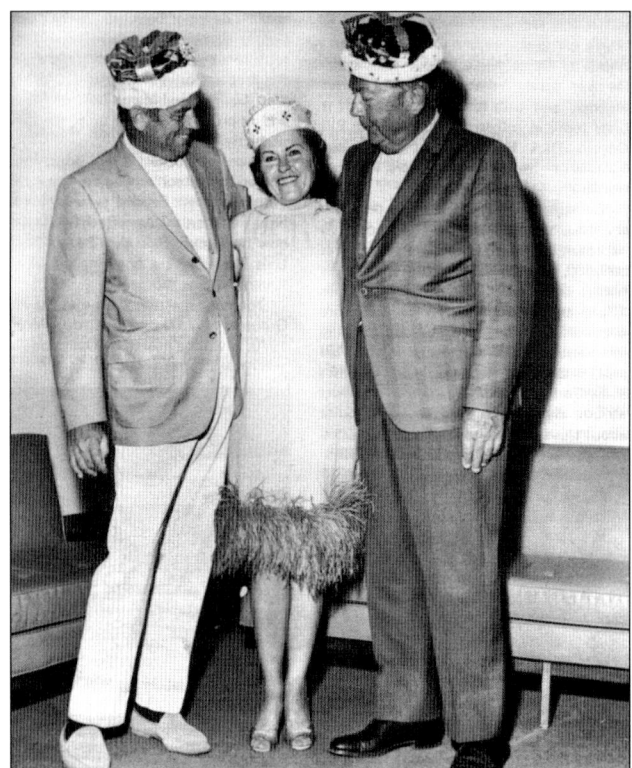

Her majesty the queen, Marcie Chace, and her two kings, Wes Steven and Bob Wallman, won the seventh annual Queen's Golf Tournament. There were 136 contestants vying for the crown, but it was this trio's spectacular net score of 57 that took the honors. Marcie had dutifully served as publicity chairman for the women's golf club for the past several years.

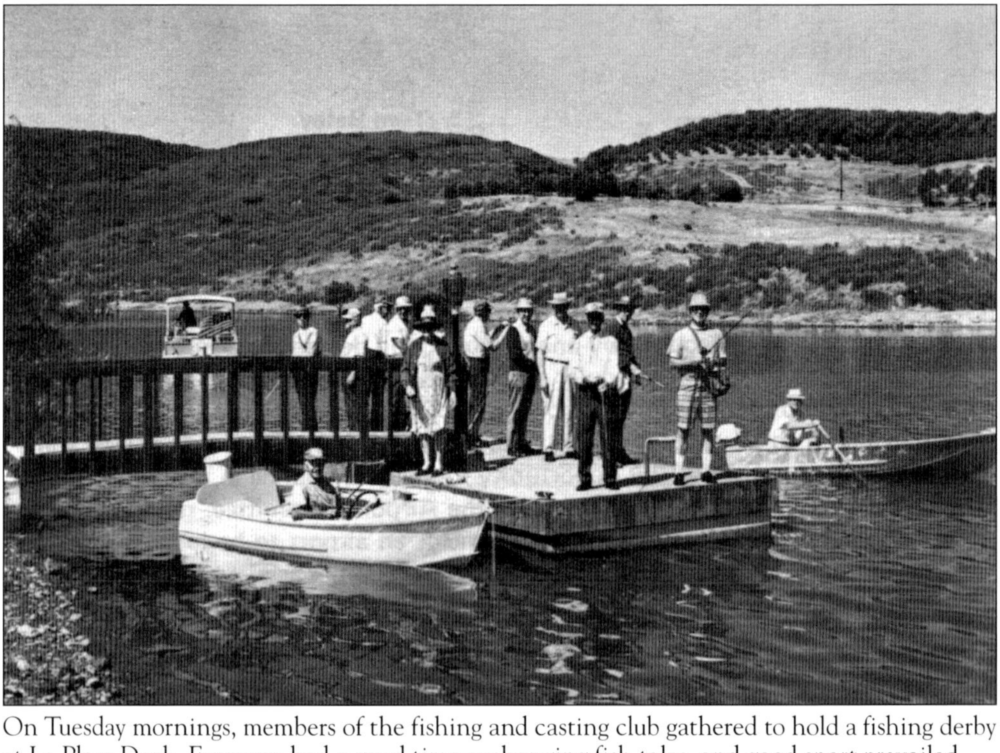

On Tuesday mornings, members of the fishing and casting club gathered to hold a fishing derby at La Plaza Dock. Everyone had a good time exchanging fish tales, and good sport prevailed.

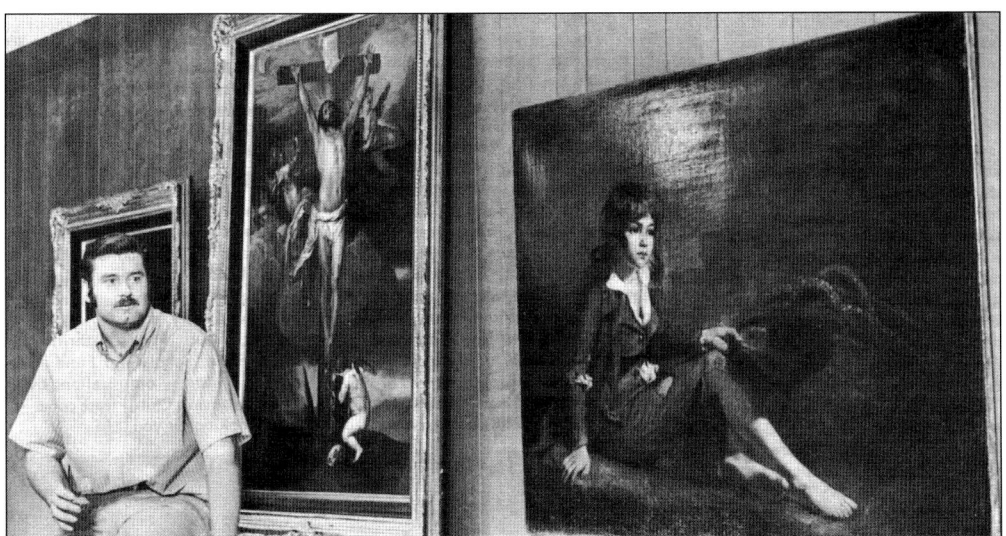

Lake San Marcos Art Gallery owner Austin Deuel displays some recent acquisitions. *The Crucifixion*, by Sir Anthony Van Dyke, dates to 1630. *The Beggar Boy* by John Rising is also displayed. Both were scheduled to be part of the annual LSM Invitational Art Exhibit.

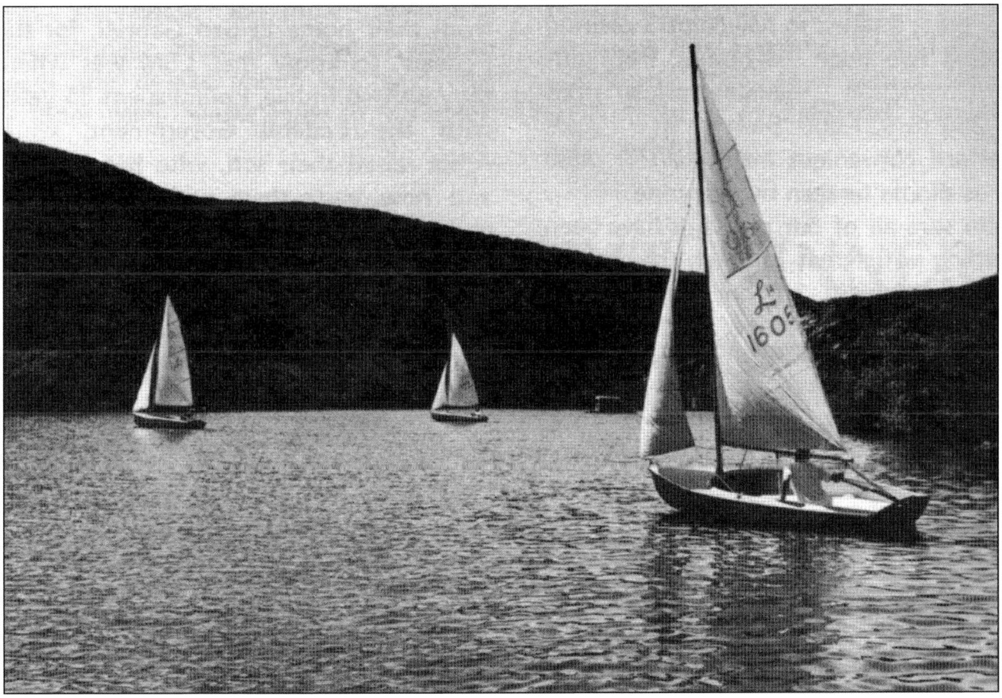

Members of the LSM Swampers got together and decided that the community should have its own America's Cup trials. The harrowing two-mile race from the bridge to the dam was won by Bill Corbin in 55 minutes.

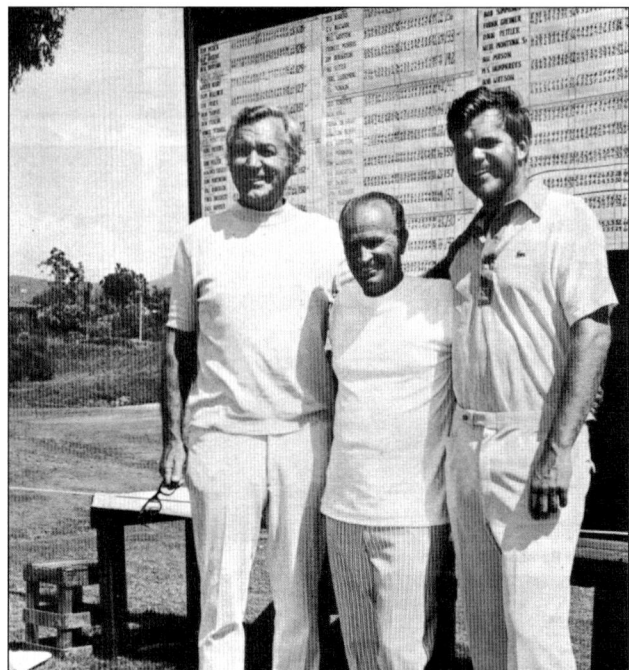

Actor Forrest Tucker (left) shared the limelight with Frazar Invitational winners Don Sharp (center) and Neal Montank (right). Everyone agreed that the "Frazar" was one of the finest tournaments held at LSM; it drew 148 contestants from 49 different clubs throughout Southern California and Arizona.

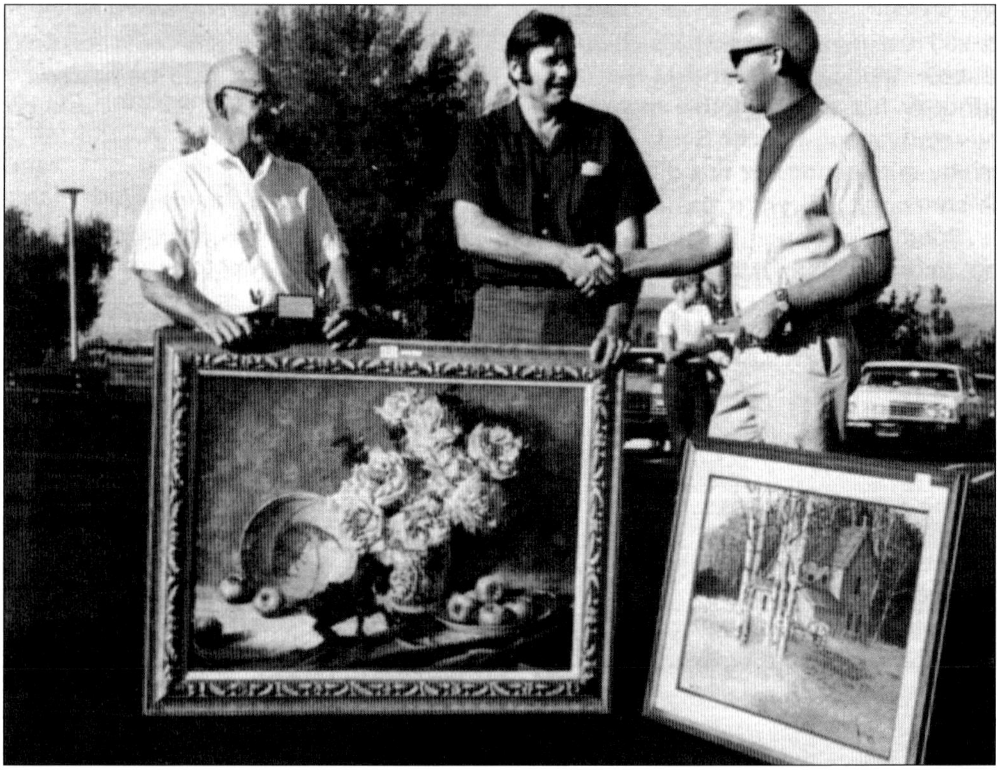

Thousands of viewers attended the two-day LSM Invitational Art Exhibit, and a popular vote once more gave the $1,000 first prize to Herbert Perrish. Placing second with a prize of $500 was a watercolor by Ray Swanson.

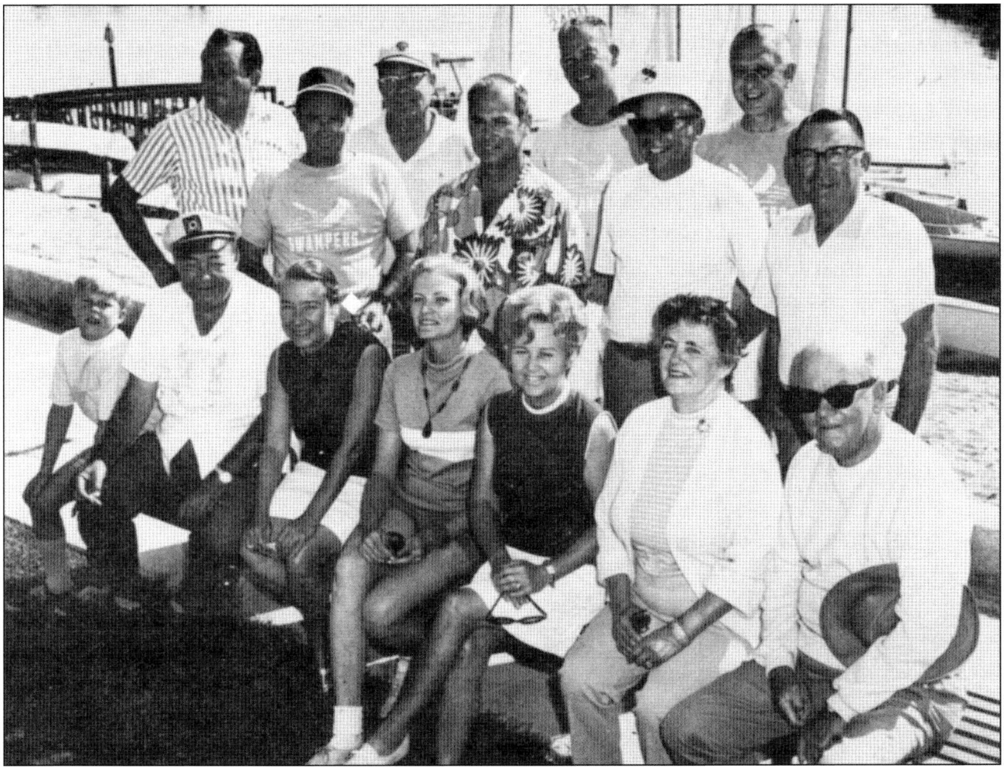

The participants of the LSM America's Cup Trials are, from left to right, (first row) an unidentified grandson of Dalt Adams, Dalt Adams, Dorothy Steven, Nancy Callison, Ellen Culp, Addie Travis, and Thornie Travis; (second row) Gordon Frazar, Don Sharp, Vernon Richardson, Bill Corbin, Dick Reed, Wendell La Belle, Harry Deuel, and Ern Culp. There was another trial scheduled for September.

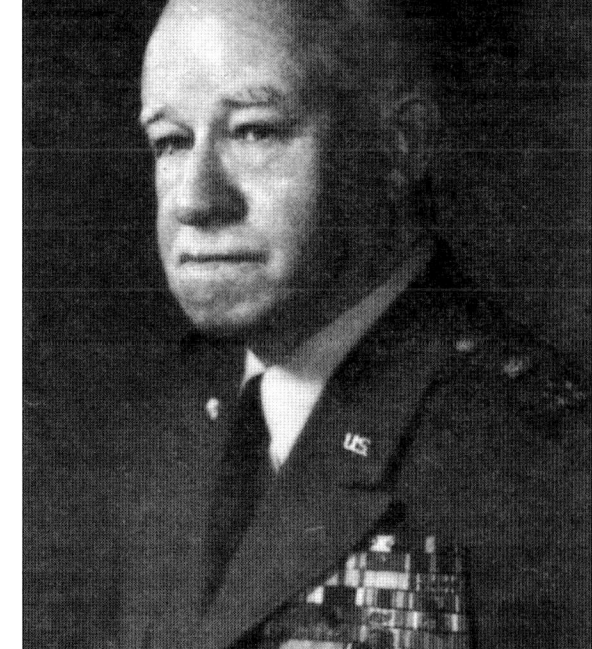

Famed visitor Gen. Omar Bradley and his wife visited the Del Mar Racetrack while on vacation and ventured out to partake in some of the community's activities. They proved to be extremely gracious visitors.

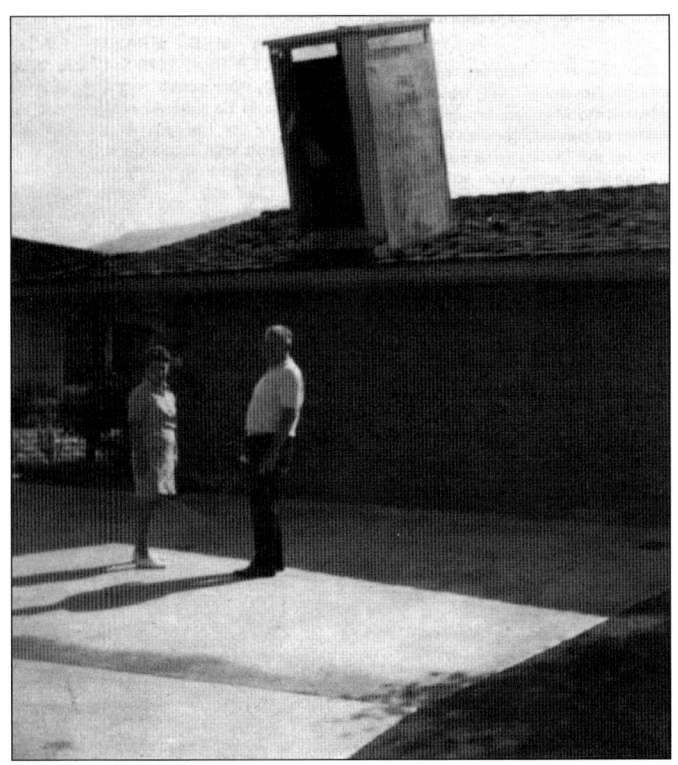

Here, a trick-or-treat prank has Mr. and Mrs. Neil Montank with the addition of an upstairs bath to their house by unknown culprits. Neil "Tank" Montank, perhaps the biggest jokester of them all, was furnished with a bit of his own type of humor. One could hear all about it on the radio the morning after Halloween.

Honorary mayor Wendell Campbell (left) and John Ainley are shown at the information center. They were urging everyone to proudly fly their flags. Wendell Campbell, previously vice chairman, was made chairman of the coordinating council for the remainder of the term after George Wieman unexpectedly passed away in November.

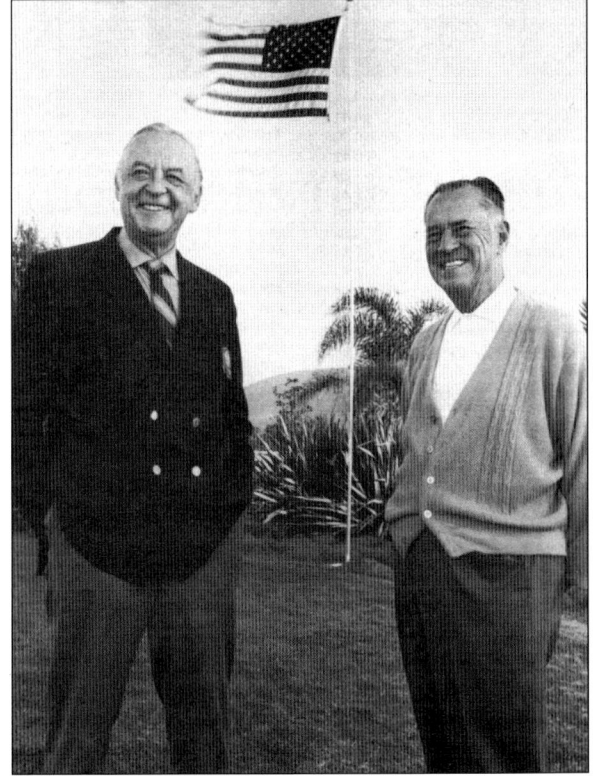

Gene Leininger (left) and Dan Deibert, new owners of the spa, invited residents to come visit. The two had a vast background in physical therapy, group exercise, and massage. Leininger was originally from West Germany. Deibert was head athletic trainer for Palomar College.

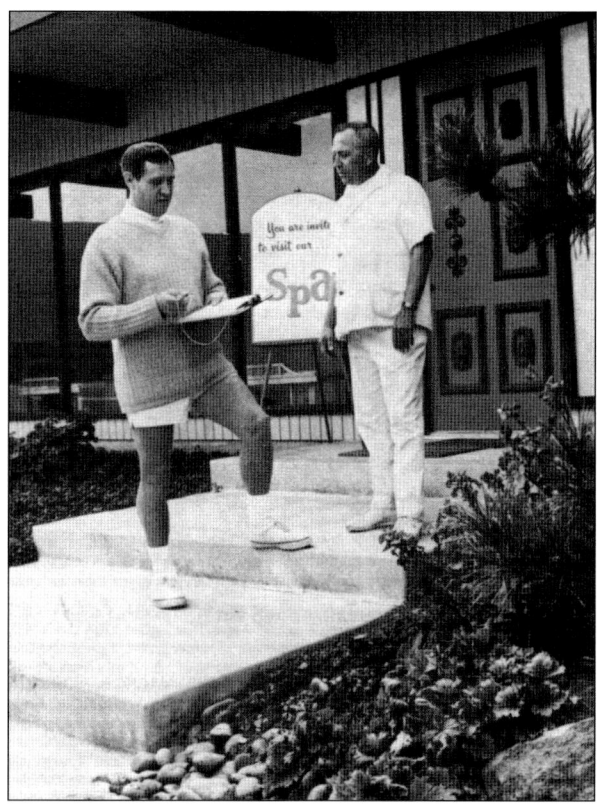

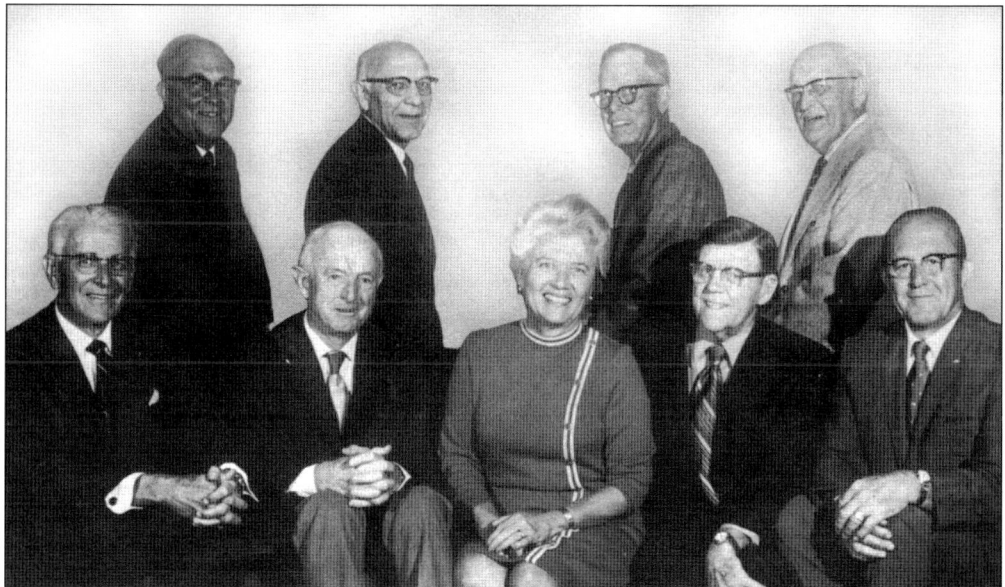

Candidates for the 1971 coordinating council election were, from left to right, (first row) "Mac" Maben, Tom Esling, Elaine Moffitt, Lea Glaze, and Neil Emerson; (second row) Charles Hahne, Gen. Fred Terrell, Adm. "Nick" Carter, and "Bud" Kendig. General Terrell was named chairman of the coordinating council for 1971. The Terrells moved to Lake San Marcos in 1967 from Wisconsin.

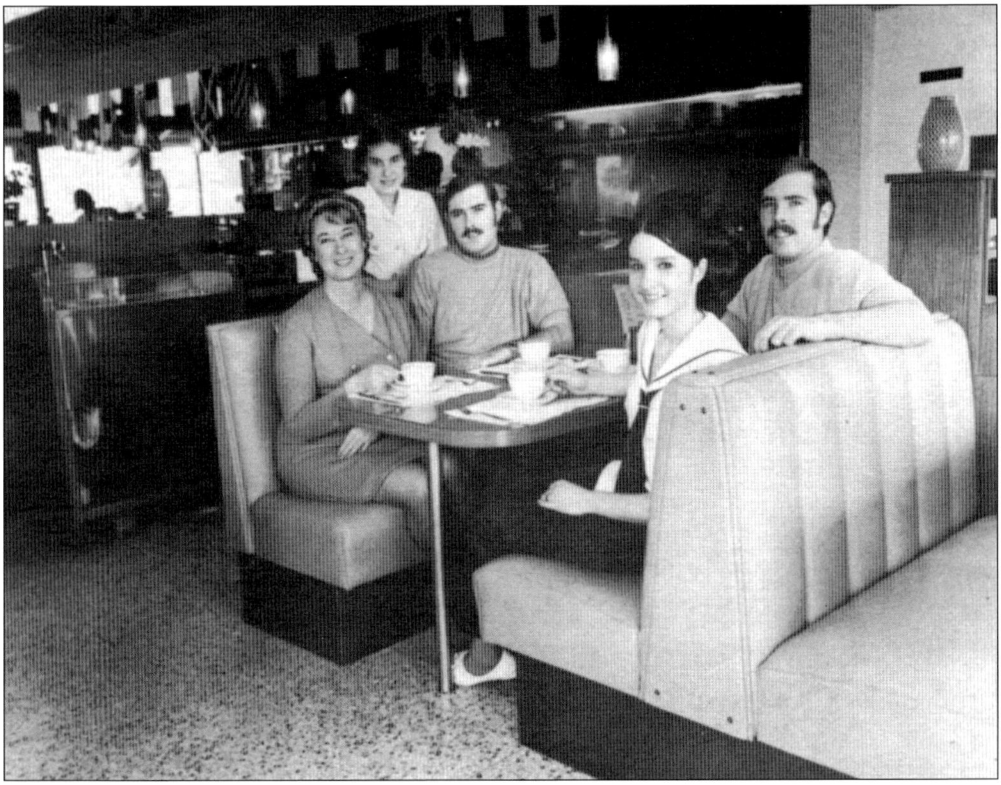

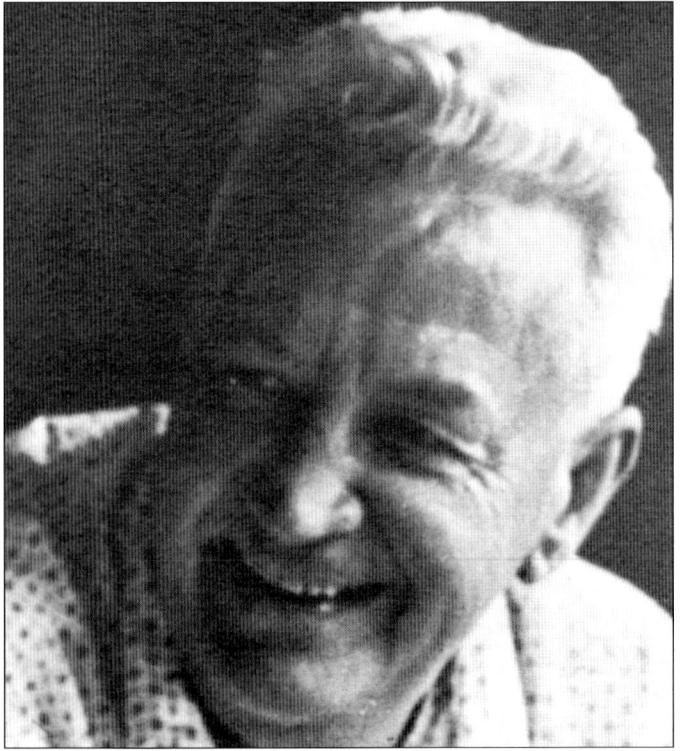

New owners of the Blue Sloop, a favorite coffee shop at the shopping center, were, from left to right, Doris Downs, Linda Downs (standing), Randy Downs, Sandy, and Craig Downs (Randy's twin and Sandy's husband). In addition to the Blue Sloop, dining at the lake could be enjoyed at the Quail's Inn Restaurant and the Trophy Room at the country club.

Lake San Marcos's own Academy Award nominee Stuart Gilmore was nominated for film editing on the motion picture *Airport*. This was his second nomination for editing.

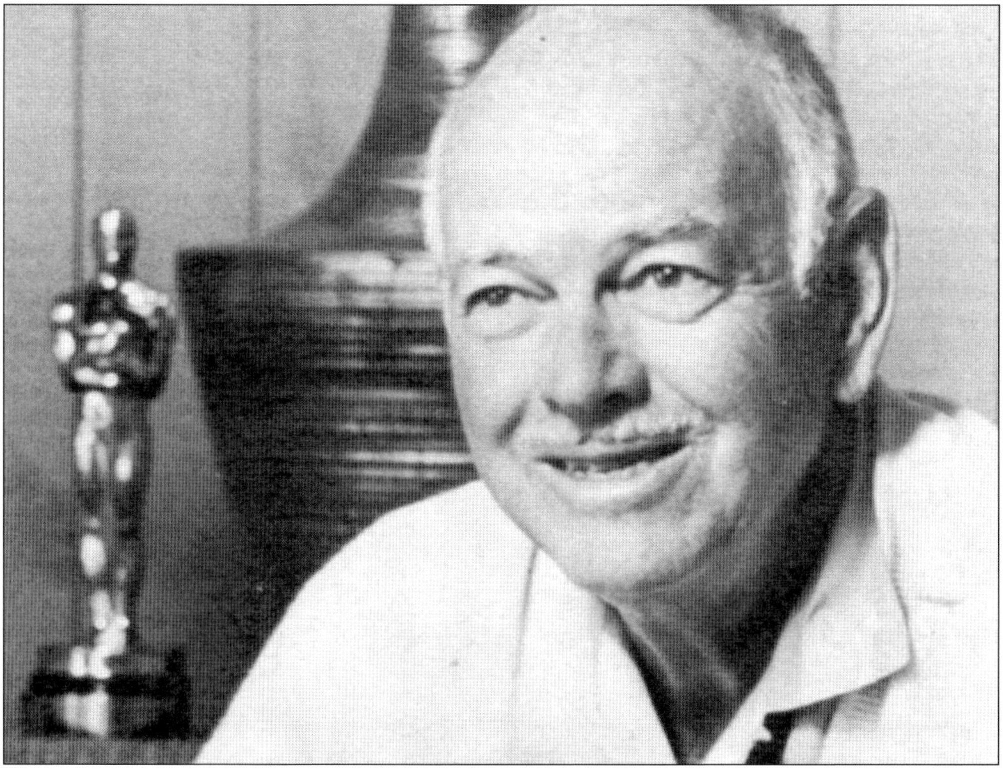

Another resident Oscar nominee was Jim Newcom, shown with his first Oscar for film editing on the movie *Gone with the Wind*. He was nominated for editing on *Tora! Tora! Tora!* This was his fifth nomination. He and Stu Gilmore had been friends for many years.

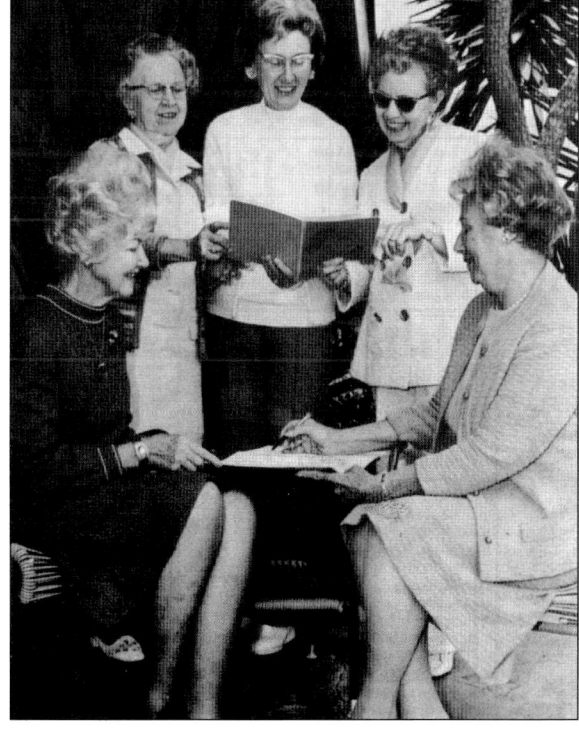

Members of the Lake San Marcos Women's Club gathered together after a fundraising luncheon. From left to right are Elberta Beum, Gladys Varenhorst, Clara Colt, Peggy Curtis, and Rhoda Grossman. One of the beneficiaries was the Dr. Strong Foundation, which received $100.

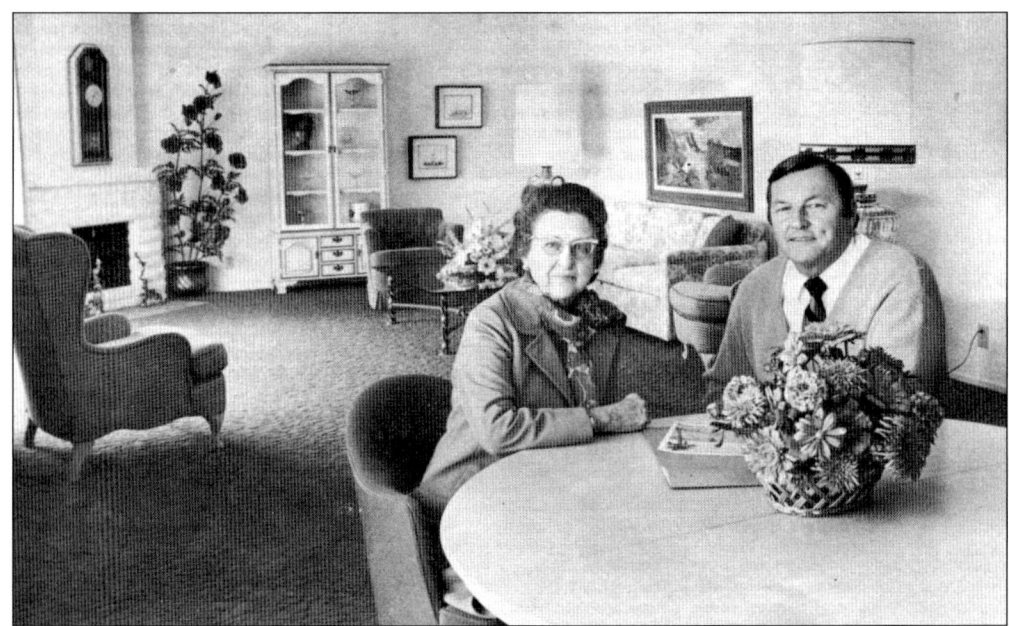

Bob Frazar is seen here discussing the details of the new condominiums with new owner Midge Wieman in the furnished model home. The two- and three-bedroom condominiums were located directly across the street from the information center at the entrance to Lake San Marcos.

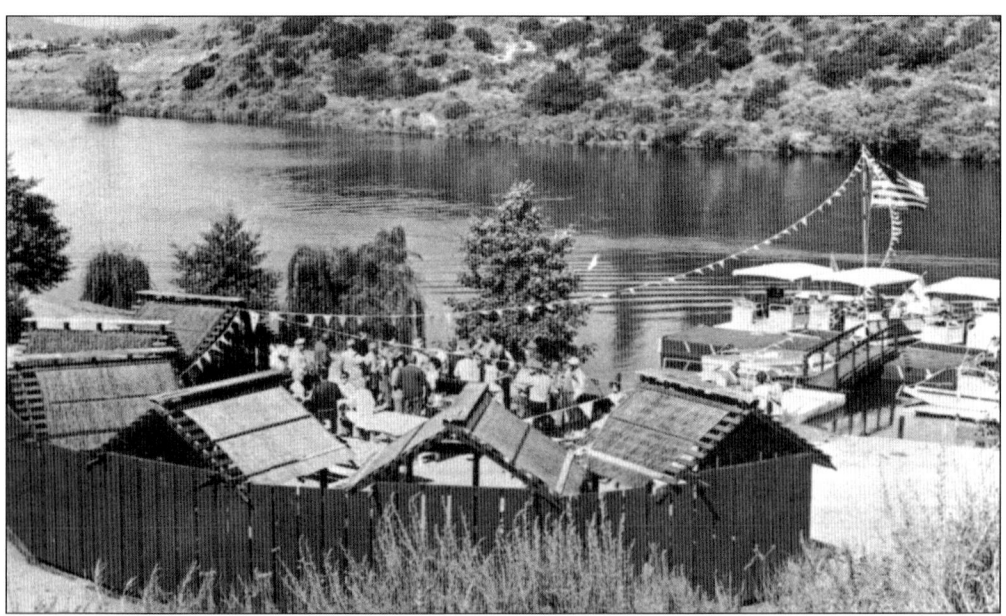

The yacht club picnic was attended by 65 members and their guests. The new cabanas encircled the picnic area at the south end of the lake. In 2014, the cabanas were torn down with plans to rebuild them.

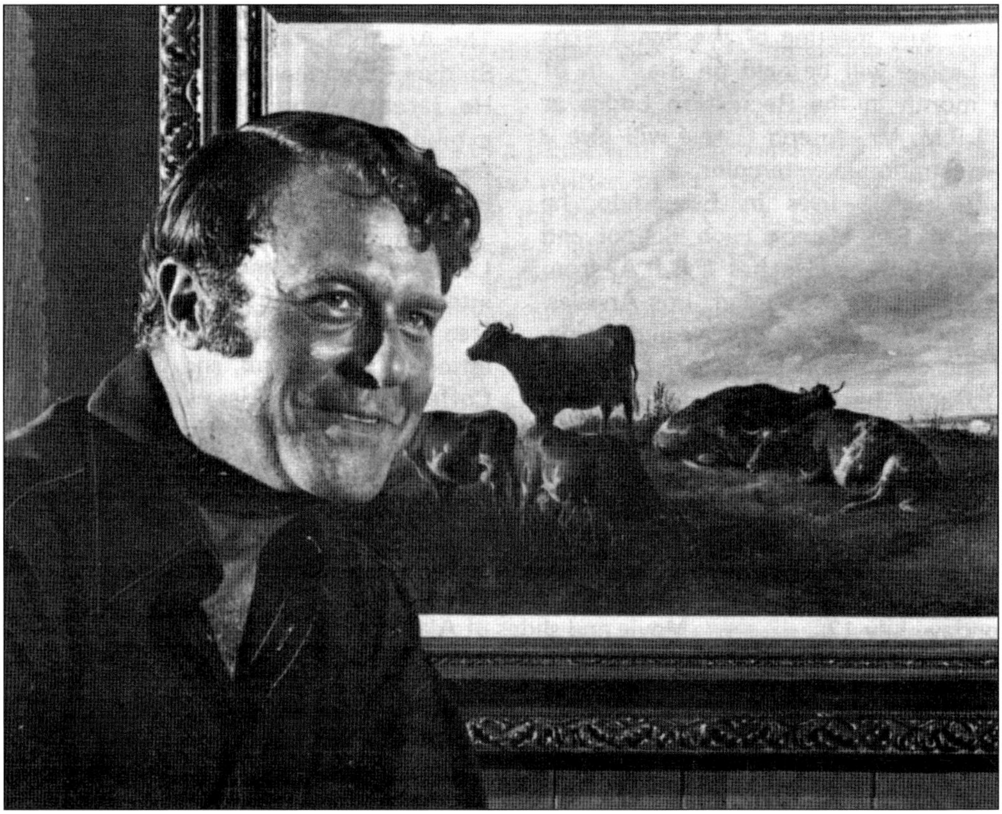

Wally McComb was the new owner of the LSM Art Gallery. Behind him is an 1887 Cooper Pastural oil from the Forthingham Collection being exhibited in the grand salon of the gallery. At another working gallery in the back, instruction was given.

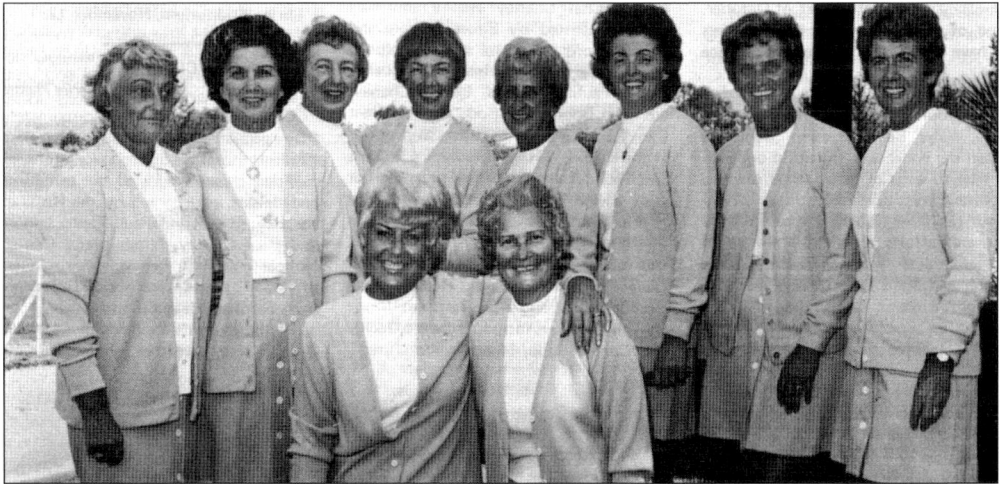

The ladies brought the trophy back to Lake San Marcos after beating the Southern Division Cottonwood team at South Torrey Pines Course. All four of the Lake San Marcos teams won their matches. Team players were, from left to right, (first row) Eddie Ream and Vi Hughes; (second row) Early Steven, Carloyn Ybarra, Irene Marcy, Isabelle Powell, Tootie Wilson, Dorothy Faulkner, Dorothy Butsch, and Pat Vanderbeck.

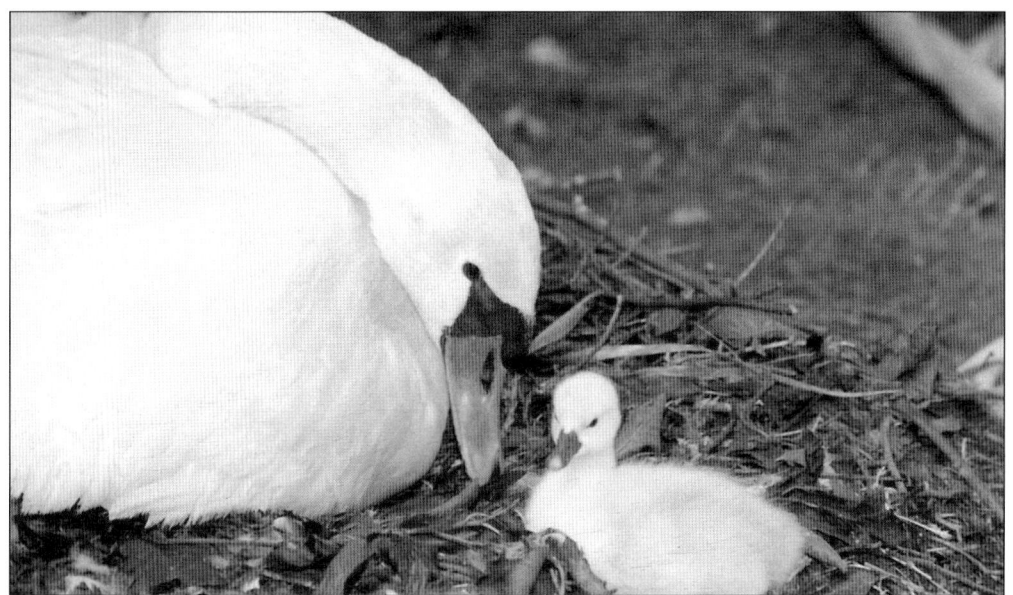

This photograph, taken by resident Bill Guier, is of a mother swan and her cygnet. Swans were introduced to the lake's ecosystem many years ago, and over time have reproduced, while others have been killed by predators. In 2014, two pairs of black swans were introduced. (Author's collection.)

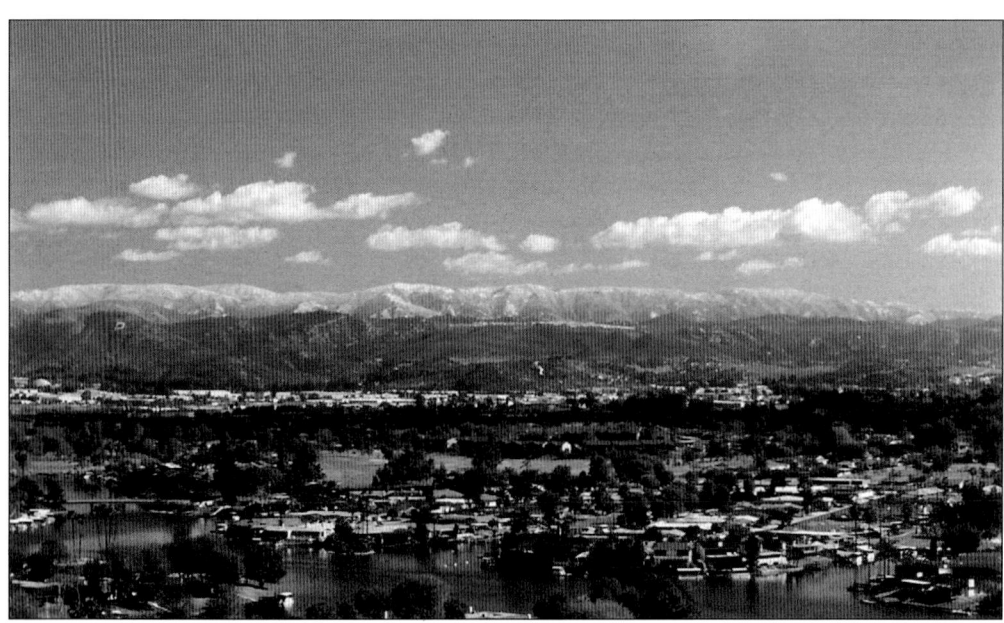

This is another beautiful photograph by Bill Guier of the winter season, showing snow on the mountains to the north of Lake San Marcos. (Author's collection.)

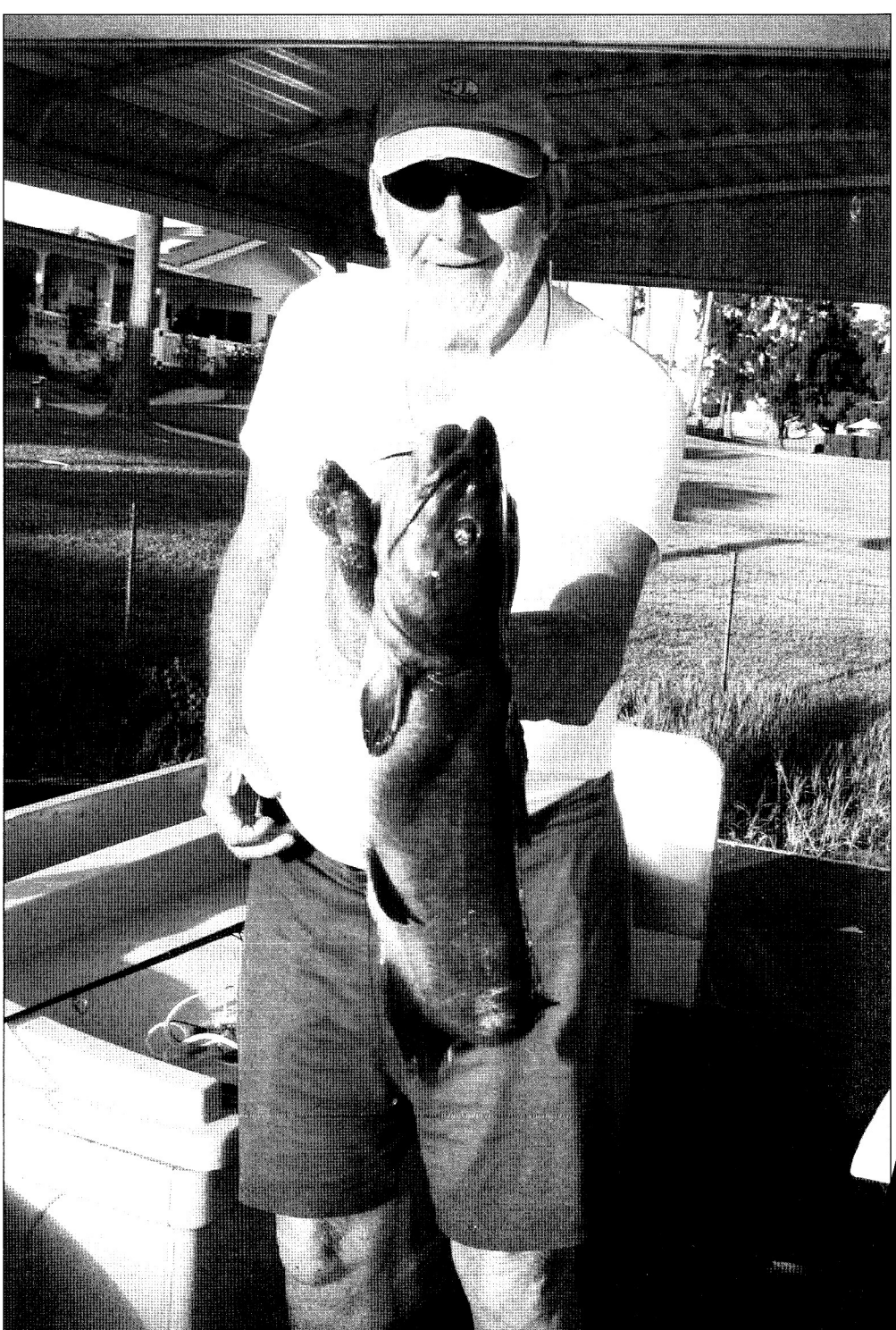

This large catfish was caught by Joe Kowasch, known on Mall 3 as "Joe the Fisherman." (and Teresa Hawker.)

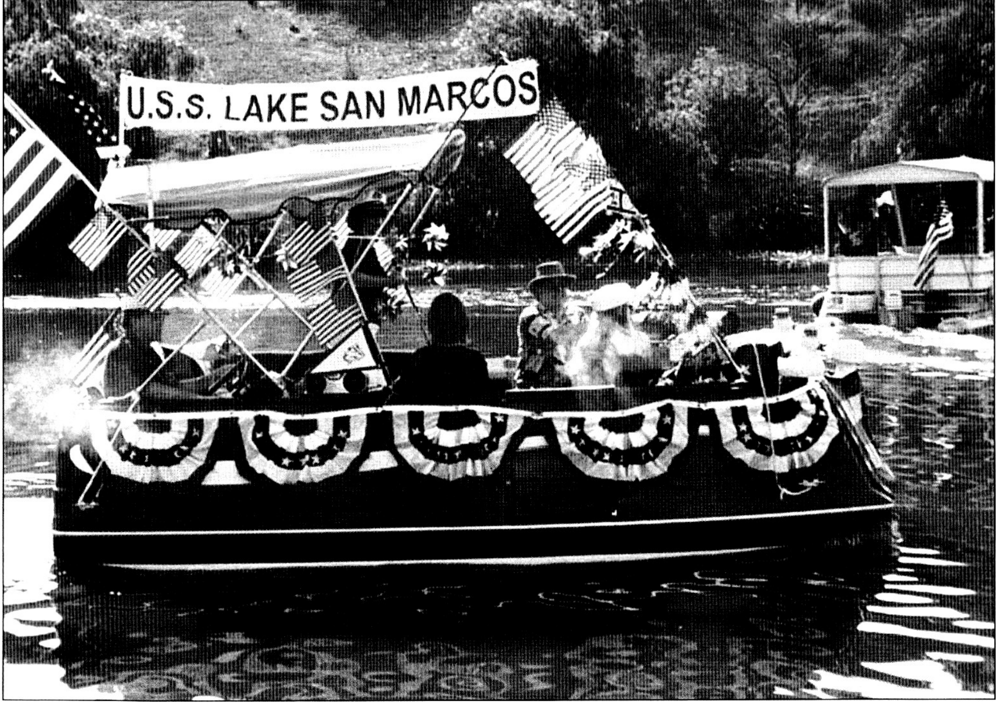

The USS *Lake San Marcos*, owned by John and Teresa Hawker, was decorated to participate in the Fourth of July boat parade. There are three boat parades held each year by the LSM Yacht Club; in them, between 20 and 30 decorated boats tour the perimeter of the lake to the enjoyment of residents and friends. (John and Teresa Hawker.)

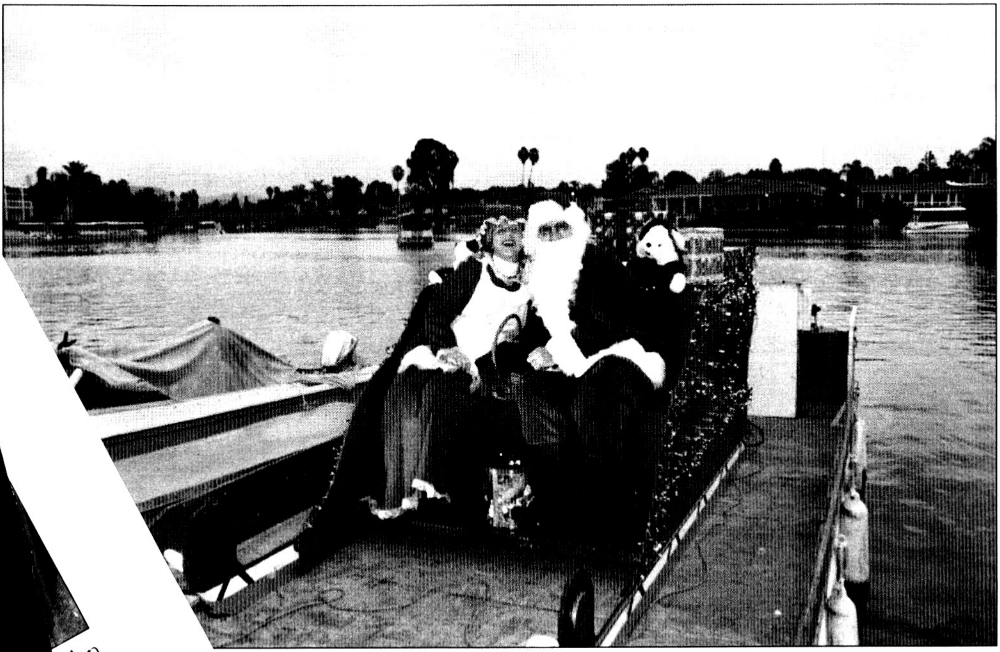

(John and Teresa Hawker) make an appearance at a Christmas boat parade ·ht Club. (John and Teresa Hawker.)

The Future of Lake San Marcos

Lake San Marcos is an unusual community that probably would not exist if the developers tried to build it today. It is wonderful in its concept, but it has not been without its controversies and growing pains. For many years, the community prospered under the management of the Citizens Development Corporation, which owned the lake and recreational facilities and leased them for use by the residents for a nominal yearly fee. The recreational facilities were not managed by the residents as most HOAs today are. When the community was in its early development, the pools, tennis courts, and recreation center were new. As time passed, they started showing their wear, and residents started complaining.

The CDC is now under new ownership and is making major improvements and upgrades to the buildings and recreational facilities. They recently purchased all-new docks for the lake. The Quail's Inn Restaurant was nationally known and very popular not only with residents but also with visitors. It is now closed and had been in bad repair for the past several years, but the new ownership is rebuilding it from the ground up.

The lake was slowly filling with sediment from the runoff of San Marcos Creek and many pollutants from the surrounding neighborhoods and cities. In recent years, several groups have joined forces to figure out a way to clean it up, including the City of San Marcos, Vallecitos Water District, and the residents of LSM. The City of San Marcos has approved a general plan for a Creek District to be built along San Marcos Creek before it flows into the lake that will have sediment catch basins and various filtering devices. This will help to control the sediment and pollutants from that source.

Lake San Marcos is still the unique community it was designed to be. The average age of its residents is over 60. Only a few of the more than 25 HOAs have age restrictions, but this community attracts active seniors due to its country club amenities and more than 25 clubs and organizations, such as golf clubs, the yacht club, dance clubs, card clubs, newcomers club, art and garden clubs, and many others.

There is something for everyone to enjoy about Lake San Marcos, and with the Creek District and new downtown San Marcos to be built, the future of Lake San Marcos looks bright.

Discover Thousands of Local History Books Featuring Millions of Vintage Images

Arcadia Publishing, the leading local history publisher in the United States, is committed to making history accessible and meaningful through publishing books that celebrate and preserve the heritage of America's people and places.

Find more books like this at
www.arcadiapublishing.com

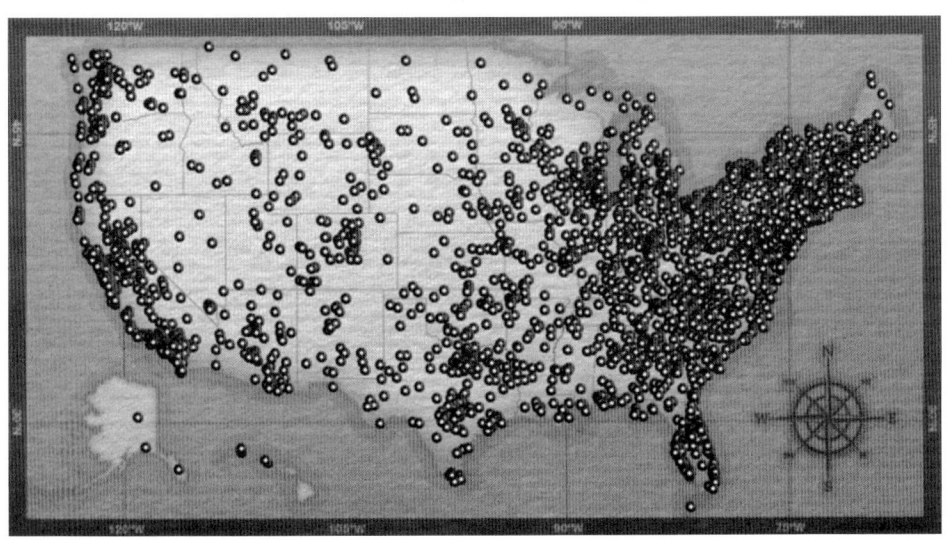

Search for your hometown history, your old stomping grounds, and even your favorite sports team.

our mission to preserve history on a local level,
ited in South Carolina on American-made
ired entirely in the United States. Products
Forest Stewardship Council (FSC) label
ent FSC-certified paper.

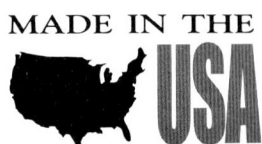